THE FUTURE OF GLOBAL FINANCIAL SERVICES

Blackwell Global Dimensions of Business Series
Series Editors: David A. Ricks, Bodo Schlegelmilch, and J. Michael Geringer

This major new series will provide authoritative international business and management material for graduate students. Each book includes focused, topic-based summaries of the key global developments in the different sub-disciplines of business. It concentrates on the strategic and practical implications in each topic area, provides material and commentary on emergent and changing trends as well as reviewing established knowledge.

Titles assigned to date include:

The Future of Global Financial Servicess	Robert Grosse
The Global Dimensions of HRM	Paula Caligiuri, Allan Bird, and Mark E. Mendenhall
The Global Dimensions of Finance	Raj Aggarwal
The Global Dimensions of eCommerce	Saeed Samiee

THE ROBERT GROSSE
FUTURE
OF GLOBAL
FINANCIAL
SERVICES

Blackwell
Publishing

350 Main Street, Malden, MA 02148–5020, USA
108 Cowley Road, Oxford OX4 1JF, UK
550 Swanston Street, Carlton, Victoria 3053, Australia

First published 2004 by Blackwell Publishing Ltd

Library of Congress Cataloging-in-Publication Data

Grosse, Robert E.
    The future of global financial services / Robert Grosse.
        p. cm. – (Blackwell global dimensions of business series)
    Includes bibliographical references and index.
    ISBN 1-4051-1700-1 (pbk. : alk. paper) – ISBN 1-4051-1701-X (hardcover : alk.
paper)
    1. Financial institutions, International.   2. Financial services industry.   I.
Title. II. Series.
    HG3881.G7284 2004
    332.1′5–dc22

                                                                            2004000866

A catalogue record for this title is available from the British Library.

Set in Rotis Serif 10/12.5pt
by Graphicraft Limited, Hong Kong

For further information on
Blackwell Publishing, visit our website:
http://www.blackwellpublishing.com

BRIEF LIST OF CONTENTS

Annotated List of Contents   vii
Preface   xiv
Acknowledgments   xvii

Part I   The Environment   1

1   Introduction   3

2   The globalization of financial services   15

3   The virtualization of financial services   35

4   Government regulation: the second key factor underlying
    industry structure   55

Part II   Competitive Strategies   71

5   The financial landscape: organizations and *allfinanz* banking
    (the status quo)   73

6   Competitive strategies of international financial institutions   87

7   Competitiveness of banks from key countries (or, Why are the
    US banks ahead?)   105

8   Responding to the challenge of the new economy   125

Part III   Where the Sector is Heading   137

9   Why insurance won't survive   139

10 Investment banking at the crossroads   153

11 Financial instruments and financial structures   167

12 The generation of long-term investment to support bond and
    stock-market growth   179

13 International financial centers   191

14 Surviving the twenty-first century   201

Index   205

ANNOTATED LIST OF CONTENTS

PART I THE ENVIRONMENT

1 Introduction

This first chapter identifies the realm of financial services – basically the provision of instruments and mechanisms to help clients hold and manage their savings, obtain funding or liquidity, transfer funds between locations and forms, manage risks, and obtain advice on their financial concerns.

The chapter discusses the range of institutions that provide financial services, as well as the technological and regulatory environment in which they operate. Financial systems in three countries – United States, Germany, and Japan – are described in some detail.

The introduction also points out that a recurring theme of the book is an examination of the "core competencies" that enable large banks, brokers, and insurance companies to survive against their rivals. These capabilities are identified and developed in later chapters. Two key environmental (external) features also are defining the competition of the early twenty-first century – the global deregulation of the sector and the global decline in cost and greater availability of telecommunications, especially via the Internet.

2 The globalization of financial services

Financial services are now provided in a highly decentralized manner, given the technological ability of institutions to market and provide their services through electronic media, and given government permission to offer such services more and more freely across jurisdictions. This chapter considers the technological changes that are driving the new structure of financial services provision. Three kinds of technology change are relevant: the use of electronic media for service provision; the use of highly automated internal management information systems within financial institutions; and the increase and sophistication of financial engineering to create increasingly adapted instruments that better service client needs.

As a result of this reality, commercial banks face new threats to their survival, coming from foreign banks as well as from nonbank competitors such as stockbrokers and investment management companies. Investment banks face the threat of being replaced by electronic securities trading and even underwriting via the Internet. And insurance companies face the greatest challenge of all – trying to differentiate themselves from the broader financial services providers. I argue that, overall, globalization of the world economy is being led by financial services globalization.

3 The virtualization of financial services

How far can the virtualization of financial services go? Will automatic tellers and Internet-based stockbrokerage replace banks and brokers? It is clear that these outcomes are not coming soon, if ever. However, the opportunities posed by electronic media are helping to shape the competitive landscape, and this chapter explores some of the implications.

The is no doubt that some banking services, such as retail withdrawals from checking accounts, can be very efficiently handled by automatic tellers, and other services can be handled by automatic tellers or Internet-based transactions. Even so, there are some activities that will remain in the domain of bankers/brokers, because the transactions involved are too complex for machines to handle, or because relationships are the basis of the business. This chapter draws up some of the strengths and weaknesses of Internet-based financial services provision and draws conclusions about which types of service will migrate more extensively to the domain of the Internet.

4 Government regulation: the second key factor underlying industry structure

In addition to the widely discussed phenomenon of the Internet, widespread deregulation of financial services during the 1990s has dramatically reshaped the industry as well. This chapter lays out the regulatory environment facing banking institutions in the USA, Europe, Japan, and a number of emerging markets. The goal is to show how generalized the process is, and what shape it is in on a country-by-country basis.

Another regulatory concern in banking worldwide is the effort to ensure that banks hold enough capital to provide support for their viability under conditions of financial difficulty. The Basle Accord of 1988 produced a set of guidelines for banks to follow in order to demonstrate their capital adequacy. Proposals to revise these rules and to deal with their failings led to repeated meetings and more revisions, such that by 2003 the new rules had not yet been finalized, but their general shape was known. This situation is reviewed, and another section is presented to consider the idea of a global lender of last resort (such as a global FDIC) to bail out failing institutions.

PART II COMPETITIVE STRATEGIES

5 The financial landscape: organizations and allfinanz banking (the status quo)

This chapter describes in some more detail the financial market structure of the USA, and adds discussion of these sectors in France, Mexico, and Korea. These commentaries supplement the more detailed analyses of competitiveness and strategies of banks in the USA, Germany, the United Kingdom, Switzerland, and Japan, in the next two chapters.

The US institutions described include Bank of America, Bank One, Charles Schwab, E*trade, State Farm, and American Express. In France, they include Crédit Agricole, Banque National de Paris, Société Générale, AXA, and CNP. In Mexico, they include Banamex-Citibank, Bancomer–BBVA, and Santander Serfin. In Korea, they include Kookmin Bank, Woori Bank, and Shinhan Bank.

The number of banking, brokerage, and insurance organizations in each country is quite distinct, though the trend is toward reduced numbers of all three kinds of financial services providers. *Allfinanz* service is clearly on the rise, while just as clearly the number of specialized niche providers is growing at the same time. Financial services in Latin America have been largely taken over by foreign institutions, based mainly in the USA and Spain.

The problems of managing a three-culture *allfinanz* organization are discussed, ranging from salary differences between banking and insurance to management styles that are more conservative in commercial banking and insurance than in investment banking. The open question of whether *allfinanz* is a viable model is presented and briefly debated.

6 Competitive strategies of international financial institutions

This chapter looks at ten major world-leading financial institutions, describes their strategies, and aims to uncover their core competencies. The goal of the chapter is to demonstrate the competencies that are needed to compete successfully at the highest level internationally, and to show where the various institutions fall on the competitiveness scale. None of the institutions is truly a global leader, though Citigroup and Hongkong Bank are the closest to that status. Most firms, such as Allianz Dresdner and Merrill Lynch, are strong leaders in their home markets, leaders in a small number of additional markets, and present in dozens of added markets. But they are far from being leaders at the global level.

The institutions are Citigroup, HongKong and Shanghai Banking Corporation, Allianz Dresdner, Merrill Lynch, Mizuho Holdings, United Bank of Switzerland,

Deutsche Bank, Internationale Nederlanden Group, Goldman Sachs, and Fidelity Investments.

7 Competitiveness of banks from key countries (or, Why are the US banks ahead?)

Taking a more detailed look at competitive factors in commercial banking, this chapter compares three of the largest banks from five countries: the USA, the UK, Switzerland, Germany, and Japan. By comparing the banks along a series of dimensions such as asset size, efficiency ratios, noninterest earnings, and others, the analysis shows which of these factors correlated most strongly with the banks' performance during the 1990s. Interestingly, one of the most significant factors was the bank's home country income growth. That is, the banks from countries that grew more rapidly had better performance, other things equal. This is a striking finding, which supports the idea that country matters; that is, that a bank's home country does indeed influence its ability to survive in global competition.

8 Responding to the challenge of the new economy

A proactive view of competitive strategy is presented in this chapter. The idea of Transformational Management is raised as a means for financial institutions to evaluate their competitive strengths and weaknesses in the competitive environment that they want to serve, and then to draw conclusions about how to stake out their turf and build competitiveness based on their core competencies. The Transformational Management concept has four stages, requiring the firm to: (1) envision the competitive domain in which it wants to compete in the future; (2) identify existing competencies for competing in that chosen context, and obtain any competencies that are missing; (3) inform the market of this vision and the firm's capabilities; and (4) implement the strategy by building the set of competencies and conveying the worldview to clients, investors, and the market in general.

This concept is illustrated with the examples of Citibank, Allianz, and Hongkong Bank, all of which have gone through wrenching changes in the past five years as a result of such transformational thinking.

PART III   WHERE THE SECTOR IS HEADING

9 Why insurance won't survive

The insurance sector has been exposed! With the change in US regulation in 1999, commercial and investment banks can now enter the turf of insurance companies. This means that the standardized policies for life insurance, auto insurance, and a number of other categories are easily copied by new competitors. Likewise, annuities can be offered by any of these financial institutions, and are not limited to insurance companies. Life insurance companies will not be able to survive unless they either become broader-scope financial services providers or, alternatively, if they focus on a market niche such as limited insurance coverage along with asset management.

This chapter makes the case for the disappearance of the insurance industry. It also describes some of the major insurance companies worldwide, along with their current product portfolios and some aspects of their strategies.

10 Investment banking at the crossroads

Investment banking appears to face a similar threat as in the case of the insurance sector. This is an overstatement, because the investment banking sector has many more major products that are not easily imitated, and which require much greater analytical skill for their success than most relatively standardized insurance products. Nevertheless, there are quite a few investment banking products that can be and are copied by commercial banks, and thus the threat of increasing competition exists here as well.

This chapter explains the major areas of investment banking, and shows how securities trading and some underwriting are subject to competition from commercial banks, and also from issuers going directly to potential investors via Internet sale of the securities. The largest investment banks are compared across product categories and according to size, demonstrating that the main competitors are full-service investment banks, and that – with a few exceptions – they tend to be US-based firms. The chapter concludes that investment banking is a viable sector because it is skill-intensive, rather than being based on characteristics such as extensive distribution or low cost.

11 Financial instruments and financial structures

The range of financial instruments available in the market is growing persistently. Even so, some of the traditional instruments, such as loans and deposits, not to speak of checks and risk management tools, are being replaced by more client-friendly alternatives. For example, electronic means of payment such as debit cards, wire transfers and Internet-based payments are inexorably eating away at the use of slow and inefficient checks. Deposits that used to be held in commercial banks are being competed away by money market accounts that offer the saver many more account features than the traditional instrument. In sum, the array of financial products is moving toward greater accessibility and lower cost to clients, much of which results from electronic methods.

This chapter explores the possible outcomes for each of the five areas of financial services: savings instruments, credit instruments, funds transfer methods, risk management methods, and financial advising arrangements.

As a separate topic, the question is raised and considered: How safe is the financial system?

12 The generation of long-term investment to support bond and stock-market growth

This chapter considers the question of why long-term financial markets are so scarce in less developed countries. The answers are several, starting from the history of high inflation and interest rates in many countries, but including more importantly today the fact that weak institutions and occasional financial crises make it difficult to operate financial contracts that extend over long periods of time.

Attention then shifts to the responses that have arisen to the problem of weak or nonexistent long-term financial markets. Governments have recently encouraged the development of mortgage markets in which mortgages can be traded in the form of bonds (CMOs). Securitization of bank loans has facilitated the development of both long- and short-term financial markets in a number of countries since this process has been permitted.

Another vehicle that has helped to build long-term financial markets is pension fund privatization, which has enabled private-sector organizations to manage pension funds and to invest part of the wealth into instruments such as collateralized mortgage obligations (CMOs) and other long-term instruments, rather than the traditional government bonds.

Together, securitization and pension fund privatization have opened a huge new market potential for the development of long-term capital markets in LDCs. The threat to these innovative policies and strategies is that financial markets tend to concentrate in financial centers. So, as emerging market borrowers look for capital, they tend to look to financial centers such as London and New York – and likewise for emerging market investors. The net result is that it will continue to be difficult for emerging markets to develop long-term financial markets, and there will be a tension between such markets and the three or four major financial centers worldwide for both funding and investment.

13 International financial centers

London and New York are the world's main international financial centers. In fact, London is the leading international financial center period – far ahead of New York in almost every measure of international financial activity. New York has the world's largest stock exchange, but even in this activity, London has more foreign firms listed on its exchange than does New York, and more trading volume of foreign stocks and bonds. London leads in foreign exchange trading, cross-border bank lending, international insurance contract origination and reinsurance, bond issue by nonlocal firms, and other such activities.

What probability is there that this situation may change, perhaps due to the introduction of the euro, or the growing use of the Internet? In fact, there does not seem to be any challenge to London's dominance in international finance, although the Internet clearly poses a threat to individual financial services providers that may not be agile enough to offer their wares through that medium when others do. New York and Frankfurt, on the other hand, have not taken market share from London in the past decade, despite the various legal, technological, and competitive changes that have occurred.

14 Surviving the twenty-first century

This chapter offers some concluding comments to the overall discussion. It begins with a brief discussion of the problem of global financial stability, noting that bail-outs of failed major institutions (Resona in Japan; Long-Term Capital Management in the USA) continue to occur, but that they have not led to a breakdown in any major country's financial market or to broader dire implications. Based on that history and other events of the late twentieth century, there is some reason to expect that existing institutions can handle the unexpected financial events of the near future without ending in global crisis.

The tendency toward *allfinanz* financial service organizations is simply a reality, rather than an unsupported trend. Most of the world outside of the United States has operated with such institutions for many years, and the problem of managing a diverse organization seems to be handled by operating separate divisions for the different services. This situation parallels the existence of diversified Economic Groups in most countries, while in the USA firms tend to be much more narrowly focused in their business lines.

Finally, some very positive results of the broad processes of technological advance and regulatory loosening are reemphasized. The range of instruments that have been developed to deal with financial risks is truly amazing, and with the possibility of transferring them around the world instantly, these hedging methods are quite widely employed today. The willingness of national governments to allow foreign institutions to provide financial services is a fascinating turn of events, that may lead to much greater consolidation of financial services providers in the years ahead. We definitely live in interesting times!

PREFACE

This book explores the future of one of the world's most important industries, financial services. The goal is to give readers an idea of the kinds of institutions and services that will survive competition in the early twenty-first century, and the reasons why. After living through the stock market crisis of 1987, and then the new crisis of 2001–2, people may wonder just how safe is the financial system, and what kinds of financial instruments are ones they want to trust their savings to. Just as well, people may wonder what kinds of institutions are going to be around in another four or five years, with all of the changes that are taking place in the United States as a result of deregulation and elimination of the barriers between banks, stockbrokers, and insurance companies.

This is not an essay in futurology. The "future" that the book explores is the next four or five years, rather than the entire twenty-first century – or even the next decade or two. This admittedly limited time horizon does not account for some possibly spectacular changes in financial methods, such as the potential complete elimination of currency, but it does consider the likely changes that we will face in the near future, such as much greater use of the Internet for banking transactions and much greater direct dealing between savers and companies that want to borrow for their own capital investment plans. And, with respect to some broad outlines of the financial sector, the discussion points out the likely disappearance of the insurance sector as a separate industry, since most of the products sold in this sector are fairly standardized and easily incorporated into a bank's portfolio of financial instruments[1].

One very important aspect of financial services that Americans tend to ignore or know very little about is the situation in foreign countries, and perhaps more important, the impact of foreign competitors on US firms and users of financial services. Just how important is the Hongkong Bank (HSBC) in global financial services? And how will Deutsche Bank's acquisition of Bankers Trust affect the US financial sector? While neither of these firms appears likely to cause a major shift in provision of financial services in the USA, they both signify the changing ownership of the financial services providers in this country.

The financial markets in other countries are themselves becoming increasingly important to Americans, given that many people invest in foreign securities (often through mutual funds), and that the London eurocurrency market is the largest money market in the world today. It is useful to understand something about the institutions and financial instruments that are used in other countries, if only to see how they may apply in the US context.

The structure of the book includes three parts. Part I describes the financial services landscape, and offers an organizing framework for thinking about financial services. This part also looks in some detail at the two most disruptive driving forces in this industry today: technological advances and deregulation of financial markets. Both of these forces are contributing to the continued globalization of financial service provision.

Part II looks at a number of financial services providers, and compares their competitive strategies. The most striking feature of the sector is that there are no truly global competitors, as there are in cars or computers or clothing. Citibank and Hongkong Bank have by far the largest spread of affiliates around the world, but neither of them is present in more than half of all countries – and neither has a leading market share in more than a handful of countries. How will this fragmented industry develop, now that barriers to foreign competition have fallen in many countries, and technology allows entry even when a domestic financial market is restricted?

The banks, brokers, and insurance companies in this industry are in many cases converging on an *allfinanz* or *bancassurance* model, which implies that the same organization provides commercial banking, investment banking, and insurance services. Is this a logical and/or likely conclusion to the growth and development of the institutions in the next few years? The answer to this question seems to be "No." With the exceptions of Allianz and Citibank, none of the other institutions has made that large a foray into all three areas – and even Citibank is spinning off some of its insurance business (the property/casualty part). Is the universal banking model then the structure of the future? Possibly, but even here the pressure is currently on in the USA to limit the interaction between stockbrokers and lenders, so that most banks and brokers may choose to remain separate, despite the successful models of J. P. Morgan Chase and Deutsche–Bankers Trust.

Part III focuses on several components of the total sector, explaining why the insurance business is likely to largely disintegrate in the near future and how investment banking likely will evolve to respond to the threat of electronic securities issue and trading. A number of financial instruments and practices likewise will disappear or be absorbed into alternative mechanisms, so this issue is discussed in some detail. Even the locations in which financial dealings are centered will probably change, basically to a more decentralized system, as a result of the mechanization and globalization of financial markets. This issue is explored in an analysis of the major financial centers of New York, London, Frankfurt, Hong Kong, and Tokyo.

A final theme is a look at the mobilization of savings through long-term financial instruments such as mortgage-backed bonds and privatized social security systems, pointing to an increasing development of financial flexibility around the world. The final chapter offers some thoughts about which institutions are likely to survive in twenty-first century competition, and why.

Robert Grosse

NOTE

1   This does not, of course, mean a complete elimination of specialized companies dealing in some insurance products that are highly nonstandardized, such as many property insurance policies and reinsurance arrangements.

ACKNOWLEDGMENTS

This project has taken a very long time to complete. This is because, almost like with an expanding jigsaw puzzle, as I was able to fit pieces together, it seemed as though new pieces were being thrown on the table almost constantly (especially due to technology changes and rules changes). The fact that *allfinanz* or *bancassurance* is and has been a fact of financial life for decades in most countries outside of the USA and the UK is difficult for a North American to comprehend, and a new mindset was needed to really try to understand, describe, and explain the conditions that exist in international financial markets. Hopefully, I have done some justice to the phenomena under study.

I would like to thank primarily the large number of research assistants who have worked on this project during the past four years. They include, but are not limited to, Xiaoyan Wang, Sangit Rawlley, Eric Grimmer, Pari Thirunavukkarasu, Andrew King, Yanfang Lei, Jayesh Ghandhi, Francis Nzeuton, Shreyas Chari, Val Pavlov, and Santiago Martello. They were very capably overseen by my two main sources of academic support during this time, Thunderbird CIBER Coordinators Marie Gant and Tania Marcinkowski.

In addition, I would like to thank my colleagues who have read and commented on various chapters and articles on these subjects during the preparation of the book. They include Alan Gart, Kumar Venkataramany, Gunter Dufey, Anant Sundaram, Taeho Kim, and Adrian Tschoegl. Their inputs have certainly improved the quality of this study, and in two cases they appear as coauthors of chapters here.

Finally, I would definitely like to thank the many managers of financial firms who have consented to being interviewed and/or making comments on chapters of the book. Many of them were participants in various executive programs that I have taught, and others I have met and worked with in the Latin American bankers' program, INTERBAN. They include Marcos Kerbel, West Lockhart, Julio de Quesada, and Darin Narayana.

Robert Grosse

PART I

THE ENVIRONMENT

Contents

1 Introduction   3

2 The globalization of financial services   15

3 The virtualization of financial services   35

4 Government regulation: the second key factor underlying industry structure   55

CHAPTER 1

INTRODUCTION

At the beginning of the twenty-first century, the financial services sector is going through an enormous and dramatic process of change. The institutions involved in providing financial services are being rocked by new competition, both domestically and internationally. Citibank, once the leading United States commercial banking institution, is now Citigroup, a diversified stockbroker, insurance underwriter, financial advisor, and finally still a commercial bank. This possibility was simply not allowed under US rules until the beginning of the new century – and now the gauntlet is down for further financial institution consolidation and convergence. The Hongkong and Shanghai Banking Corporation (Hongkong Bank, or HSBC) has metamorphosized from an Asian giant to a global financial services provider, with its headquarters now in London and with a huge US network of affiliates, based on its acquisitions of Republic Bank of New York, Marine Midland Bank, and other smaller institutions. And even insurance companies are finding it necessary to enter other financial services in a major way – witness the acquisition by Allianz of Dresdner Bank, Germany's second largest, and its rapid global expansion through acquisitions of insurance companies in the Americas and Europe.

The definitions of financial services themselves are changing, as electronic methods replace people and physical documentary activities. Internet banks have not replaced traditional ones – but Internet-based banking services are now necessary for large competitive banks to stay in the game against their technology-driven rivals. This volume tries to make some sense out of the rapidly evolving sector and the competition within it.

The current chapter sets the stage. First, it answers the question: What does the financial services sector do? Next, it describes the current structure of the sector, so that competitors, partial competitors, and even noncompeting groups can be seen in the proper context. With these bases in place, it is possible to interpret the technological, legal, and strategic changes that are shaping the new environment.

WHAT ARE FINANCIAL SERVICES?

What is it that banks, stockbrokers, and insurance companies – among other financial services providers – do that creates the "sector"? Traditionally, we think of the two sides of financial intermediation: namely, (1) taking in people's savings and giving them financial claims such as time deposits that reward them for giving up the current use of those savings; and (2) providing financing to people, firms, and governments who want to invest in activities that will enable them to pay back the financing (plus some charge for the use of the funds) in the future. These functions clearly are necessary in any society that advances beyond exchanges based on barter, and commercial banks have generally provided such functions during the past two centuries.

A third category of financial service is the use of money or other financial instruments to realize payments for purchases of goods and services. One of the classic justifications for the use of money[1] is to provide a clear and manageable means of exchange – to set prices of different items and to carry out payment when purchases are made. Thus the financial services sector provides the means of payment (money and its correlates) and the mechanisms for carrying out that payment (such as electronic transfers, checks, and smart cards). In most societies, a main institution such as a central bank is given the role of creating money (cash), and then financial institutions such as banks and others are able to take the initial money supply and move it around, change its form, and generally leverage it to provide the various additional financial services that we know. However, the starting point is the creation of the money and its insertion into the economy.

One could debate the significance of the central bank's role in creating money, versus alternative mechanisms that could be imagined. That would take the discussion too far from its intended focus on the near future, the first decade of the twenty-first century, which is our target time frame. Instead, the discussion focuses on the financial services sector with central banking as a given – though even here the issue is interesting, given the direction of many countries to create new joint central banks (in the European Monetary Union, for example), and thus to shift the money creation activity from a national function to a multinational one. Again, we will begin here with the assumption that a central bank produces new money, and that it is the role of the financial services sector to mobilize that money and optimize the benefits from it.

The third role of the financial sector in dealing with this money is thus to mobilize it for payments of purchases of goods and services. This means offering users the ability to make purchases and receive payment for sales in an efficient, low-cost, and low-risk manner. Toward this end, financial sector participants have developed checks, wire transfers, credit, debit and smart cards, and various other instruments. This can be considered the payments mechanism of the economy.

A fourth role of the financial services sector is to provide guidance to savers on the use of their savings, as well as to investors on their sources of funding. This service ranges from the advising itself to the provision of asset management and treasury management, and additional services beyond. Both investment advising and asset management have grown to be enormous industries on their own in recent years.

Finally, a fifth role of the financial services sector is to provide risk management to both savers and investors. Traditionally, risk management meant insurance – of buildings, workers' lives, and property. Today, the scope of risk management has broadened greatly, to the point of including property, casualty, and life insurance; financial derivatives to manage price, interest rate, exchange rate, and even credit risks; portfolio design to mitigate risks; and even self-insurance.

The sum of these parts thus defines the financial services sector as the provider of:

1 Mechanisms/instruments for savers to store their savings.
2 Mechanisms for investors/borrowers to find funding for their projects.
3 Mechanisms for carrying out payments.
4 Advice and management for savers and investors to deal with their financial needs.
5 Mechanisms for managing and protecting against risks.

In a schematic view, the set of financial services can be grouped as shown in figure 1.1, which lists some of the instruments that are used to provide each type of service, as well as showing the links of the services to the relevant users.

These are the areas of financial service that must be covered by institutions in the sector. The questions for the future are: What kinds of institutions and instruments will they be? Which ones will provide what services? And how will the services be provided? Before trying to answer these questions, it will be useful to take a look at the institutional structure that currently exists in the sector.

WHO PROVIDES FINANCIAL SERVICES?

This question can probably best be answered on a national basis first, and then the global reality can be envisioned from that initial point. The financial systems of the USA, Japan, and Germany are sketched as key examples today.

The United States

The US financial system is comprised of an array of institutions that provide some of the five types of service, but only a tiny number (such as Citigroup, J. P. Morgan Chase, and Bank of America) that provide the whole array of services to a wide range of clients. And only Citigroup is present in a major way in the insurance sector, which was just opened to bank entry in 1999.

In the early twenty-first century, the US financial system is the most developed and extensive in the world. The number of financial services providers and the range of their services exceeds those in any other country – with the United Kingdom in second place overall, and in first place with respect to the provision of some of the

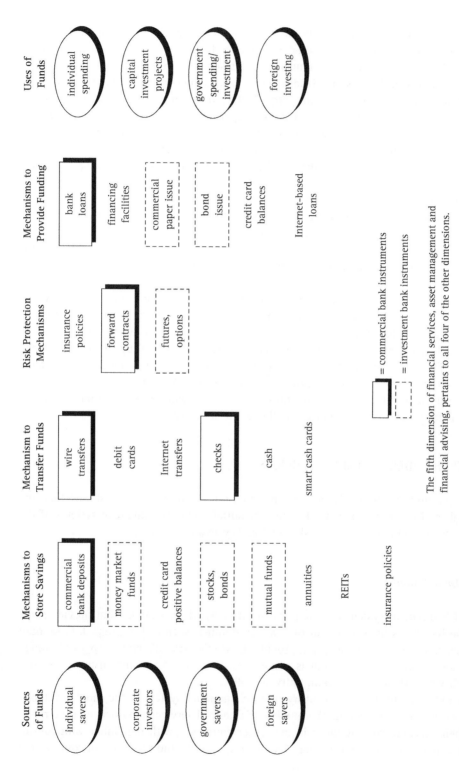

Figure 1.1 The financial services landscape.

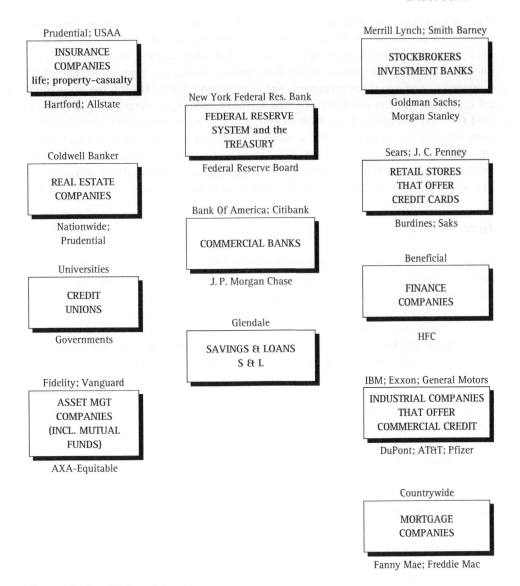

Figure 1.2 The US financial system.

major international services such as foreign exchange, reinsurance, and international bond issuance and trading. The US system has broadened to the point at which banking institutions provide only 20–30% of savings and credit instruments in the economy, with the rest offered by investment banks, insurance companies, fund management companies, and other providers. These service providers and the array of services are described in subsequent chapters.

The US system is shown in figure 1.2 as having a core set of banking institutions, located in the central vertical column and regulated by the Federal Reserve System.

Then, a wide range of additional providers offer further and overlapping financial services, as shown in the major categories listed around the central base. On the right-hand side are listed types of financial services provider that are largely seen as financing sources: investment banks that arrange financing, companies that offer commercial credit to their customers, and specialized lenders. On the left-hand side are organizations that are more oriented toward managing savings, such as mutual fund management companies, credit unions, and real estate companies. These institutions are only the main financial services providers; for every category listed there are even more specialized firms that offer more limited services along the same lines. Overall, the US system is extremely broad in the array of services offered and specialized in terms of the myriad of instruments that are tailored to individual users' needs.

Japan

As in the United States, Japan's government limited the expansion of banks, insurance companies, and stockbrokers into each other's business until the late 1990s. This situation was rather significantly different in reality, since the Japanese firms generally operated within the structure of broad industrial groups, or "keiretsu," which included one or more of each kind of financial services provider in the same group. While the keiretsu remain a dominant force in the Japanese economy, half of the city banks are now not members of a major keiretsu. The structure of the Japanese system, shown in figure 1.3, looks very much like that of the USA, and in the early twenty-first century this appearance has become more of a reality.

The Japanese financial system is based on the commercial banking core, regulated by the Bank of Japan, the Ministry of Finance, and – since the financial crisis of the 1990s – by the Financial Supervisory Agency. This system operates much like the Federal Reserve System in the USA, though with the banks typically involved in cross-ownership and control within the economic groups. The "city banks," with nationwide branch networks, dominate the system. Also key to the provision of financial services are the major securities firms and the deposit-taking Postal Savings system, with its 24,000 branches.

Japan went through a "Big Bang" financial deregulation process in the late 1990s such that, by the end of 1999, insurance companies were allowed to offer banking products, and banks were allowed to operate through subsidiaries in investment banking activities such as stockbrokerage and underwriting. Even with these reforms, an overhang of bad debt remains with most large financial institutions from the bursting of the financial bubble economy in 1991, so that, in the early 2000s, Japan's financial system is quite weak by industrial-country standards.

Germany

Historically, the German financial system has been much less extensive than that of the USA or Japan. In particular, since universal banks have been permitted to offer

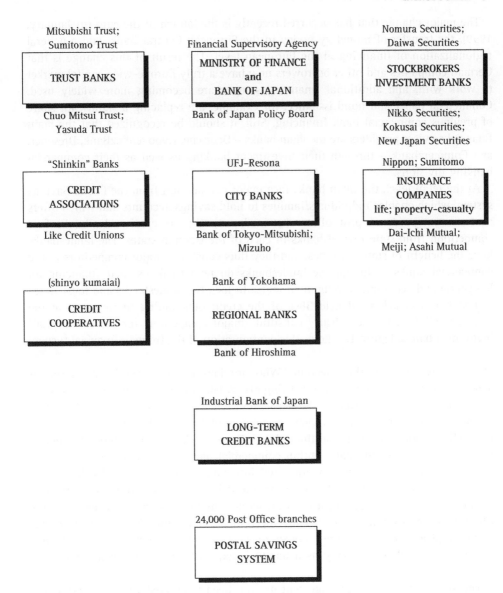

Figure 1.3 The Japanese financial system.

both commercial and investment banking products for many years, the wide range of financial institutions in those other countries is not repeated in Germany. Additionally, with banks allowed to own shares in commercial and industrial companies, the financing needs of some of the major borrowers tend to be serviced by related banks. In overall terms, bank financing provided the vast majority of credit in the German system at the end of the 1990s.

The major change that has occurred recently is the launch of the euro (in January, 1999), the transfer of monetary policy to the European Central Bank, and a general regionalization of financing at the European level. The result of this change is that German companies and other borrowers now have a truly Europe-wide capital market to work with, and additional financing sources are becoming more widely used. Commercial paper and bond issuance, for example, are replacing a significant share of previous commercial bank financing. Still, it should be recognized that the main financial services providers are the main banks – Deutsche, HypovereinzBank, Dresdner, and Commerzbank – through their investment banking as well as their commercial banking divisions.

At the retail level, the main banks face major competition from the Postal Savings system, which enables individuals/families to hold savings accounts and which offers access countrywide at post offices (as in Japan). On the credit side, banks face competition from state-owned banks in each of the German states. The landesbanks have the benefit of state subsidies, and they thus constitute major competitors to the commercial banks – though the landesbanks do tend to focus their financing on long-term and economic development loans. In fact, the landesbanks and local state-owned banks (*sparkassen*) held 38% of the credit outstanding in Germany at the end of the 1990s, so they clearly constitute major competitors for the commercial/investment banks. Figure 1.4 shows this configuration of the German financial system.

Thus, the response to the question "Who provides financial services?" is that it depends greatly on which country is being discussed. While the move to globalization of financial services is well under way, and some competitors from other major financial centers are present in every major national financial market in the world, the reality is still more national than global. In the USA, insurance products remain to be integrated institutionally within commercial banks (or vice versa). Investment banking products have been incorporated into large commercial banks during the 1990s, and a number of mergers have produced financial institutions that provided both commercial and investment banking services by the year 2000. In Germany, the UK, and Japan, insurance products have been incorporated into financial institutions, though typically through the mechanism of an insurance company subsidiary owned by the same holding company as a parent bank, rather than within a commercial bank itself.

The area of investment management has not been integrated very well into either investment or commercial banking in the USA. The mutual fund companies have created a market segment which they dominate, and which the commercial banks are only now entering significantly. This is not necessarily a huge challenge, since the large banks are much larger than most mutual funds companies, so that – in principle – the banks can buy market share in the fund management segment fairly readily. It remains to be seen, however, how quickly and in what institutional structure this will happen.

The area of risk management has, just in the past few years, become an integrated field, comprising not just insurance products for life, health, property, and casualty

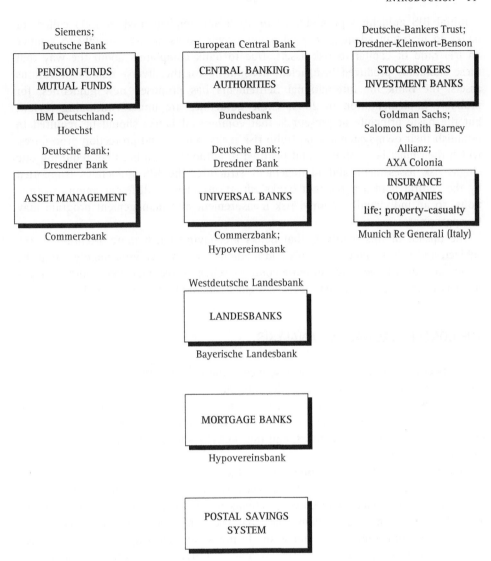

Figure 1.4 The German financial system.

risks, but also products to deal with financial market risks (interest rates and exchange rates) as well as credit market risks. Commercial banks have become greatly concerned about this subject, since the rules for prudent management that are established by national regulatory authorities (typically by central banks) are moving toward a harmonized structure under the leadership of the Bank for International Settlements. And the BIS is pursuing more flexible, risk-based guidelines for capital adequacy determination in commercial banks.

Initial BIS guidelines promulgated in 1988 and implemented in 1993 called for banks to maintain adequate capital against their assets at risk, broadly to achieve an 8% ratio of capital to risk assets. Due to bank complaints about the way that these standards produced insufficient accounting for the diverse quality of various assets, the Bank for International Settlements has proposed new guidelines, for probable implementation in 2005. These guidelines are under continuing review, but the basic principle at present is that commercial banks should be required to establish their own systematic portfolio risk measurement and protection procedures, which then must be explained and justified to authorities. Rather than requiring one single risk assessment and management structure, the BIS guidelines (supported by the central banks) agree that banks' situations may be different among institutions, so an individually tailored risk measurement and management program may be appropriate[2].

The upshot of this reality is that banks are paying much more attention to the subject, and risk management tools and methods are now evolving rapidly. From the basic value at risk measure[3], to more complex schemes, risk assessment and management is creating almost a new market segment in financial services today.

THE CONCEPTUAL BASE OF ANALYSIS

In the twenty-first century as just described, what are the characteristics of financial services providers that will enable them to survive? The building blocks for competitiveness will be labeled "competencies," following the terminology of Prahalad and Hamel[4]. Competencies are business activities that the firm carries out in a manner superior to its competitors, and thus activities that give the firm an ability to compete successfully.

In commercial banking, a competitive edge may be gained by a bank that can provide financial services more cost-effectively than its competitors, or by a bank that can get its services distributed to clients more widely than its competitors, or by a bank that can make clients feel that they are receiving more personalized service than from competitors, and so on. In investment banking, a competitive edge may be gained by a stockbroker that is able to provide less costly transactions to retail clients, or by an underwriter that is able to offer better distribution of securities to corporate clients. In insurance, a competitive edge can be gained by offering a more extensive network of affiliates to sell policies and provide claims responses. All of these advantages are examples of activities carried out by financial services providers in which one firm can establish a competency that is superior to that of its rivals.

Initially, we will look at existing competition among financial services providers, to try to discover the competencies that enable individual providers to survive and prosper. The sectors of investment and commercial banking and insurance are explored. Then attention will shift to the new environment that is evolving today, to try to anticipate the competencies that will be most important in that context.

LEGAL AND TECHNOLOGICAL SHIFTS

The financial services sector is key to the prosperity of nations, and so governments are vitally concerned with the viability of the financial system and with their abilities to impose economic policies through that system. The legal/regulatory environment surrounding the sector is therefore crucial to the strategic direction of banks, insurance companies, and other providers. And it is just this legal environment that has been undergoing radical changes in the recent past, such that competitors are being faced by major new threats from rivals – and by *reduced* limitations from regulators.

On the technology front, the Internet has brought huge changes to competition in financial services, so this mechanism, which provides a channel of distribution of financial products, a means of internal information transfer within firms, and even a new source of competition from "virtual" firms, is explored in some detail.

AN OVERVIEW OF WHAT IS TO COME

The rest of this first part of the book takes a broad perspective on the financial services sector. The next chapter looks at the globalization process that is under way in financial services. After that, the two main environmental challenges to the sector are analyzed: technology changes and regulatory changes. These conditions are the terms of reference in which financial services providers are operating.

The second part of the book looks at competition among financial services providers. First, the array of financial services providers and their relative positions in major markets are described. Next, some of these competitors are described in some more detail, and their broad strategies are sketched. Then an attempt is made to identify key competencies that have enabled financial institutions and brokers to survive and flourish in competition during the recent past. A suggested means for establishing competitive strategy is offered, the idea of Transformational Management.

The final part looks at two of the sector's key businesses – investment banking and insurance – analyzing the existing competition in each one and pointing out the features that are leading toward the future structure of the sector. This section also describes the financial instruments and structures that are defining the financial services landscape, and then looks at some specific issues in this context. One such issue is the generation of long-term investment to support capital market development worldwide. Another is the role of financial centers in the current context of electronic banking and virtual institutions. The final chapter recaps the expected changes in financial services provision that we should see in the next few years, and draws some conclusions about the direction of the sector as the twenty-first century unfolds.

NOTES

1   The three classic uses of money are:
    1   As a unit of value, to denominate all other goods and services in an economy.
    2   As a means of exchange, providing some instrument such as cash to carry out exchanges of goods and services.
    3   As a store of value, such that the money itself, or money transformed into financial instruments, can be held for future purchases.
2   The BIS capital adequacy requirements based on the 1988 agreement are listed at http://www.bis.org/publ/bcbs04a.htm. The proposed new requirements are listed at http://www.bis.org/publ/bcbs504.htm. The new requirements are expected to take effect in 2007.
3   Value at Risk is a concept developed by J. P. Morgan in the late 1980s. The basic measure is the maximum amount that a project or a company/bank can be expected to lose in 99 out of 100 periods (days). See, for example, Philippe Jorion, *Value at Risk*, 2nd edn. (New York: McGraw-Hill, 2000).
4   See C. K. Prahalad and G. Hamel, "The core competence of the corporation," *Harvard Business Review*, 68, May–June 1990.

CHAPTER 2

THE GLOBALIZATION OF FINANCIAL SERVICES

INTRODUCTION

In 1998, Citibank merged with Travelers Group to form Citigroup, a global financial services firm that was not permitted by existing law in the United States at the time[1]. In 1999, three of the largest Japanese banks (Dai-Ichi Kangyo, Fuji, and Industrial Bank of Japan) joined to form a new entity, Mizuho Group, which is by far the largest financial institution in the world. In 1998, Deutsche Bank acquired Bankers Trust, and established a full-service universal bank with bases in the USA and Germany. And at the same time more than 7,000 independent banks operated in the United States, mostly in local communities with limited geographic and service reach. Where is the world of financial services headed?

These mega-mergers are indicative of the responses of financial services providers to the challenges of operating in a world of low-cost communications, incredible computer processing power, and client awareness of services from many different markets around the world. The thousands of local banks still operating in the USA (and similarly in Germany and in Japan) are also indicative of the retail pressures that require decidedly local and personalized service in some segments of the total market. We are unquestionably experiencing a two-directional path of financial services provision, which may in fact leave the way open to many local, small, but inter-connected institutions in the future, alongside a small number of huge megabanks that have global clients and compete aggressively for market share. One necessary step toward understanding the direction of financial services provision in the future is to understand the impact of globalization on this business.

The financial services industry comprises a wide range of financial intermediaries and institutions, from commercial banks to insurance companies, from investment banks to real estate investment companies. Technology was the principal driver of change in the financial services sector in the 1990s, as the process of deregulation largely was in the 1980s. It could be argued that the lack of regulatory intervention today also plays a tremendously important role, and this logic would not be wrong

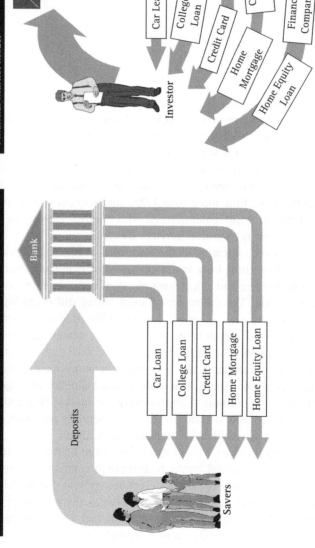

Figure 2.1 Banks versus nonbanks.

– but the emphasis would be misplaced. It remains that the dramatic changes in technology, from banking on the Internet to global real-time trading in financial instruments, are defining the direction of financial services in the early twenty-first century.

The time horizon considered in the present analysis is from now to the year 2008. The conditions and trends in financial services that are discussed below either exist already today, or they are imminent during the next four or five years. This time frame is consistent with the strategic planning horizon used by many large banks and other corporations, and it enables the analysis both to extrapolate current industry trends and to take some degree of futuristic license toward anticipating the conditions ahead.

The process of change that brought US financial services to the current situation began in 1977, when Merrill Lynch launched its money market fund and Cash Management Account. This innovation offered investors (or quasi-depositors) the opportunity to put their money into short-term money market instruments that earned money-market interest rates, along with gaining access to the funds through a checkbook that functioned exactly as with access to a traditional bank deposit. At that time, commercial banks were not paying interest on checking accounts and were limited to a maximum of $5^{1}/_{4}$% per year interest on savings accounts[2]. This phenomenon, and similar efforts that soon followed from other investment banks, as well as the reactions of the Federal Reserve and other US regulators, pulled the US financial system into a new constellation of instruments and participants. The change is depicted in figure 2.1[3].

Note that the fundamental process of passing savings into investment has not changed, but the means for carrying out this process have multiplied enormously. Funds have passed out of the commercial banking system to the point at which less than one-fourth of US financial assets are held in commercial banks; and, similarly, less than one-fourth of credit extended in the US economy goes through commercial bank credit instruments today[4]. This dramatic shift, or process of *disintermediation*, still has not fully played out in the US financial system, and it is well under way in other countries as well.

In Germany, the process of change had much more to do with European economic integration than with domestic regulation and competition among banks and brokers. In fact, in Germany it has been legal since the 1950s for commercial banks and investment banks/stockbrokers to be part of the same organization. And, as a result, the German financial services sector was dominated by the Big Three banks[5] – Deutsche, Dresdner, and Commerzbank – so that change was not as rapid as in more widely competitive countries. (It is difficult for Americans to see this point, since US banks were until 1994 prohibited from setting up branches through the whole country, and were limited to one state, or to a handful of multi-state regional banking areas. Banks in most other countries have been free to operate nationwide, and German banks have done so for many decades.)

The main factor that is pushing German financial services toward globalization is the establishment of trans-European competitors within the European Union (EU).

The combination of deregulation in several countries, along with the creation of the European Monetary Union (EMU) at the beginning of 1999, has pushed banks, brokers, insurance companies, and so on, to operate regionwide and to offer a broad range of financial services. Thus, moves such as the acquisition by Hongkong Bank of CCF (of France) and Banco Santander's acquisition of Banco Totta & Accores (of Portugal) are stimulating the German banks to become more global.

And, of course, the acquisition of Bankers Trust by Deutsche Bank in 1998 gave Deutsche a global presence immediately. This is not to say that the German banks failed to offer global service before – all of the Big Three were present through branches and representative offices in much of the world, and through correspondent relationships in the rest. However, now the emphasis is on major presence and direct offering of broad financial services in multiple countries, within the EU and even more widely.

In Japan, the driving force for globalization has been the decade-long recession of the 1990s, which caused the failure of some institutions (e.g., Hokkaido Takushoku Bank, Yamaichi Securities, Nippon Credit Bank, and Sanyo Securities) and the significant restructuring of the sector as a result of the Financial Reconstruction Commission (Japan's equivalent of the US Resolution Trust Company) buying bad loans from major banks and demanding recapitalization and management reforms in return. By 2003, the Japanese banking system had been transformed into a handful of enormous financial institutions, merged and acquired from the greatly debilitated original banks. These include Mizuho (Dai-Ichi Kangyo Bank + Fuji Bank + Industrial Bank of Japan), Mitsubishi Tokyo Financial (Bank of Tokyo + Mitsubishi Bank + Nippon Trust Bank), Sumitomo Mitsui (Sumitomo Bank + Sakura Bank), United Financial of Japan (Sanwa Bank + Tokai Bank + Toyo Trust Bank), and Resona (Daiwa Bank + Asahi Bank).

These phenomena have produced an openness of the Japanese financial system to foreign participation, with results such as the purchase of Long-Term Credit Bank by US-based Ripplewood Holdings, that of Tokyo Sowa Bank by US-based Asia Recovery Fund, and that of Nikko Securities by Citibank. Nevertheless, the Japanese banking system is the most inward-looking and largely anti-foreign among those of the industrial countries.

Even before the economic crisis had taken hold, the Japanese government began a process of opening the sector to greater competition. In 1993, the banking rules were changed to allow commercial banks and investment banks (but not stockbrokers) to be part of the same organization. This produced a wave of consolidations between these two subsectors – though, realistically, most of the changes were mergers of investment and commercial banks that were previously members of the same keiretsu. The real globalization, separate from domestic deregulation, has just begun in the past few years.

The discussion to this point has described some of the structural changes that have occurred in recent years in three major national financial markets. In all three of these countries, as well as elsewhere in the world, the globalization of financial services has advanced dramatically in the past decade due to the technology revolution. The general aspects of this revolution are the continually expanding capabilities of small computers to perform greater tasks more efficiently and less expensively, along with the equally continuing series of advances in telecommunications, such that information can be transferred among locations rapidly and inexpensively. The specific aspect of this revolution is the use of the Internet to carry out both internal and external activities of financial services providers. Here, we describe the main elements of this revolution's impact on financial services, and then in chapter 3 we look at the subject in more detail.

FUNDAMENTAL TECHNOLOGICAL FACTORS

There are three fundamental technological shifts that are defining the competitive landscape of the early twenty-first century in financial services provision. First and foremost is **distributed service provision**. This term refers to the fact that both deposit-taking and credit provision – as well as financial advising, insurance sales, and other services – are becoming more and more dispersed geographically, with less and less need for service providers and service users to meet face to face. From loans on the phone to Internet shopping[6] to automatic teller machines, simple financial services are being provided along with many other products, through increasingly numerous and ingenious methods. The principal enabling technology is advanced telecommunications, which allows for operation of widely dispersed automatic teller machines, videoconferencing, and Internet operations.

Visa International already provides a service (Visa Interactive) to member commercial banks through which they can use the VisaNet transaction processing network. This access allows the member bank to offer clients the ability to pay bills through the network, to inquire about their account balances, to transfer funds through the network, and to use e-mail for communications. The idea of this service is to try to capture part of the market for electronic bill paying, without having existing bank customers look to outside providers of this service (such as telephone companies)[7].

Internet-based bill paying, funds transfer, and other account access is already a reality in the United Kingdom, through the service called First Direct, offered by Hongkong Bank. In the USA, over 1,000 banks are offering various Internet-based services, but the vast majority are waiting for a more conclusive resolution to the problem of guaranteeing security in Internet transactions before developing transaction services. The waiting period may be over before this study comes into print but, regardless of the exact timing, Internet banking transactions will become a reality and a significant force in bank activity within the next year or two in most industrial countries and in many emerging markets[8].

A perhaps less obvious aspect of Internet-based transactions is that they may be carried out instantaneously (or within a few seconds, after inter-bank verifications are completed), without any float of funds. This means that banks are finding another intrusion into their use of float, which has historically been a major source of funds in the banking system. Without the one or two days – or sometimes even a week – allowed to banks to clear payments, clients obtain much more rapid access to their funds, while banks lose those funds from their repertoire of financing sources. This pressure has been growing for years, and the banks will find that float becomes almost nonexistent in the twenty-first century. This implies, of course, that other means will be needed to generate the funding and income that are lost from this source.

Another impact of the increasingly more electronic means of financial services provision is that the new distribution methods make it less important for banks to maintain offices in numerous locations, and that there is thus excess capacity in the banking market. Simultaneously, the cost-saving nature of the new technology produces a need for banks to realize greater economies of scale to benefit optimally from their ATMs, videoconferencing, and Internet/intranet facilities. Both of these factors have led to pressure for consolidation of the banking systems worldwide, especially in the USA[9].

While the emphasis here is on the technological advances, it should not be forgotten that the basic products being produced and sold are essentially loans, deposits, insurance policies, and so on. If we identify services such as deposits and securities transactions as commodities, then it becomes more obvious that the terrain on which the competitive battle is taking place is one in which *marketing* is crucial, and in which customer service will become an even greater part of the package. This simply follows the trends in automobiles, consumer electronics, and even traditional commodity businesses. The telecommunications advances allow financial services providers to achieve higher levels of service to clients, even though the underlying products do not change fundamentally. These advances also help reduce labor costs, allowing banks and other providers of financial services to improve their efficiency ratios.

The second huge technological change that is under way concerns internal **management information systems**. Financial institutions are now able to put relevant data from all affiliates and activities into real-time accessible form. This means that loans booked in Singapore in yen can be included instantly in the bank's global records, and be instantly known to decision-makers throughout the organization. When constructed and managed properly, this information system provides a powerful tool to decentralized organizations for the purposes of managing risks, as well as informing each part of the organization about the activities of the whole.

A global management information system can enable a bank or other financial services provider to arbitrage interest rate and exchange rate differences between locations, thus lowering the firm's cost of funds and raising returns. It can also potentially enable the firm to avoid unsupervised speculation by its traders (except for fraudulent transactions), since the firm's position in any market, currency, or instrument will be readily observable.

In a more mundane context, the management information system can allow the bank to keep closer track of customer relationships around the world. In this way, a customer can receive optimal service from the bank/institution, since all appropriate employees are able to see the full relationship in the record. As large banks move to service major clients on a global or regional basis, this ability of all bank managers to know the details of the bank's relationships with such clients will become increasingly important as a decision-making device. In sum, the ability of the bank can be greatly extended to observe and intervene in the activities of far-flung affiliates.

The third technological change is **financial engineering**. This shift is not constituted by new machinery or necessarily new software but, rather, by the design of new financial instruments that provide services tailored to the needs of clients. These instruments, such as options, futures, and swaps, offer clients the ability to hedge against unexpected changes in interest rates, exchange rates, and prices. Additional financial innovations include instruments for producing credit or liquidity, such as financing facilities (RUFs, NIFs) and derivative instruments such as depositary receipts (ADRs, GDRs). None of these instruments is "high-tech" in the sense of requiring advanced electronic equipment for its production, but all of them are quite high-tech in providing up-to-date hedging/financing services to clients. The development of new financial products has progressed to the point at which the instruments listed above are now considered "plain vanilla," and many more complex instruments, such as swaptions, multi-currency financing facilities, and others, are being introduced at an extremely rapid pace[10].

The credit or liquidity-producing instruments in particular are enabling the global interconnection of savers and borrowers at a very rapid speed and with very low intermediation costs. Issues of American Depositary Receipts alone have enabled non-US borrowers to gain direct access to investors in the US market, such that in 2000 alone $US 29.5 billion of funding was provided. This linkage both reduces costs of financing for the non-US borrowers over alternative sources of funds and expands the investment opportunities to US investors, such that they can diversify their portfolios more globally. This instrument, along with Global Depositary Receipts (typically issued in London) and other innovations, will bring capital markets into much greater integration over the next five years.

This final technology is the most widely discussed of the three, since the instruments themselves are visible on a day-to-day basis to clients and banks alike, and they have led in some cases to spectacular risk-taking and losses (e.g., in 1995, the demise of Barings Ltd. from trading in futures on the Nikkei 225, the 10-year Japanese government bond, and three-month euroyen; the huge losses and market manipulation at Sumitomo Bank in trading copper futures in 1996; the losses of Procter & Gamble that were produced in interest rate swap contracts with Bankers Trust and ultimately absorbed by that bank in 1994; and the demise of Long-Term Capital Management and the loss of more that $US 4 billion by its shareholders due to speculation on the difference between bonds and bond futures prices in 1998).

In spite of the small number of catastrophic failures, financial engineering in a systemic context allows market participants to share risks according to the parties that are best able to bear them, thus improving efficiency of the market. Large banks are actively pursuing this business as a noncredit service and, as shown below, such business is growing faster than traditional credit activity. Because of the sometimes insufficient ability of financial institutions to ensure prudent behavior of all of their employees, institution-crashing risks still may be incurred – so there is room for increased supervision of financial services providers to try to reduce the occurrence of this behavior.

All three of the kinds of technology change described here contribute to the globalization of financial services by breaking down borders to movements of information and funds. These changes are not international but global, since they do not recognize national borders in the first place. This is a particularly challenging concern of national governments that want to supervise if not regulate the activities of the financial services providers operating within their borders.

IMPLICATIONS OF REGULATORY CHANGE

Several likely outcomes emerge from the process of deregulation that has spread around the world during the past decade and a half. For one thing, capital markets are much more exposed to speculative movements of funds. As countries such as Mexico and South Korea open their markets to foreign investors, foreign portfolio managers are moving – and have moved – more of their funds into such investments, to improve their total portfolio performance. This investment is at once increasing the size of the emerging capital markets and raising the risk of massive capital flight from them in times of instability or loss of confidence. Thus the technological changes that enable investors to move funds more easily, coupled with the deregulation of financial markets that opens opportunities for new investment, paradoxically make emerging markets more risky rather than less, other factors being equal. The 1997 Asian financial crisis demonstrated this reality quite starkly.

Of course, other factors will not remain equal. One major change will be in government policies, to try to hold on to the foreign capital that supports market growth. The way to keep foreign (and domestic) capital satisfied and not subject to speculative outflows is fundamentally to operate a stable and growing economy with transparent regulation and a minimum of surprising policy shifts. To produce this kind of environment, governments will be forced to follow more "traditional" or "neoliberal" monetary and fiscal policies and policies toward foreign investors. The net result is that the combination of policy and technology conditions presses very heavily on governments to follow the rest of the world in maintaining open borders and in aiming at a low-inflation, balanced-budget (or low-deficit) growth path. If a government tries to avoid this convergence, technology allows saver/investors to move their funds fairly readily into more attractive environments.

This reality already exists, and it is evidenced by the problems of governments in industrial countries such as Canada, which needs to improve its budgetary situation relative to that of the USA in order to lower its interest rates and compete for funds with users in the USA. Spain is an excellent example in which the effort to achieve convergence with the most stable EU countries was followed very emphatically in the run-up to EMU; and today Spain's interest rates and government budget deficit are very similar to those of Germany, The Netherlands, and other previously more stable EMU countries.

Perhaps this point is better illustrated at present by the situation in Venezuela, the only medium-sized or large Latin American country that has *not* embarked on a path of sustained economic opening and fiscal conservatism. Venezuela has, since 1990, been the odd man out in Latin America, as a result of its on-again/off-again program of foreign exchange market opening (and closing), privatization of state-owned enterprises (and reversal of such plans), and other liberalization measures that have been reduced or reversed. As a result, the economy has suffered continued capital flight and deep economic recession. The unwillingness or inability of the government to move to a policy regime that is consistent with those of the main players in the rest of the hemisphere has taken a huge toll on the country and continues to do so.

Possibly the most striking outcome of the global deregulation process and techno-logical advances is the growth of global stockholding and issuance. It is now possible for firms from many, if not most, emerging markets to issue shares on the New York or London Stock Exchange and to attract investors from around the world. This globalization does not mean that any firm from an emerging market now has access to global capital markets – by far the preponderance of emerging market firms do not and will not attract investment from the institutional investors who buy ADRs and GDRs. However, the larger and more successful local firms from Indonesia to Peru are able to finance some of their capital needs through direct access to industrial country investors[11]. ADR issues by Latin American borrowers grew significantly during the 1990s, from just a handful of programs in 1990 to almost 100 total programs by 1999. In 2000, Latin American borrowers issued new ADRs worth $US 6.3 billion[12].

The regulatory impacts above relate to the globalization of financial activity. There are also major impacts on the global expansion of financial services providers. In most countries, there still remain some kinds of limitation on foreign institutions. Even within the EU, national governments are imposing or trying to impose restrictions on foreign takeovers of domestic banks, brokers, and insurance companies. The 1999 example of Portugal's effort to disallow the takeover of Champalimaud by Banco Santander Central Hispano from Spain is only one of many such instances. It appears that the barriers are coming down, but the reality still is that most consolidations are within-country in the EU rather than between countries. Obviously, this situation is poised to change dramatically once the first few major cross-border M&A deals are accomplished.

THE IMPLICATIONS FOR COMMERCIAL BANKS

There is an ongoing process of consolidation of large commercial banks in the USA due to the spread of nationwide banking (relaxation of the McFadden Act and the Bank Holding Company Act), and in Europe due to the EU's opening of the commercial banking sector among the member countries, as well as worldwide due to greater deregulation of the sector. This process is causing the number of large banks to decline, as mergers and acquisitions take place. The process certainly will not lead

Table 2.1   The 20 likely multinational banking survivors in the year 2006

No.	Bank	Country
1	ABN Amro Bank	The Netherlands
2	Bank of America	USA
3	Bank of Montreal	Canada
4	Bank of Tokyo-Mitsubishi	Japan
5	Banque National de Paris (BNP) Paribas	France
6	Barclays Bank	UK
7	Canadian Imperial Bank of Commerce	Canada
8	Citibank	USA
9	Commerzbank	Germany
10	Credit Suisse	Switzerland
11	Dai-Ichi Kangyo Bank (Mizuho Group)	Japan
12	Deutsche Bank	Germany
13	Goldman Sachs	USA
14	Hongkong Bank (HSBC)	UK
15	Industrial & Commercial Bank of China	China
16	J. P. Morgan Chase Bank	USA
17	Lloyds TSB Bank	UK
18	Merrill Lynch	USA
19	Royal Bank of Canada	Canada
20	United Bank of Switzerland	Switzerland

This table is based on current bank size, international scope of activities, competitiveness, and home country bank market size and its competitiveness. Compiled by the author.

to the concentration of all banking activity in a few hands by the end of our time frame, but the number of truly large and international competitors may indeed drop to less than 20 institutions. Table 2.1 suggests the list of 20 multinational competitors that are expected to be competing in many countries and market segments in the year 2006.

At the same time as the large banks fight to be members of this exclusive club, there will be hundreds or even thousands of niche providers that survive and even thrive right beside the mega-banks. This is evident in the process of consolidation in the USA, though perhaps most noticeable in the divergence of large banks from community banks. The providers of particular services such as home loans or trade financing or foreign exchange trading may become much fewer in number, but as technology changes these providers also may be shaken out and replaced by newcomers or more adaptable existing competitors.

The one underlying attribute of commercial banks that assures their survival as financial services providers is their ability to offer government-backed insurance on deposits. Without this guarantee, there would be nothing fundamental to separate commercial banks from their nonbank rivals. Whether banks would offer adequate

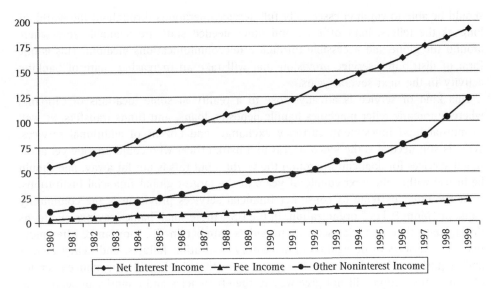

Figure 2.2   The net income of US commercial banks, 1980–99 (in $US billions).
Source: FDIC, http://www2.fdic.gov/qbp/qbp.cfm?report=%2F

service to attract clients from other providers would be an empirical question. Under the current and probable future rules, government-backed deposit insurance will continue to justify the existence of commercial banks.

Lest bankers feel too complacent based on this last point, it also needs to be recognized that the way in which banking services will be provided is shifting more and more to electronic media, and away from people. The employment trend alone supports this logic, and it implies that bankers will need to develop skills that differentiate themselves from machines. Clearly, personalized service is the principal differentiator, so banks more and more will be seeking personnel with such a capacity.

Even with deposit insurance, commercial banks are seeing their percentage of total financial assets in the USA decline, to less than one-fourth of the total today. This trend, which may stabilize, implies a need for the banks to seek out additional kinds of business more aggressively. A quick review of bank activity in the past few years indicates that banks indeed recognize this need, and in fact many are moving to replace interest-based earnings (mainly the margin between lending and deposit-taking) with *fee-based services*. These services range from money management, funds transfer, and foreign exchange, to credit analysis and funds placement. Figure 2.2 shows this trend among US banks.

When considering the **consumer** segment of financial services provision, it is not hard to see the reality of 24 hour per day service provision for a wide range of activities beyond the automatic teller deposits and withdrawals. For example, through Internet transactions, most financial services will be available anywhere at any time of day. And through videoconferencing, banks and other financial services providers should be able to conduct essentially full-service operations throughout the world, as long as the tellers, loan officers, and other needed staff are available somewhere around the globe and accessible through a telecommunications medium. This is one form of distributed service provision that will take an increasing share of banking activity in the next several years.

This kind of service is already close to a reality at some locations of Citibank, where automatic teller machines handle deposits, loans, and funds transfers, as well as mutual fund investment, currency exchange, and dozens of additional services. What is still needed is the video-access to a bank officer who could provide yet additional services for application around the world – but this is not far away, and should be in use within the next couple of years in the largest global financial institutions.

At the other extreme of consumer financial services provision is the community bank, or "Mom & Pop" organization. In the USA these small banks, savings and loans (S&L), and other financial services providers number in the thousands, after more than two decades of deregulation, depository institution failures, and heavy merger and acquisition (M&A) activity. It appears clear that the highly personalized service of a local institution will not give way to the efficiencies and quantity of services of the mega-banks. And so the horizon of financial services provision, in the USA at least, appears to hold continued opportunity for the small provider, with successfully differentiated service provision based on knowing the customer and providing easy-access, high-quality interaction between the retail customer and the bank[13]. In this way, banking services will be distributed via small community banks, at the same time as these services are being provided by large banks through electronic media.

From both of these kinds of institution, global and local, it is likely that we will see the provision of new services such as "smart cards," credit card lookalikes that are actually charged with cash in limited amounts. A smart card can be used to make purchases from locations where reader machines are available, without exposing the card user to risk of having mistakes made in his or her bank account or having any kind of electronic thievery take place. The smart card, once it is charged, operates independent of a bank account. The card may be charged by debiting a bank account or by exchanging cash or another means of exchange for it. Once charged, the smart card is effectively plastic cash, whose value declines as purchases are made with it. The limit at present to this technology is the low availability of machines that can read the cards. Heavy promotion of the cards at the Atlanta Olympic Games by Visa was expected to provide a stimulus for rapid growth of smart card use in the United States, but that step had still not advanced five years later[14]. This outcome in the USA appears to be due to various competitors' efforts to build the market using incompatible technologies, as well as some consumer resistance to the instrument. In Europe, the opposite is true. Smart cards have proven quite attractive, with widespread availability of card-reading machines and vendors willing to accept such payments.

At the **wholesale** level of commercial banking, there is no question that the trend is toward declining numbers of large-scale providers. The number of very large banks in the USA has been steadily declining since the early 1980s, and there is no end in sight to this process. There could easily be a half dozen fully national banks by the year 2005, with another 20 or so super-regional banks that serve large multi-state portions of the country without being completely national. This would leave the other 100–200 large regional banks in limbo, with the tendency to see them either absorbed into the very large competitors, or allied among themselves to achieve economies of scale and be able to respond to the threat of the super-regionals and money center banks – or forced out of the market.

Since the process of bank realignment is not one that occurs overnight, it is quite possible that the outcome will be a continuation of the fairly steady erosion of the number of banks. From 1980 to 1999, the number of commercial banks in the USA fell from more than 14,000 to just over 8,000[15]. Those that remain fall more and more clearly into the two ends of the spectrum.

THE IMPLICATIONS FOR INVESTMENT BANKS

The new environment facing investment banks in the early 2000s holds a challenge of rapidly increasing competition, from investment banks in emerging markets, from commercial banks entering the field, and from other financial services providers that are permitted to enter this segment of financial services. With respect to distributed financial services, the investment banks work heavily through electronic means, with far fewer physical offices than their commercial banking counterparts. This reality implies that the investment banks will be more rapid to implement the electronic means for handling assets and liabilities and financial information for retail clients, since they have less direct exposure to these clients than do the commercial banks. We see this phenomenon taking shape in the USA through the multi-purpose accounts (e.g., Financial Management Account; Cash Management Account) that clients can use via telephone or Internet to buy and sell securities as well as to pay bills and hold funds in interest-bearing accounts.

The function of **stockbroking** in investment banks already has been attacked, first by discount brokers, then by commercial banks offering discount brokerage service, and now by Internet-based brokers such as E*Trade and Ameritrade. As early as 1983, the Federal Reserve permitted Bank of America to acquire Charles Schwab discount brokerage[16]. This strategy has been followed by an increasing number of super-regional and money center banks during the past decade, and of course is now completely open with the repeal of the Glass–Steagall Act in 1999.

The function of **underwriting** was initially attacked by a few commercial banks such as Morgan Guaranty (later renamed J. P. Morgan), which was able to obtain permission to function as primary issue underwriter for bond issues. In subsequent years, the specific entry into this market segment was allowed to Citibank and Morgan Guaranty in 1987, when they requested permission to underwrite and deal in commercial paper issues. This permission was extended to all types of debt and equity securities in 1989, when Morgan Guaranty was given authorization to underwrite a large bond issue[17]. Then the floodgates were opened completely with the Financial Services Modernization Act of 1999.

The function of **portfolio management** has long ago been entered and dominated by portfolio management companies in the USA, especially those that sell mutual funds, such as Vanguard and Fidelity. Nevertheless, the investment banks in the USA are active in this segment of financial services, though their positions are under attack now by commercial banks as well.

Outside of the USA, the phenomenon of commercial banks fighting for stock-brokerage business or underwriting opportunities has been far more common, since most countries operate some kind of universal banking rules, rather than fully separating the two services. Many countries – such as Japan, Colombia, and Spain, among many others – require that investment banking activity be segregated into one legal entity in a bank holding company, while commercial lending and deposit-taking must be segregated into another.

The competition among banks in European countries is producing a consolidation reasonably analogous to that in the USA by the early 2000s. One key difference is that each country in Europe has relatively few full-service commercial banks – typically 15 or 20 in total (with many more branches of course), in contrast to the US population of almost 8,000 banks. Nevertheless, the consolidation is taking place, generally within countries rather than across borders. For example, in Spain, the eight large banks in 1986 have become three large banks in 2000, with mergers of Banco Central with Banco Hispanoamericano, and then with Banco Santander (which earlier acquired Banesto) and Banco Bilbao with Banco Vizcaya, and subsequently with Argentaria. In addition, investment banks have combined with commercial banks, such that today each of the commercial banks owns an investment bank. Likewise in the UK, the number of British commercial banks declined from 171 in 1992 to 42 in 2000; and in France, the number of domestic banks declined from 300 in 1992 to 172 in 2000. The story is similar throughout Europe, with fewer major commercial banks in each country than the number from ten years ago, and with a trend to even more consolidation[18].

THE IMPLICATIONS FOR INSURANCE COMPANIES

In the march to globalization of financial services, insurance companies are surely the endangered species. With their relatively standardized products and their glacial response to the changing environment, these financial services providers stand to lose the most in the new context. Not only can online providers offer the same products much more efficiently, but even the commercial banks and perhaps other distributed-service firms can duplicate the insurers' large numbers of agents and offer wider service in addition. It is clear that insurers will have to move into other financial services or die.

Looking at the life insurance part of this sector, the picture could not be clearer. Life insurance policies are largely standardized, with term life insurance having become the standard in many countries including the USA. The "whole life" policies that require policyholders to invest more than the death benefit related premium function like portfolio investments offered by mutual funds and some banks. This kind of instrument has become relatively unattractive in the past two decades, as other providers have offered more desirable instruments for portfolio investment. The insurance companies could in principle respond by improving these investment management products, but thus far they have not done so successfully in terms of building market share. The net result is that life insurance is a commodity service that will be offered by banks in the newly opened US environment, and which already is offered as a segment of "*allfinanz*" providers in many countries.

The property insurance segment is less commoditized, but it also is subject to invasion by banks and other service providers who are allowed to offer such risk-management tools. That is, property insurance depends to some extent on property characteristics that may be highly nonstandardized – but the provision of such policies is not complex, and can be added to a set of financial services offered by other kinds of providers. The inexorable trend is toward marginalization of the insurance-only providers.

An interesting example of this problem and a possible solution is the German company, Allianz. This company is the third largest insurer in the world after AXA from France and Nippon Life from Japan. Allianz has decided, in the ongoing tempest of financial services consolidation in Europe, that it needs to build a major presence in multiple financial services. To go beyond its shareholdings in Deutsche Bank and Dresdner Bank in the late 1990s, Allianz attempted to build a jointly owned retail banking network through Germany along with these two allies. Given the failure of a proposed Deutsche–Dresdner merger in early 2000, Allianz shifted its gears and moved to acquire the three-fourths of Dresdner Bank that it did not already own, and now is aiming at global competition in full-range financial services provision. Allianz saw clearly the need to offer services beyond insurance, since that base alone will not be adequate for survival in the new environment.

Other segments of the insurance sector do offer some product diversification, but still inadequate for competing against more widely diversified firms. The annuity business was originally in the domain of insurance products, but such instruments have now been copied by commercial and investment banks to the point at which annuities are just one more investment product. The reinsurance business may turn out to be a viable segment of the sector that is not subject to intrusion by commercial and investment banks. However, even here, the new providers of "risk management" services may tear away this segment as well. Given that insurance is only one means of protecting against various business risks, the providers of a variety of risk management products (such as insurance policies, futures, and options) may add reinsurance to their portfolios of instruments sold in the market.

The process of virtualization of the insurance sector in the USA will continue to be slowed by the fact that regulation of the sector is imposed by individual states. This means that insurance rules differ somewhat between many states, and that single policies cannot fit all applications at present. This barrier will prove transient, since the ability of virtual insurance providers to reduce costs and add alternatives to clients will inexorably push regulators to harmonize their rules.

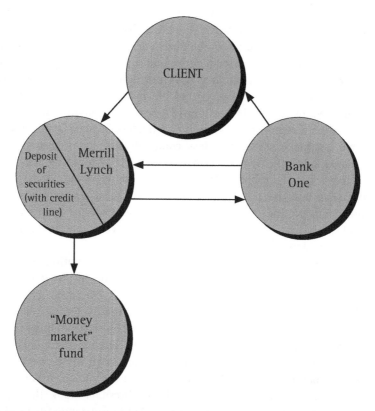

Figure 2.3   The "CMA" account of Merrill Lynch. (Goal: establish the firm as leader in the retail financial market throughout the entire USA.)

THE OVERALL PICTURE

In terms of a picture of financial services provision at the beginning of the twenty-first century, figure 1.1 gives an indication of the main participants and activities involved.

This figure shows that the two sides of credit-giving and deposit-taking remain the linchpins of financial services, with funds transfer, risk management, and asset management and advising constituting additional key pieces of the puzzle. More and more firms from other industries are entering and will enter various segments of the financial services sector, so that the net result will be a frequently changing constellation of service providers.

The instruments used to provide the various financial services are changing as well, with many competitors for traditional bank deposits. For example, the quasi-deposits that were innovated by Merrill Lynch in the late 1970s – that is, money market funds – have become severe competitors to traditional deposits. Figure 2.3

shows this innovation. This instrument alone has led to disintermediation of former bank-managed funds in the United States at the level of $US 1.845 trillion by year-end 2000[19]. In addition, the development of "smart cards" to replace cash may soon produce a wave of movement into that instrument – it has already done so in Europe, but not yet in the USA. Likewise, the growth of payment means through the Internet will certainly shift a large amount of deposit-type activity to that medium.

In terms of moving funds between buyer and seller, or saver and borrower, the instruments are rapidly expanding beyond wire transfer and checks. The use of checks may easily be driven down to almost nothing as a result of debit cards, Internet transfers, and more alternatives for carrying out wire transfers. Indeed, checks themselves could become obsolete in a period of between 10 and 20 more years, though not in our time frame before the year 2008.

Referring finally to the credit extension vehicles listed in figure 2.2, it is very easy to imagine a point at which traditional bank loans are marginalized by the direct extension of credit from savers to borrowers through commercial paper issue, commercial firm credit card balances, and other "financing facilities" that have quasi-loan characteristics but are not structured as bank loans. This tendency does not necessarily leave out the commercial banks, which can enter the market for the new instruments and serve as intermediaries (and/or underwriters) just as other competitors may do. However, it does mean that traditional bank loans will have to become more competitive in their terms and flexibility to match the convenience of the other credit facilities. (This, of course, has happened in the recent past, as US domestic loans have become closely comparable to unrestricted euroloans – as competition forces banks to offer these conditions or lose business.)

At the global level, the number of financial services providers is expected to decline due to the pressures for consolidation to achieve economies of scale in producing and delivering the services. The technology-driven innovations in telecommunications and data processing in many cases can best be utilized in large organizations, across which the costs can be distributed. At the same time, the fact that monetary policy takes place through banks requires that national governments maintain control as much as possible over their banking systems. This fact will lead to government protection of domestic banks to some degree, so that Citigroup or Deutsche Bank has no chance of achieving global dominance of the kind realized by IBM in computers during the 1960s and 1970s, or Microsoft in computer operating systems and business software in the 1990s. There will be "national champions" everywhere, in addition to the competitively determined global banks.

By the same token, in countries such as the United States, there is great room for entry by foreign banks to acquire US banks and to build competitive networks that may challenge Citigroup and Bank of America in all types of services and all across the nation. It would not be at all surprising to see Barclays Bank acquire a large US financial institution, as has Deutsche Bank with Bankers Trust, or for Hongkong Bank to expand beyond its acquisitions of Marine Midland Bank and Republic Bank of New York into other US banks. By the year 2005, it is very likely that half a dozen foreign financial institutions will be among the 30 largest US commercial banking firms.

Within the USA, bank functions will continue to be eroded as nonbank firms find it in their interest to enter segments such as credit extension (e.g., General Motors Acceptance Corporation and General Electric Capital Corporation, two of the largest lenders in the country today). The Federal Reserve has demonstrated a strong commitment to allowing market forces to determine the direction of financial services provision, so it appears certain that banks will face more severe competition and thus have a greater need to fall back on their secure base of offering insured deposits, plus their abilities to offer either differentiated services or less expensive ones due to their abilities to achieve economies of scale.

The trends in technology essentially allow for more convenience to savers and borrowers around the world. The challenge to commercial banks is to offer competitive services that can respond to the innovations of investment banks, insurance companies, and even commercial firms that are entering the financial markets with their own instruments and services. The challenge for all of the financial services providers is to keep up with the technological changes that will continue to offer new means for capturing savings, transferring funds, and making credit available.

FURTHER READING

Baig, Edward 1997: Your friendly banker, the Web. *BusinessWeek*, May 12, pp. 150–1.

Freeman, Andrew 1996: Technology in finance. *The Economist*, London, October 26.

Hannan, Timothy, and Rhoades, Stephen 1992: Future US banking structure: 1990–2010. *The Antitrust Bulletin*, Fall, pp. 737–832.

Javetski, Bill, and Glasgall, William 1994: Borderless finance: fuel for growth. *BusinessWeek*, November 18, pp. 40–50.

Lee, Peter 1996: Eat or be eaten. *Euromoney*, August, pp. 28–34.

Pearlstein, Steven, and Knight, Jerry 1993: Banks lose out as depositors go elsewhere. *The Washington Post*, August 22, pp. A1ff.

Shull, Bernard 1994: Banking and commerce in the United States. *Journal of Banking and Finance*, January, pp. 255–70.

Smith, Roy C., and Walter, Ingo 1997: *Global Banking*. New York: Oxford University Press.

Spiegel, John, Gart, Alan, and Gart, Steven 1995: *Banking Redefined*. Burr Ridge, Ill.: Irwin.

Sutton, Brent, and Glorieux, Guy 1992: The future of financial services: industry and regulator perspectives. Report #89–92. Toronto: The Conference Board of Canada.

Swary, Itzhak, and Topf, Barry 1992: *Global Financial Deregulation*. New York: Blackwell.

NOTES

Thanks to Sangit Rawlley and Xiaoyan Wang for their excellent research assistance in the development of this chapter.

1   That is, Citibank and Travelers Group received conditional approval to merge, subject to subsequent divestiture of the insurance business if US law had not changed within two years of the approval.

2   Through Regulation Q, the Fed established maximum interest rates on bank deposits of less than $US 100,000 (and on deposits in S&L associations, which were permitted to pay $1/4$% higher rates than the banks). During the late 1970s, a 5% interest rate was often below the rate of inflation (due to the oil crisis). In 1980, the US Congress passed legislation to reduce the limitations on commercial banks in this competition with nonbanks. Banks were subsequently allowed to pay market interest rates, and thus to compete better with the money market funds. Banks still could not offer clients the ability to invest in securities as their stockbroker competitors could.

3   The author acknowledges a similar figure that inspired figure 2.1; the prior figure appeared in Steven Pearlstein and Jerry Knight, "Banks lose out as depositors go elsewhere," *The Washington Post*, August 22, 1993, p. A1.

4   Based on Federal Reserve "Flow of Funds" tables, *Federal Reserve Bulletin* (various issues).

5   They have become the Big Four banks, with the merger of two major banks to form HypoVereinsbank in 2000.

6   Gary Silverman, "The mixed blessings of online banking," *BusinessWeek*, May 10, 1999, p. 114.

7   Although banks are also forming strategic alliances with telephone companies to provide this service. See, for example, "Telecoms and banks tie the knot," *BusinessWeek*, March 13, 2000, p. 140E2.

8   Paul Beckett, "Online banking: Will it click?" *Wall Street Journal*, January 21, 2000, p. C1. See also William Schaff, "CheckFree Holdings Corp," *Informationweek*, March 20, 2000, pp. 146-7.

9   Paradoxically, there was an *increase* in the number of bank branches in the United States consistently in the 1990s, at the same time as the number of banking organizations is declining. The argument here projects a decline in the number of branches as well.

10   Financial innovations are described in many recent publications. A leading text on the subject is: John Hull, *Options, Futures, and Other Derivatives*, 4th edn. (Englewood Cliffs, NJ: Prentice-Hall, 1999). Another useful one is Philip McBride Johnson, *Derivatives: A Manager's Guide to the World's Most Powerful Financial Instruments* (New York: McGraw-Hill, 1999).

11   This is not to ignore the issues of eurobonds and Yankee bonds by emerging market firms, which likewise grew dramatically in the 1990s.

12   ADR data from Bank of New York at http://www.banofny.com. In 2000, Telmex made a secondary offering of $US 1.7 billion, and Grupo Televisa also issued GDRs worth $US 1.1 billion in another secondary offering. See http://www.citibank.com/corpbank/adr/.

13   Many people, especially senior citizens, like the individual attention and specialization available from the small community banks. As this segment of the market grows in the United States, greater opportunities will arise for these small banks.

14   Visa, along with NationsBank, Wachovia, and First Union Bank, provided smart card service in and around Atlanta for the summer 1996 Olympic Games. See IntelliSeek for Business, "Prepaid Card Products," July 1995, S-12.

15   This does not mean that the number of bank *offices* will decline, but just the number of independent banks. Additional branches may be established, though this analysis argues that there will be more automatic teller locations, as the smaller number of banks try to position themselves to offer maximum service to clients. The number of branches may actually rise if stockbroker and insurance agency locations are merged into banks as universal banking offices.

16   Federal Reserve Board of Governors, "Order approving acquisition of retail discount brokerage firm," *Federal Reserve Bulletin*, February 1983, pp. 105–17.

17   See Bernard Shull, "Banking and commerce in the United States," *Journal of Banking and Finance*, January 1994, pp. 255–70, for a discussion of this issue and relevant citations of the laws and rules involved.

18   These numbers are collected from the France and UK sections of Economist Intelligence Unit, *Financing Foreign Operations*, 1993, and from the *Thomson Bank Directory* for 2000.

19   *Federal Reserve Bulletin*, January 2001, Table 1.21. See also http://www.ici.org/aboutfunds/money_market_faqs.html.

CHAPTER 3

THE VIRTUALIZATION OF FINANCIAL SERVICES

INTRODUCTION

The financial services sector is, like quite a few others, an industry that has been dramatically affected by the explosion of Internet services since the mid-1990s. From deposit-taking and lending on the Internet, to stock trading, to provision of huge quantities of current financial information, to supermarket-type selling of insurance policies, to the introduction of new financial services, the Internet is transforming this sector. The transformation is especially striking in the context of such a (historically) highly regulated business, which stores the wealth of societies and provides the payment system for business transactions.

The present chapter looks at the ways in which the Internet (along with reductions in regulatory barriers) has changed and is changing the landscape of financial services provision. The scope of the analysis is broad – considering traditional commercial banking functions such as deposit-taking, lending, and funds transfer, plus investment banking activities such as trading of financial instruments and funding arrangements, and insurance products. This is generally called "*allfinanz*,"[1] but due to regulatory differences, the legal structures of institutions are somewhat different across countries. The scope of countries considered is largely limited to North America, Europe, and Japan, but emerging markets in Latin America and Asia are also discussed.

The Internet has already produced a new and rapidly growing structure in investment banking, with more than one-third of the stock trading in the United States passing through electronic brokerage accounts by mid-1999. While electronic-only intermediaries such as Ameritrade and E*Trade have taken huge chunks of this business, the no-frills brokerages such as Charles Schwab have built large Internet-based services, and even Merrill Lynch has now joined the online brokerage business[2]. At the international level, the ability of firms from around the world to put their funding requests (e.g., solicitations for bond issues or for global equity offerings) on line makes it that much more likely that the long-term capital market will continue the integration process linking savers and investors across national borders[3].

In commercial banking, the electronic-only services such as Net.B@nk and Security First Network Bank have built up substantial customer bases, but the traditional banks that have set up Internet divisions (e.g., Bank One with Wingspan.com and Hongkong Bank with FirstDirect.com) have vastly more online customers. Of course, if one considers electronic banking versus use of branches with human employees, the picture is much more striking – by far the majority of commercial banking today is done through electronic means, whether it be automatic paycheck depositing, obtaining cash through automatic teller machines, or making retail purchases with debit cards[4].

The main product/service area that will permit a major expansion of Internet-based banking is provision of the payments mechanism for electronic commerce. The initial steps were taken in the late 1990s, but even in 2000 the amount of purchasing done over the Internet using electronic means such as credit cards or account transfers ($US 190 billion in 2000; $US 590 billion in 2002) was still small relative to payments through other means. The concerns of safety in passing account information and privacy in the use of financial information were substantial barriers to the growth of an Internet channel for carrying out payments for e-commerce at that time. Both of these concerns are likely to be resolved in the near future, so that banks and other intermediaries will be able to offer payments mechanisms to e-commerce participants on a much more extensive basis. This one service will probably become the most significant kind of financial service provided through the Internet in the near future.

The lines of virtual competition have not become clear at all in universal banking and more broadly in *allfinanz* at this point. The E*Trade online brokerage firm now operates the Telebanc (which it bought in 2000) commercial banking service on the Internet, along with LoansDirect mortgage lending (acquired in 2001), and thus has become a broad virtual service provider (minus insurance thus far). This situation is changing almost daily, especially as firms such as Citigroup and Hongkong Bank move into greater service provision on the Internet.

The introduction of *new* services on the Internet is a phenomenon that remains to be developed, but which likely will affect the competitive landscape enormously in the next decade. The new services appear likely to come from bundling existing services that have been previously available only from multiple sources, but the territory is relatively uncharted at this point. (For example, the bundling of quotations from a variety of financial services providers has produced the new service of "aggregating," in which firms such as LendingTree.com and Quotesmith.com operate.)

In addition to the external services that institutions provide to their clients, the Internet has greatly altered the internal information systems that banks and other intermediaries are able to use. Financial services providers now are able to operate internal information systems that allow any point in the firm's network of affiliates and locations to obtain information about any activity of the entire firm, from client information to internal controls to performance comparisons among affiliates. This is

not very different from the situation in other sectors, but it bears careful considera-
tion, because some of the internal processes that financial institutions carry out may
very well be better done through outsourcing – as many institutions have done with
check clearing and other back-office operations.

One aspect of the nature of financial services provision that likely will develop
much further is the use of strategic alliances for providing a greater array of services
across the spectrum of universal banking. Banks that do not merge with stockbrokers
or insurance companies will certainly link up with them to provide online access for
their clients to a more extensive array of services. The banking sector has historically
been very active in alliances, from correspondent banking relationships around the
world to the common use of two major credit cards, Visa and MasterCard, to shared
networks of automatic tellers in regions, nations, and even globally.

The impacts of the technological changes are felt not only by competitors in the
financial markets, but also by the regulators. In this highly regulated sector, the rules
of financial services provision are under heavy pressure for change – to permit the
provision of more efficient services and to supervise the providers. Commentary on
the regulatory situation and changes that are under way is offered briefly here, and
then given in more detail in the next chapter.

The rest of this chapter is structured as follows. First, an analysis of the limitations
and opportunities of virtual financial services is presented, to give a perspective on
the way in which such electronic services have changed and may change the competition in financial services. Next, a commentary on the extent of virtualization in
banking in several parts of the world is presented. The empirical evidence on the
global scope of financial services virtualization is followed by a discussion of how
the sector can assign some activities to centralized hub operations and disperse
others to market locations. This strategy may achieve the benefits of virtualization
and diminish the negative impacts where costs or client resistance make electronic
services uncompetitive. And, finally, the direction of competition in global financial
services is sketched as an extension of the kinds of strategies that are observed.

LIMITS AND OPPORTUNITIES FOR VIRTUALIZATION OF FINANCIAL SERVICES

In the heat of the debate about whether or not the Internet is going to replace "bricks
and mortar" financial institutions, it is helpful to sit back and reflect on what
features of the Internet do indeed offer a competitive or preferable means of providing
financial services, and what features create barriers to service provision.

First of all, it has to be recognized that the Internet is not a new financial service
but, rather, a channel of distribution (within financial institutions, as well as between
financial services providers and their clients and suppliers). This reality is often
missed in popular discussions of how the Internet is going to replace banks or
insurance companies. The Internet makes it possible for more agile institutions to
offer more customer-friendly services and more economical services, due to its rapid

Table 3.1   Strengths and weaknesses of Internet-based financial services

Strengths	Examples
Low cost	Internal management information systems (SAP); stockbroker accounts are very active
Rapid delivery	Retail funds-transfer transactions
High-capacity information storage	Client and internal any time, anywhere access
Weaknesses	*Examples*
Lack of personal client interaction	Most bank clients have not embraced Internet banking thus far
Lack of visibility in target market	Attracting clients requires a large marketing cost
Potential legal restrictions	Some governments do, or want to, restrict Internet financial transactions
Lack of client trust in virtual financial service security	Account information may be leaked; Internet transactions may fail if the server goes down, the phone line is lost, and so on

operation and its extremely low cost. But it does not replace the need for clients to interact with financial intermediaries, except in the extreme cases where borrowers and lenders can connect through the Internet, and realize direct transactions without intermediation.

The key to understanding the Internet's impact on financial services comes from comparing what it can and cannot do for clients. For example, the Internet cannot offer the same level of face-to-face service that a banker can – even though in principle the Internet-transmitted, electronically stored information might be superior to that offered by a single human being. The Internet cannot offer the same level of trust as the bricks-and-mortar bank – and this trust is at the heart of financial services. On the other hand, the Internet can certainly enable clients to reduce their costs of obtaining many financial services, as long as the services are able to be carried out electronically. Table 3.1 shows the major strengths and weaknesses of Internet-based financial services provision.

An absolutely fundamental concern of Internet-based financial services provision is **trust**. This trust is multi-layered, having to do not only with clients' trust in the safety of transferring financial information on the Internet, but also with their trust in a virtual institution that has no visible means of support. It is dramatically easier to convince clients to trust an Internet-based deposit or withdrawal of funds from a "real" bank account, as compared with a deposit account at a virtual bank, where there is no obvious physical place either to have recourse in the case of nonperformance or to talk with someone in the event of any problem. The basic issue of trust is fundamental to any financial institution, which must convince clients that it can be counted on to deliver services as promised and to safeguard the client's wealth; the Internet only compounds this problem[5].

The problem of trust can be subdivided into two categories: trust in the use of the Internet for financial transactions; and trust in the reliability of the service supplier

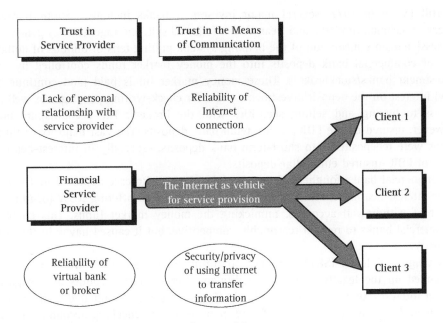

Figure 3.1   Trust in Internet financial services provision.

to deliver as contracted. Trust in the Internet as a delivery vehicle in turn has two components: first, the doubts that people have about the security of using the Internet to transfer financial information without having it escape to unauthorized parties; and second, the doubts that people have about the ability to successfully carry out Internet transactions without having problems such as a service provider's Internet server going down, or the client's phone line being lost momentarily, or the client's computer having some problem – any of which could lose all or part of a transaction in progress. Trust in the reliability of the service provider to deliver also has two components. First, there is concern about the credibility of a financial services provider that has no visible means of support (which seems to be *the* main source of resistance to retail Internet-only banking today). And, second, the lack of any personal links between the service provider and the client disallows the personal trust between human beings that is generated with face-to-face contacts. Dealing with each of these concerns is a necessary condition for financial services providers to build business on the Internet (see figure 3.1).

CURRENT SUPPLY CHAINS OF FINANCIAL SERVICES

The United States

In the USA, the financial services sector has undergone several revolutions during the past 25 years. Beginning with the launching of a money market mutual fund by

Merrill Lynch in 1977, several major investment banks including Smith Barney, Shearson Lehman Brothers, and Dean Witter followed suit, and together they generated a massive disintermediation of the banking system, pulling tens of billions of dollars out of commercial bank deposits into the money market funds controlled by the investment banks/stockbrokers. These money market funds paid (and continue to pay) interest on the deposit/investment, and offer check-writing privileges as well as access to buying and selling securities with the brokers. The accounts are not, however, insured by the FDIC, as are retail bank deposits. The vast majority of these funds were redeposited into short-term bank deposits, especially in interest-bearing but not FDIC-insured eurodollar deposits.

Commercial banks fought back by obtaining Federal Reserve approval in 1980 to offer interest-bearing checking accounts. They then began offering NOW (negotiable order of withdrawal) accounts, mimicking the money market funds. This enabled commercial banks to remain reasonably competitive, but it caused havoc in the S&L industry.

Savings and loans (S&L) were not so fortunate, in that their whole existence depended on the legally mandated ability to offer savings accounts at a slightly higher interest rate than commercial banks (5$\frac{1}{2}$% per year, as compared with 5$\frac{1}{4}$% at the time). Once the banks began offering interest-bearing checking accounts, and no longer faced the $\frac{1}{4}$% interest rate disadvantage, the whole S&L system became nonviable. Within three years a massive wave of S&L failures and mergers and acquisitions by banks began, ultimately costing US taxpayers a bail-out cost estimated at over $US 90 billion[6].

Banks lost additional ground when stockbrokers began offering financing facilities and commercial paper and other credit structures that knocked out bank loans. Indeed, by the end of the 1990s, banks only accounted for a little more than 20% of credit offered in the USA, as shown in table 3.2.

The total number of banks in the USA has dropped from more than 14,000 in the 1980s to about 8,000 in the year 2002. Most of the banks that have disappeared were small ones that were overwhelmed by pressures to merge and grow, or even large ones that were merged into yet larger ones. Changes in the rules that permitted first regional interstate banking (in 1990) and eventually full nationwide banking (in 1994) produced a handful of truly national commercial banks (e.g., Citibank, J. P. Morgan Chase, Bank One, and Bank of America) and another handful of very large regional or specialized banks (e.g., First Union, Deutsche–Bankers Trust, and Wells Fargo). Even with this trend at the national level, there appears to be room for the "Mom & Pop" type small community bank, that offers limited but personalized services in small geographic areas.

Internet-based banking in the United States was a reality by the end of the 1990s, despite initial concerns about security of the electronic transactions involved. (Thus far, it has turned out that the Internet banking transactions have had no more problems than use of automatic tellers in terms of either errors or hacking into accounts.) The number of banks offering Internet-based transactions in the USA was only 376 by the end of 2002, according to the Federal Deposit Insurance Corporation,

Table 3.2 Relative shares of total financial intermediary assets, 1960–2001

	1960	1970	1980	1990	1995	2000	2001
Insurance companies							
Life insurance	0.1964	0.1427	0.1053	0.1115	0.1145	0.0924	0.0910
Property and casualty	0.0288	0.0252	0.0338	0.0338	0.0338	0.0242	0.0227
Pension funds							
Private	0.0366	0.0299	0.0414	0.0482	0.0517	0.0333	0.0317
Public (state and local government)	0.0351	0.0405	0.0402	0.0432	0.0383	0.0383	0.0346
Finance companies	0.0452	0.0446	0.0491	0.0463	0.0380	0.0404	0.0370
Mutual funds							
Stock and bond	0.0037	0.0047	0.0047	0.0354	0.0556	0.0522	0.0537
Money market	0.0000	0.0000	0.0115	0.0365	0.0393	0.0614	0.0674
Depository institutions (banks)							
Commercial banks	0.3714	0.3720	0.3526	0.2725	0.2539	0.2379	0.2285
Savings & loans and mutual savings	0.1938	0.1935	0.1976	0.1156	0.0659	0.0517	0.0496
Credit unions	0.0084	0.0124	0.0145	0.0164	0.0190	0.0180	0.0185
Asset-backed securities							
Federally related mortgage pools	0.0004	0.0039	0.0312	0.1002	0.1133	0.1184	0.1241
Asset-backed security issuers	0.0000	0.0000	0.0000	0.0248	0.0471	0.0762	0.0827
Other	0.0802	0.1305	0.1182	0.1154	0.1296	0.1555	0.1587
Total percentage	100%	100%	100%	100%	100%	100%	100%
Total financial sector debt ($US billion)	537.7	1,223.8	3,658.1	10,174.5	13,863.9	21,040.1	22,807.4

Source: Board of Governors of the Federal Reserve System, Flow of Funds Accounts (Total Credit Market Assets).

while about 40% of all US banks and thrifts had websites and offered some degree of Internet banking information.

Insurance policy provision had been segregated into a separate industry since the Depression, and has only been allowed to banks and brokers since 1999. After years of proposals and debate among commercial banking interests, insurance companies, and investment banks, the US Congress was finally able to pass legislation that eliminated the Glass–Steagall barrier to combining investment and commercial banking, and allowed insurance policies to be provided under the same holding company as well[7]. The insurance industry remains regulated by individual US states, but the ownership of insurance companies is now permitted to national or global commercial and investment banking organizations.

There were just over 5,000 insurance companies in the USA in 2002, of which about two-thirds were involved in selling property/casualty policies and one-third were in life/health insurance. The major competitors are fairly split between property/casualty (State Farm, AIG, Allstate) and life/health (Prudential, Metropolitan, TIAA–CREF) insurance. Both kinds of insurance are sold at the retail level, and both kinds of companies have extensive agent networks. In 2000, in the USA and in Europe, there was only one major insurance company that offered policy sales on line in each region. The European exception was Prudential, which operated the Internet bank called Egg, that sold both banking and insurance services on the web. The US exception was Lincoln Life, which marketed discount products over the Internet.

Europe

In European countries, the division between commercial and investment banking has not been as strict as in the USA, and financial institutions have provided universal banking services for many years. In fact, the financial conglomerates in most European countries have followed the commercial banking + stockbroking + insurance, or *allfinanz*, model since before the 1990s. Throughout Europe, it has also been common for banking institutions to own shares of industrial companies, and even to exercise decision-making authority in those companies. For example, the largest shareholders in Daimler Benz are Deutsche Bank (with 12% of outstanding shares) and the Kingdom of Kuwait (7%); and in BASF, German banks and insurance companies own 55% of the firm's outstanding shares. In France, the same kind of model has existed for many years; today, the key shareholders of Renault include the French government and three large banks; in St. Gobain, they include the Banque National de Paris and the AXA insurance company; and in Alcatel they include the Société Générale banking group.

This industrial structure is less common in the United Kingdom, where industrial groups tend to be separate from financial ones, and banks are involved almost exclusively in financial services investments. That is, in the UK, the universal banking model is followed, with Barclays, Lloyds TSB, Hongkong Bank, and other smaller institutions providing the full range of services. Industrial shareholdings are permitted under the EU's Second Banking Directive (up to 15% of the bank's primary capital may be invested in an individual firm, and up to 60% in total), but still the industrial groups with their captive or preferred financial institutions have not developed as in most of continental Europe.

In the UK, electronic banking has been stimulated by the traditional banks' slow response to technology that permits faster and cheaper transaction processing and more efficient service provision in general. To protect their margins, traditional banks have not moved rapidly into online services, other than offering clients account accessing through the Internet. As a result, the online banking subsidiary of the Prudential life insurance company, called Egg, gathered 22% of new bank deposits in 1999[8]. And MBNA bank from the USA took a major share of credit card business from the local banks by offering lower transaction charges (and specializing in this niche market). This same kind of process is occurring throughout the European Union as well.

There have been different rates of change in the USA and Europe, where for example debit cards have been much more widely and quickly accepted, and where the number of financial services providers is much smaller. The Internet is causing cross-border consolidation of the European sector much faster than it would have from just following the process of European monetary integration. Because the national stock markets have already been found inadequate in a financially open EU, the electronic stock trading is now being centralized in London and Frankfurt, along with the part of securities trading that is going through online-only brokers.

Internet-based brokerage in Europe at the beginning of the decade is far behind that in the United States. The largest online broker in Europe in 2001 was the German firm Comdirect, A.G., with just over half a million accounts, followed by ConSors, A.G., with a similar number of accounts. In the UK, the Charles Schwab affiliate led all others by a wide margin in 2001. Overall in Europe, it was estimated that about 3.3 million online broker accounts existed in early 2001[9], compared with over 20 million in the USA.

In another area of investment banking, namely underwriting, Internet-based public offerings are now taking significant market share. In 2000, Deutsche Bank claimed to be selling about 10% of its equity offerings on line[10]. This is a potentially very large market segment that may become virtualized in the near future in the USA as well. As long as new equity and debt issues can be presented in a sufficiently standardized format and with adequate information to potential investors, then high-quality issuers should be able to find investors through Internet-based issuance essentially immediately. This, of course, will reduce the margins earned by investment banks on such issues, and simultaneously greatly expand the exposure of issuers to a broader array of investors.

Internet-based banking in Europe at the end of the 1990s was still less than in the United States. Even with Hongkong Bank's First Direct virtual bank, the volume of Internet-based banking in European countries was quite limited in the year 2000. Certainly this situation is poised for rapid change, as use of the Internet grows in Europe, but the reality is that the initial push into Internet-based banking is still occurring more rapidly and extensively in the USA.

The major multinational insurance providers, AXA and Allianz, were doing very little via the Internet by the year 2000. AXA had announced a joint venture with Woolwich Ltd. to provide AXA's insurance and investment management products along with Woolwich banking services in the UK. Allianz had not unveiled any Internet-based insurance program by the end of 2000. The firm was actively pursuing global expansion of insurance affiliates, and growth of its funds management business, but the Internet was not being used as a major vehicle for marketing Allianz services.

In emerging markets

In emerging markets, the spread of Internet-based banking is much slower than in any of the industrialized countries or regions. With much less-developed banking systems and services overall, the arrival and spread of the Internet has proceeded much more slowly – except for banks' internal use of the Internet for passing information between branches and the home office, and generally for internal management of banking activities.

In Chile, for example, the first significant provider of Internet-based commercial banking services at the end of the 1990s was T-bank, an affiliate of Banco de Crédito e Inversiones. By the end of that decade, Banco Santander and a few others were also offering Internet access to bank services for their clients. In all of these cases, the services were primarily account information and some simple transactional activities such as moving funds from one instrument to another for the same client[11].

In India and China, with state-owned banks dominating the financial system, Internet-based banking was almost nonexistent at the turn of the century. In India, HDFC Bank and ICICI Bank were exceptions to the rule. As private-sector banks, they were more agile than their public-sector rivals, and both had begun to offer clients access to financial services through the telephone and the Internet. Nevertheless, this electronic provision of services lags far behind what is found in the industrial countries. Likewise, in China the four main state-owned banks were entering into Internet-based service provision in 2000, but the number of potential clients with access to Internet service was extremely limited. Publicly traded China Merchants Bank announced in mid-2000 that it expected to carry out more than $US 50 billion of transactions over the Internet for the year, almost all for corporate clients rather than retail accounts. These numbers are quite small relative to the levels of activity in Western European countries, North America, and Japan.

MODELS OF VIRTUAL BANKING

There are two basic categories of virtual banking: the first is the replication of existing bank services through electronic means such as the telephone and the Internet; the second is the creation of new services that are offered in virtual form without having been offered previously through the traditional bank outlets.

One example of the latter category is the Citibank virtual branch, which was tried in Singapore but not introduced worldwide. This virtual branch acted as the combination of an automatic teller machine with fairly sophisticated options that allowed clients to utilize their accounts for depositing, bill paying, transferring funds, and so on, plus a videoconference-based live bank officer, who could serve many client locations from one central location, to assist clients with more complicated transactions. The use of interactive video enabled Citibank to offer a "real" person to deal with such issues, while still conserving office space and machinery, by just transporting the bank manager through interactive video to the client locations[12].

Examples of the first model of virtual banking (viz., replication of existing services) include all of the more than 1,000 US banks' web pages that offer some degree of access to the bank via the Internet. In some cases this includes the ability to carry out transactions, but in most cases it is just an information source.

When the cost of the same deposit or withdrawal to the bank is on the order of $1.03 for each transaction carried out by a live bank employee, versus $0.01 doing it through the Internet, the logic is clear for pushing greater Internet banking. This is just a continuation of the trend toward use of automatic teller machines and telephone-based bank transactions, which the banks discovered to be likewise much less expensive than the live ones (on the order of $0.07 per transaction in the same study carried out by the New York Federal Reserve Bank in 1999)[13].

At this point in the development of electronic banking, the enormous potential savings from the low transactions costs have been largely eroded by the costs of promoting the Internet-based services and the costs of employing real people to handle client questions and client problems that arise with Internet communications, from bank servers that go down to home computers that lose power or lose ISP connections.

It is clear that the main approach taken by financial institutions for their virtual banking activities is to reproduce services that are already offered through real offices or through automatic tellers and just to use the Internet as an additional delivery vehicle. Given the transition costs of setting up Internet service programming, assigning responsibilities, controls, and so on, this is not unexpected. Still, in a world moving at the speed of the Internet, it is highly likely that new services will be introduced quite rapidly once the basic infrastructure is in place.

Perhaps the most logical direction of this expansion will be the provision of complementary services through the Internet. In *allfinanz* institutions, the logic should be to provide bank deposits, transfers, and so on, side by side with securities transactions, asset management, and insurance product sales from the various divisions of the institution. By the year 2002 this was not yet a reality in any major way, although institutions such as Deutsche Bank, Citigroup, Hongkong Bank, and others were developing exactly such services.

This idea of providing a portfolio of services is one way for the institution to avoid being pulled into a cutthroat competition for standardized services, in which margins could easily be driven down to unprofitable levels. No doubt this exact problem will occur for many banks, as their more rapid competitors move first, and as their more diversified competitors do offer broader portfolios of services. The cost-minimizing strategy cannot prevail for too many institutions, and most will either move into broader service provision or get out of the mainstream competition and look for niche markets (e.g., client bases without easy access to the Internet – if they can be found!).

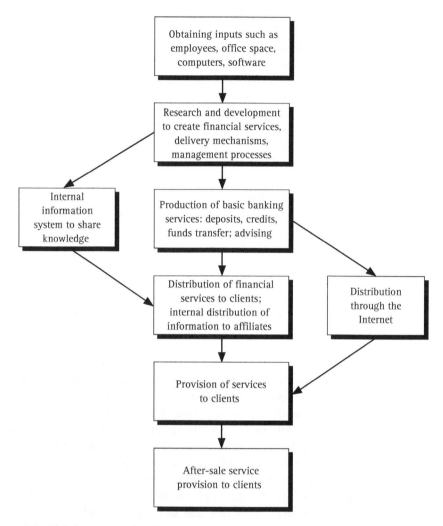

Figure 3.2   Global structures for virtual service provision.

Figure 3.2 shows a pair of configurations through which financial services providers can utilize virtual means along with "real" means to serve clients and operate internal activities to pursue competitive advantage.

A key point to recall in this discussion is that financial services providers have both wholesale and retail clients, and that much of the emphasis here has been placed on retail service provision, since that is easier to visualize for most people. If we switch to consider the *wholesale* side of commercial and investment banking and insurance provision, the issues remain the same, but the significance levels change, often dramatically. For example, a bank may offer retail services with branches and automatic tellers throughout a country to achieve full market penetration. But to achieve the same degree of wholesale service to large-scale clients, it may not be necessary to have more than one or two physical locations, plus virtual access through telephone and Internet. Citibank in Mexico, for example, operates hundreds of retail branches in every corner of the country, while only carrying out large-scale corporate lending and service provision through the Mexico City office and occasionally through one of five other branches in key major cities, including Guadalajara and Monterrey. (This was before the acquisition of Banamex in 2001.) We shall consider the wholesale side of commercial banking in a bit more detail.

CORPORATE BANKING AND THE INTERNET

In this key segment of the banking industry, major bank clients include other banks, large corporations, and government agencies. To keep the discussion relatively simple, this section just comments on the activities of major money center banks in corporate banking. In this context, the major applications of Internet technology have been in foreign exchange trading and in payment mechanisms.

The largest value of business carried out through the Internet is foreign exchange dealing. Until the past couple of years, inter-bank foreign exchange dealing (more than $US 1 trillion per day) took place through telephone transactions, often involving foreign exchange brokers. With the availability of the Internet to post bids and offers of currencies, the business has passed largely to the Internet, where banks trade directly with each other and through an Internet-based broker, Fxall. Since this business is highly impersonal and based on price quotes, the switch from telephone to Internet has been relatively smooth. Of course, the issue of security of the transactions is paramount, but the same kind of processes used to verify telephone transactions are being applied to Internet transactions.

The second major application of the Internet in corporate banking is the provision of payments mechanisms. Banks may have lost large percentages of wealth holding (as deposits have been replaced by mutual funds and other investments) and of credit extension (as bank loans are being replaced by securities issuance and other nonbank credit facilities), but they remain central to the transfer of funds and realization of payments globally.

Banks function at the center of payments for transactions, whether the payments occur through wire transfers, credit cards, or even smart cards. The major banks are looking for ways to offer their services to clients such as large business-to-business purchasing networks, in which the industrial firms arrange the computerized systems for making price quotes and product descriptions available, while the bank(s) offer the mechanism to carry out payments.

A third important area of corporate banking that is growing rapidly on the Internet is the issuance of securities. In addition to the trading of stocks and bonds, as described above, corporate issuers of securities now are finding that Internet-based issuance can allow a much wider range of potential buyers at a much lower cost of presenting the relevant information. Even so, unless the documentation is able to be standardized, stock and bond issue on the Internet will be limited to high-quality, well-known issuers and very simple securities. As one would expect, the banks are developing ways to better standardize documentation and to broaden the scope of issuers and types of issue that can be handled through the Internet.

THE GLOBAL DISTRIBUTION OF VIRTUAL FINANCIAL SERVICES ACTIVITY

When a financial services firm looks to globalize its activities, this clearly does not mean that all globally dispersed activities need to follow the virtual model. In fact, given the drawbacks of virtual service provision as shown in figure 3.1, the optimal global service structure will have to respond to mitigate those problems.

Regulatory aspects

As the facilitator of the real and the virtual economies, the financial services industry will continue to face significant regulation that limits competition to some degree among institutions worldwide. Even with this reality, however, the sector has been opened widely to more competition in the 1990s and beyond, and the number of financial services providers is declining in most countries. The survivors at the national or large-size end of the spectrum are increasingly multi-function institutions, offering insurance products as well as commercial and investment banking services. Both policies to ensure adequate prudence in banks and policies to limit monopolistic behavior of the very large institutions will continue to shape the competitive landscape in this sector.

Thus far, Internet-based banking activities have not run into severe regulatory constraints on either ground. The Internet-based banks are either operating as part of existing institutions whose overall activities are supervised by the national banking authorities, or they are very small competitors that have not yet caused any problems in the financial system. Given that the Internet is just another kind of financial mechanism that produces accounts and transactions that are either existing in nonvirtual banks, or that can be recorded in the same kinds of electronic records that banks use for existing transactions, there is no inherent problem that Internet banking should present.

The concern for privacy and protection of account information that has been raised frequently with regard to Internet banking has simply not produced any important problems thus far. Just as electronic fraud and illegal account access can occur in a physical bank, so they can also occur in a virtual bank. It does not appear that there are major additional problems being generated by this transaction structure.

CONCLUSIONS

The impact of the Internet on the financial services sector has been enormous in terms of improvement of internal efficiency in banks and other financial firms. Its impact on competition among commercial banks has been minimal, as virtual banks have gained little headway in the last five years, and well-established banks have been able to quickly attract large numbers of clients when they move to offer Internet banking.

The Internet's impact on investment banking, particularly on competition in retail stockbroking, has been much more striking. Internet-based competitors such as E*Trade have made major inroads into the customer base of traditional stockbrokers, and Internet-based trading has become the dominant form of retail stock trading in the USA at the start of the new century.

The Internet's impact on the insurance industry may be much more telling, as insurers make their policy information known on the Internet, and various services (integrators) offer customers the ability to comparison shop for the best rates. Much more important, however, has been the congressional decision in the United States to allow single financial holding companies to offer commercial bank loans and deposits, investment bank stockbroking and underwriting, and insurance policies, under the same roof. This regulatory change will very likely end the era of independent insurance companies in the USA, and may prompt a global consolidation of financial services firms. The early indications of the impact are definitely consistent with this assertion.

Internet-based financial services provision will certainly grow, and perhaps grow dramatically, in the next few years. It appears that Internet-only institutions will not replace traditional ones but, rather, that the Internet will be an increasingly important mechanism for carrying out financial transactions and for providing financial information. Table 3.3 summarizes the extent of the "virtualization" of financial services that has occurred up to now.

The kinds of competitive strategies that will succeed in this environment will require a real transformation of the financial services providers. The new reality in the USA for the next several years will require broad-scope financial services provision and maximum use of the Internet to reduce costs and make services available most widely. The new reality in Europe and Japan does not need to cross the first bridge, since universal banking has existed in those countries for quite some time. Even so, the new environment is making it more difficult for European and Japanese financial institutions to hold investments in industrial firms, and so a new financial ownership structure is very likely to develop in those countries. Figure 1.1 has presented much of the array of financial services that successful providers will have to offer their clients, directly or through strategic alliances, to succeed in the new competition.

The kinds of competitive advantages that appear likely to serve in this environment are networks of existing clients, who can utilize the new Internet-based services; scope of services, including those from all three areas of financial services; flexibility to move into the provision of services through these new and developing electronic

Table 3.3   Providers of electronic finance

Type of financial service	United States	Europe	Asia	Latin America
Online banks	Telebanc, Net.B@nk, X Bank, Wingspanbank	Egg Bank, Smile Advance Bank, Bank Girotel, Comdirect, Diba, Entrium, First E., Santander, Augsburger Aktien-bank	OUB (Singapore, to be established), Dah Sing (Hong Kong, to be established)	Banco1
Online lenders	E-Loan, Mortgage.com, NextCard, Finet, Intuit/Quicken	EuropeLoan (Belgium)		
Aggregators	InsWeb, AnswerFinancial, Lending Tree, Quotesmith.com, Intuit/Quicken	InsuranceCity (Germany), Interhyp (Germany)	DollarDEX (Singapore, Hong Kong, soon in Malaysia, Taiwan, and China), Eisland.com (Singapore), Admortgage.com (Hong Kong), e-finance.com (Hong Kong)	Dineronet (Argentina), Zonafinanciera
Online brokers	Schwab.com, E-Trade, TD Waterhouse, DU Directs, Fidelity.com, Ameritrade	Consors (Germany), Direct Anlage (Germany), Avanaz (Sweden)	Boom Securities (Hong Kong), Polaris, Kong Chen, Masterlink (Taiwan, China), Daishin, LG Sec., Samsung Securities (Korea)	Patagon (Argentina, Brazil, Chile, Mexico), Socapa Souza Barros, Novacao, Hedging Griffo, Coin Valores (Brazil), CB Capitales (Chile)

Table 3.3 (cont'd)

Type of financial service	United States	Europe	Asia	Latin America
Financial portals	Yahoo!Finance, Microsoft Network, Intuit/ Quicken, America Online, Motley Fool, TheStreet.com	eXchange Holdings (UK), bfinance (France), FTYourMoney (UK)	Quamnet, Baby Boom, asiabondports (Hong Kong), quicken/SPH (Singapore), PaxNet, Thinkpool, Net Invest (Korea), 99stock.com, stockstar.com, homeway (China)	Investshop (Brazil), Patagon Dineronet (Argentina), Zonafinanciera, LatinStocks, LatinInvestor, Consejero
Enablers	Security First (S1) Sanchez, Corrillian, Digital Insight, iXL Enterprises, Online Resources, Alltell, Bixyx, Fiserv, EDS, M&I, 724 Solutions		eBiz solutions, Finese Alliance, I-ayala, System Access, The Edge Consultancy, S1 Singapore, Ebx.com	
E-payments	CheckFree, Spectrum, CyberCash, Mondex, Cybersource, Entrust, Verisign, Intelidata, Sterline Commerce, DotsConnect, First Ecom		QSI (Australia), First Ecom (Hong Kong), V-check (Singapore)	

Source: Stijn Claessens, Thomas Glaessner, and Daniela Klingebiel, "Electronic finance: a new approach to financial sector development?" World Bank Discussion Paper 431 (World Bank, Washington, DC, 2002), p. 33.

means; and perhaps the ability to anticipate client willingness to use newly developed services that are electronic.

FURTHER READING

Allen, Franklin, McAndrews, James, and Strahan, Philip 2002: E-finance: an introduction. *Journal of Financial Services Research*, 22(1–2), pp. 5–27.

Allen, H., Hawkins, J., and Sato, S. 2001: Electronic trading and its implications for financial systems. Working paper, Bank of England, London.

Buckley, Eileen 2000: Green Revolution. *The Industry Standard*, May 15, pp. 186–94.

Camp, Jean 2000: *Trust and Risk in Internet Commerce*. Cambridge, Mass.: MIT Press.

Claessens, Stijn, Glaessner, Thomas, and Klingebiel, Daniela 2002: Electronic finance: reshaping the financial landscape around the world. *Journal of Financial Services Research*, 22(1–2), pp. 29–61.

Clark, Theodore, and Sviokla, John 2000: Security First Network Bank: the world's first Internet bank. In Christopher Westland and Theodore Clark, *Global Electronic Commerce*. Cambridge, Mass.: MIT Press.

Credit Suisse First Boston 1999: *Special Internet Banking Review*. New York.

Hunter, William C. 2001: The Internet and the commercial banking industry. In Zuhayr Mikdashi, *Financial Intermediation in the 21st Century*. New York: Palgrave, pp. 17–28.

Pyun, Chong Soo, Scruggs, Les, and Nam, Kiseok 2002: Internet banking in the US, Japan, and Europe. *Multinational Business Review*, Fall, pp. 72–81.

Rexha, Nexhmi, Kingshott, Russel, and Aw, Audrey 2003: The impact of the relational plan on adoption of electronic banking. *Journal of Services Marketing*, 17(1), pp. 53–67.

Wilhelm, William 1999: Internet investment banking: the effects of information technology on relationship banking. *Journal of Applied Corporate Finance*, Spring.

NOTES

Thanks to Xiaoyan Wang and Sangit Rawlley for their excellent research assistance on this project.

1 The combination of commercial banking, investment banking, and insurance under one corporate roof is called "*allfinanz*" in Europe, based on the German model. (It is also called "*bancassurance*" in France.) We will use this terminology as well.

2 While the Internet-based brokers took the lion's share of Internet-based stock-market trading initially, the traditional brokers had made a major comeback by 2000. By the end of the year 2000, it was estimated that the six largest traditional brokers would have more online accounts than all of the Internet-based brokers combined – though the traditional discount brokers would have twice as many as either of these groups (*BusinessWeek*, July 10, 2000, p. 58).

3 Clearly the regulatory/supervisory setting is tremendously important in this context, where potentially massive investment by savers from one jurisdiction will be made in firms located in another jurisdiction. At most, some of the key regulatory elements needed to ensure reasonably safe operation of such cross-border financial intermediation can be sketched here.

4   Still, it is interesting to note that when checks are not deposited automatically, 73% of a group of 1,200 US adults surveyed in 1999 made deposits in a branch through a (live) teller. See Paul Beckett, "Online: E*Trade joins a packed field of web bankers," *Wall Street Journal*, June 2, 1999, p. B1.

5   In a survey of 2,000 retail bank clients in ten countries, Deloitte Research found that the two characteristics most important to clients were (1) responsive service and (2) the feeling of being a valued customer. The former could be produced through electronic means, but it is unlikely that the latter could be. See *Myth vs. Reality in Financial Services* (New York: Deloitte Consulting, 2000).

6   George Steiner and John Steiner, *Business, Government and Society*, 8th edn. (New York: McGraw-Hill, 1997). A total of 747 institutions were sold or paid off by the RTC as of October 23, 1995. Total asset sales and collections were $US 392 billion. This left $US 13.7 billion of assets (book value) to be sold. The net cost to the taxpayer of the S&L debacle, as of October 23, 1995, was $US 90.1 billion.

7   These changes are embodied in the Financial Services Modernization Act of 1999.

8   This example and others concerning British banks' slow response to the new economy appear in "British Banks in the Balance," *The Economist*, July 8, 2000, pp. 75–6.

9   http://singapore.cnet.com/news/2001/01/22/20010122o.html.

10 As noted in Deloitte Research, "Year 2000 banking and securities top ten" (p. 12), at http://www.deloitte.com/industries/financial.

11 A key problem for e-commerce in general in Latin America is the distrust of electronic payments. This continues to be a problem even without moving to Internet-based payments. For example, credit cards are not widely used in the region, and payments for e-commerce purchases are often required to be made only by dollar-based credit cards, since domestic ones in each country can only assure payment in local currency.

12 Apparently, this model was not sufficiently successful to warrant a larger roll-out, and Citibank has not pursued this means of virtual banking.

13 The apparent low costs of Internet-based banking transactions are not actually as clear as it may seem. The Internet transactions alone are quite inexpensive. The costs of dealing with client questions about Internet transactions, marketing the Internet-based services, and other costs involved with operating an Internet-based service have thus far not enabled banks to achieve dramatically lower costs. And what is worse, the Internet-based competition has forced banks to lower their prices, so that margins have been reduced on these services.

4

GOVERNMENT REGULATION: THE SECOND KEY FACTOR UNDERLYING INDUSTRY STRUCTURE

In the 1990s, deregulation was clearly the watchword of financial services authorities around the world. From Latin America to Europe to the USA, major regulatory changes took place, almost all in favor of less restriction on the sector. This dramatic change was partially related to the victory of the open-market model and the demise of Soviet communism, partially to the attempts by emerging markets to escape the external debt crisis of the 1980s, and partially to the technological changes that made industrial country governments realize that competition was becoming truly global whether they liked it or not.

The end of the communist alternative produced fledgling market systems in Central Europe and the former Soviet republics. These new and liberated countries were faced with strong pressure to reverse decades of centralized decision-making and regulation. They moved, for the most part, quickly to allow private-sector banks and other institutions to participate in the national economies, and placed relatively loose restrictions on their activities. Not all of this openness produced miraculous results – plenty of crises and bankruptcies, and corruption, have occurred during the past decade under this new system. Still, the regulatory environment has been and remains relatively open, with a clear role for private-sector institutions as producers of financial services.

Emerging markets, particularly in Latin America and Asia, had lived through a "Lost Decade" in the 1980s, with huge burdens of external debt and various rounds of debt restructuring and renegotiation, until finally achieving some degree of closure in the early 1990s. Some of the debt was forgiven, much of it was restructured with longer payment terms and sometimes lower interest rates, and finally a good deal of it was converted into bonds (especially Brady bonds) or into local investment in companies (debt/equity conversion). Since the governments and government-owned companies were the main borrowers whose loans had defaulted during the 1980s, a tremendous lack of credibility developed in these institutions. The upshot of this painful process of dealing with the debt was to make the countries involved broadly more receptive to private-sector firms, including those in financial services. Thus, in Latin American countries and East Asian countries in particular, the banking sector was privatized (if it had been in state hands), and financial markets were liberalized in general.

Technological changes such as electronic banking (from extensive networks of automatic teller machines to the use of telephones for carrying out banking transactions) and Internet-based stockbrokerage, and the reduced cost of both computing and telecommunications, have also pushed forcefully against government regulation on financial services. These factors have made it more difficult for governments to restrict the provision of financial services (for example, between US states), as well as making it more logical to allow banks and brokers to offer their low-cost electronic services to a wide array of customers.

Along with this wave of deregulation and technological change came a concern for overall financial system stability that has resulted in efforts to establish capital adequacy requirements on commercial banks and demands for improved risk management by the banks[1]. This concern was clearly raised during the debt crisis of the 1980s, when several major banks from the USA were shown to have loans outstanding in several Latin American countries that had a face value of more than the value of the bank. (Citibank, for example, had almost 200% of its capital loaned in the region, with three-fourths of the total capital on loan in Brazil alone.) The concern was amplified in October 1987 with the crash of the New York Stock Exchange, which happily was resolved by massive short-term lending and an overall return of investor confidence in less than one year. Nevertheless, the fragility of the system was highlighted by the enormous loss of value that occurred in that incident, which could have led to more bankruptcies and much wider panic.

The system-wide stability was called into question again in late 1994, when Mexico's government once again encountered an exchange rate crisis that led to many bankruptcies and a wholesale failure of the nation's domestic banks, almost all of which were ultimately rescued by foreign purchasers during 1995–9. Although some analysts did call for abandoning emerging market debt and investments, this event did not lead to a regional or global crisis as in the 1980s. There was, however, just over two years later, another crisis – this time in Thailand in July 1997 – that produced more widespread investor panic and that led to crises in several neighboring countries. This latter event was followed by financial crises in Russia in August 1998 and in Brazil in January 1999, and then by the Argentine crisis at the end of 2001. Whether they were related or not, the series of crises once again led to questions about the viability of the global financial system. And this time the questions were about the viability of the open system, rather than criticisms of the earlier highly restricted national systems.

In the early years of the twenty-first century, the regulatory climate has remained largely open, with repeated calls for improved bank supervision and overall systemic safeguards, such as a lender of last resort or a global deposit insurance program. It seems reasonably clear that despite the problems that have occurred due to deregulation of financial markets, the overall benefits of greater availability and lower cost of financing, plus higher returns and lower risk of investments, have exceeded the costs of rate volatility and occasional financial crises[2]. Nevertheless, the search is on for policies and mechanisms that might reduce the frequency and severity of these crises.

The next few sections of this chapter examine the regulatory settings in several countries whose financial systems are important in the overall global system and whose experiences shed some light on both the benefits and the costs of economic opening and of open capital markets in particular.

THE UNITED STATES

In the 1990s, the USA was transformed from a highly geographically restricted banking market to one that is now nationally integrated and largely open. In addition, the country moved from strict separation of the three financial subsectors to a situation in which insurance, investment banking, and commercial banking services may now be offered within the same holding company – with some firewalls and other limits on activities between the segments, but general freedom for one institution to operate in all three areas.

Banks

Commercial bank regulation in the USA comes from the Federal Reserve system, in the case of nationally chartered banks, and from individual state authorities in the case of locally chartered institutions. In addition to the Fed's regulations, commercial banks are subject to Federal Deposit Insurance Corporation rules (for FDIC-insured banks) and additional supervision by the Controller of the Currency. The rules are generally similar across state jurisdictions, although some reporting requirements and other items make it attractive for banking institutions to choose one or another legal charter, depending on the state and the nature of the organization (for example, foreign-owned versus domestic banking firms).

Since the end of 1994, banks have been allowed to establish branches or to own other banks throughout all 50 states, whereas before that inter-state banking rules prohibited such expansion[3]. Since the end of 1999, commercial banks have been permitted to enter into insurance and investment banking, through separate subsidiaries, under the Financial Services Modernization Act of 1999 (also known as the Gramm–Leach–Bliley Act). These changes have produced more competitive intermediation in the USA, at least as measured by the loan/deposit interest rate spread, which dropped from about 4.39% in 1993 to about 3.87% in 2000[4].

Commercial banks have been permitted to enter into limited securities underwriting since 1987, when the Federal Reserve permitted Bankers Trust, Morgan Guaranty, and Citibank to underwrite municipal revenue bonds, commercial paper, and mortgage-related securities in separate subsidiaries, deriving up to 5% of their revenue from that activity. These subsidiaries were expressly permitted under Section 20 of the 1933 Banking Act, and the Federal Reserve interpreted the new activity as consistent with the rule. In 1989 the Fed expanded this authority to commercial banks in general, and to underwrite corporate debt and equity securities, still subject to the 5% limit. Later that year, the limit was raised to 10%. In 1996, the limit on Section 20 subsidiaries underwriting was raised to 25% of their gross revenues. Thus, by the time of the Gramm–Leach–Bliley Act in 1999, commercial banks already had a partially open door to this aspect of investment banking activity[5].

Perhaps surprisingly, nationally chartered commercial banks have been allowed to own insurance affiliates since 1986. In that year, the Office of the Controller of the Currency decided that "a previously overlooked section of the 1917 National Bank Act (Section 92) allowed a national bank to sell insurance anywhere under the condition that one of its branches be located in a town with less than 5000 people." In 1993 a US Court of Appeals upheld this ruling, and in 1996 the US Supreme Court reaffirmed it, forcing state legislatures to allow nationally chartered banks to sell insurance products. The upshot of this legal activity was not very striking, since banks first refrained from extensive expansion into insurance during the legal appeals processes, and ultimately did not move actively into the market even with full permission in 1996. It was estimated that banks held less than 2% of total insurance policies by 1999[6].

The main concern of regulators in the USA has been for system-wide stability during the past several years. Once the gates were opened for nationwide banking, attention has shifted toward ensuring that systemic crises such as that affecting Japan for a decade, and those in many emerging markets during the 1990s, do not hit the US system. This has led to review of FDIC insurance provisions, and a move, for instance, to consider raising insurance premiums for banks holding more risky asset portfolios.

Likewise, the regulators have moved to increase supervisory attention to bank operations, to seek to uncover problems before they result in crises, and also to pursue other goals such as to reduce the amount of money laundering that takes place through the banking system.

Investment banks

Regulation of investment banks and stockbrokers comes primarily from the Securities and Exchange Commission. Although this sector holds a very significant part of total US household savings, there is no insurance protection as in the case of FDIC insurance on commercial bank deposits. The number of major institutions competing in this sector is relatively small, and perhaps the ones that hold the bulk of household savings are "too big to fail." This hopeful view is certainly held by most people who trust their savings to the stockbrokers and investment banks, but it is untested and probably wrong. Nevertheless, since the investment banks have most of their clients' funds invested in securities issued by commercial and industrial firms, government securities, and bank deposits, there is not a concentration of risk in the investment banks themselves[7].

Regulation of these investment banks generally follows concerns of fair pricing of services (especially to smaller clients) and other issues common to all corporations in the USA. The investment banks are not subject to the rules of the Federal Reserve, since they in fact are not depositary institutions. Their basic business is finding buyers of securities to link up with corporate and other borrowers/issuers, leaving the investment banks with no client deposits on their own books. (Of course, investment banks do sell their own securities, so that some, generally small, portion of their channeling of client funds does go into their own business.)

Future regulation of investment banks in the USA does not appear to present any expected barriers to entry of domestic or foreign competitors, whether through merger of similar institutions or through diversification of commercial banks or insurance companies into investment banking. Anti-trust concerns seem to be relatively limited, given the Justice Department's lack of any action on acquisitions/mergers of large US investment banks, such as Dean Witter merging with Morgan Stanley and Smith Barney with Salomon Brothers, as well as Deutsche Bank's acquisition of Bankers Trust, UBS Warburg's acquisition of Dillon Read (and the subsequent acquisition of Paine Webber) and Dresdner Bank's acquisition of Wasserstein Perrella, among others.

Insurance companies

For insurance companies in the USA, regulation is largely imposed by the insurance commissions of the individual states, with each state's regulators allowed to establish local rules as desired (except that banks and other institutions *cannot* be kept out or restricted as owners of insurance companies). The net result of this reality is a hindrance to provision of standardized insurance policies nationwide, but no fundamental restriction on entry and exit from the sector.

Given the rules under the Financial Services Modernization Act of 1999, the insurance sector is rapidly consolidating, both from within through mergers and acquisitions and from entry by banks and stockbrokers. Huge mergers since the deregulation include Aegon's (The Netherlands) acquisition of Transamerica, Allstate's acquisitions of CAN and American Heritage Life, and AIG's acquisition of American General. Cross-sector consolidations include the merger of Citibank and Travelers, and the acquisitions by several insurers of small commercial banks or savings and loans (e.g., Metropolitan Life Insurance Company's purchase of Grand Bank, Allstate's creation of Allstate Federal Savings Bank in July 1998, and State Farm's creation of its own savings bank in May 1999).

As noted in chapter 9, the insurance sector faces a similar crisis to that in the S&L industry in the 1980s. Once the artificial legal barrier to entry by broad-scope financial services providers was eliminated, there is no justification for narrowly focused insurance companies to exist. It is the same idea as a bank that would offer only time deposits, while competitors offer a much wider array of products and services. While banks and brokers have not moved rapidly to acquire insurance companies, they have moved into offering insurance products through their own branches.

Certainly the offering of *life* insurance policies is very simple, based on actuarial benefit payout values that are equal across insurers, and thus subject to low-cost sale as with bank deposits, credit cards, and other fairly standardized financial products. Life insurance companies will only be able to survive independently if they build value-added activities in funds management (which they necessarily either do or contract out to manage their policyholders' funds)[8] or some other area.

Property/casualty insurance companies may find that their knowledge is more differentiated, and that premiums and policies are more able to be tailored to individual client needs. This reality may mean that such companies can maintain competitive positions against new entrants such as banks – but their generally smaller size makes them likely acquisition targets for banks and brokers. These insurers (such as Travelers Group and Allianz) have been more active than their life insurance counterparts in seeking to broaden their product lines to include bank and stockbroker products.

Annuities, an investment product once limited only to issue by insurance companies, have been under attack by commercial banks since the 1995 US Supreme Court ruling that state laws could not prohibit the sale of annuities by national banks (*Nationsbank* v. *Vatic*). The court ruled that both fixed and variable annuities were not substantially different from products offered by savings banks, and thus were not subject to state insurance regulators' jurisdiction. This opened a floodgate of bank issuance of annuities, to the point that within five years banks were approaching a share of about 15% of the national annuity market[9].

THE UNITED KINGDOM

Banks in the UK are supervised by the Financial Services Authority, an agency created in 1997 to oversee banks, brokers, and other financial institutions. The Authority replaced the Securities and Investments Board and then took on additional functions (from the Bank of England in 1998) as principal supervisor of commercial banks. It was given added functions as principal supervisor of insurance companies (from the Insurance Directorate of the Treasury) in 2001 as well. The rules are highly nonrestrictive, allowing domestic and foreign owners to operate *allfinanz* institutions, offering commercial and investment banking and insurance products under one roof.

The British system has been open to *allfinanz* corporate structures for many years; hence the Big Four clearing banks – Barclays, Lloyds TSB, National Westminster ("NatWest," now part of the Royal Bank of Scotland) and Midland (now fully acquired and integrated into Hongkong Bank, HSBC) – all have insurance affiliates and major commercial and investment banking businesses[10]. Indeed, these four institutions control well over half of the domestic financial market in the three areas, and they are active in other areas such as funds management, factoring, leasing, and so on. Just as in the continental European Union (EU) countries, UK banks may own shares of nonfinancial companies (up to 15% of the bank's regulatory capital in one firm and up to 60% in all such investments), thus allowing the banks to be involved with control of industrial firms[11]. Nevertheless, the major UK banks do not have a great deal of nonfinancial business diversification. Lloyds TSB owns an auto dealer/repair company (the UK-based Camden Motors). NatWest (now itself owned by the Royal Bank of Scotland) owns only financial services firms such as Coutts private bank and the Direct Line insurance company. Barclays likewise owns a controlling interest only in financial services firms, as does Hongkong Bank[12].

The greatest competition in the UK financial services sector comes in the international arena, since London serves as the financial center of Europe. In addition to bank lending and wholesale deposit-taking, London also dominates the worldwide reinsurance business and global foreign exchange trading, and it rivals Chicago in global derivatives trading. London accounts for approximately one-half of world turnover in nonlocal share trading, including both global equity issues and global depositary receipts (GDRs). It is also the market in which two-thirds of global bonds are issued and three-fourths of global bond trades take place. In the year 2000 there were more than 200 international banking institutions allowed to take domestic deposits and over 500 total foreign banks active in the London market.

The regulatory environment in London basically fosters competition and seeks to ensure prudence in managing financial wealth of clients. There are no restrictions on foreign or domestic ownership of commercial banks, or on their lending activities, other than supervisory rules on capital ratios to avoid systemic financial crisis.

Investment banking is open to competitors from any country, and in fact the leading underwriters are mostly from the USA (Goldman Sachs, Morgan Stanley, and Merrill Lynch) and continental Europe (Dresdner Kleinwort Benson, UBS Warburg, and Credit Suisse First Boston). The London-based investment banks were historically the world leaders in underwriting debt and equity issues, arranging mergers and acquisitions, and general financial advising. In the past 20 years, as the financing needs of major corporations outstripped the funding capabilities of even the largest independent investment banks, they began to be acquired by commercial banks with much larger balance sheets and hence much larger in-house financing capabilities. Given that the investment banks are not involved in deposit-taking, their regulation has been and continues to be unrestrictive.

Insurance firms are dominated by British-owned institutions – affiliates of the four clearing banks and another half-dozen major insurers. Insurance firms are major participants in investment management in the UK. Lloyd's of London is the main insurance exchange worldwide[13], and includes participation from many foreign as well as domestic insurers and investors. Because of the enormous losses at Lloyd's of London in 1997–9, supervision of the insurance sector has increased since then. Still, the sector remains highly unrestrictive, with ownership of insurance companies open to banks and other firms and investors, and with few restrictions on insurance policies. The insurance companies in the UK are the main institutional investors in the financial markets, so these firms are seen by regulators more as needing to operate prudently in this aspect of their business, rather than in insurance activity specifically.

SWITZERLAND

The Swiss banking system is dominated by the Big 2 banks, United Bank of Switzerland (UBS) and Credit Suisse. These two make up more than half of the domestic commercial and investment banking business in Switzerland. Credit Suisse is also a leader in the insurance markets, operating the country's second largest insurer, Winterthur. UBS formerly owned the second largest life insurance company, Swiss Life, but divested that interest in 1999 along with two other insurance company holdings. In 2001, UBS had no internal insurance business, but was involved in an alliance with the largest insurer, Zurich Financial Services[14].

Bank regulation in Switzerland is very unrestrictive, permitting domestic and foreign owners to own commercial and investment banks, as well as insurance companies. Despite this openness, the domestic financial markets are dominated by the Big 2, as noted above. There were no capital controls or restrictions on foreign direct investment in Switzerland in 2002.

The main focus of international financial services provision in Switzerland is in the area of private banking and asset management. The two big Swiss banks have each more than $US 800 billion under management. Foreign banks – almost all investment banks rather than commercial banks – also operate major asset management businesses in Switzerland. The long history of bank secrecy in Switzerland makes this country a very attractive target for deposits and investments of wealthy individuals and organizations.

Swiss law permits *allfinanz* organizations, and in this case the organizations are permitted to own shares in industrial companies as well as financial ones. Thus, as in Germany, large Swiss banks hold significant shares in some key industrial companies. Swiss Bank Corp. (now part of United Bank), for example, has major holdings in the Electrowatt and Fides corporations, and in 1998 invested a major share in Ace Technology of Korea. Credit Suisse, through its investment banking arm Credit Suisse First Boston, owns major interests in several high-tech companies. In addition, since the banks are world leaders in the asset management business, they hold large quantities of corporate shares in the portfolios of their clients as well.

GERMANY

The German financial system has been largely open to foreign banks since the EU called for region-wide opening for banks from any of the member countries to establish full-service operations in any other. The EU's Second Banking Directive of 1989 provided this legal basis to banking organizations incorporated within an EU member country. US banks could take advantage of this situation by setting up a subsidiary in any EU country, and thus expand on that base throughout the region. In fact, no US bank had a major presence in Germany by 2001, except for Bankers Trust, which had merged into Deutsche Bank in 1998, and Citibank, which operated several affiliates there in commercial and investment banking.

Although monetary policy has been passed to the European Central Bank, the Bundesbank (Germany's central bank) retains the function of bank supervision. That is, the decisions on money supply and interest rates are now taken by the European Central Bank (which is in fact located in Frankfurt); the Bundesbank continues to monitor bank performance and systemic stability in Germany.

Investment banking is subject only to the same kinds of rules as other business in Germany, with no specific regulation from the central bank. All of Germany's Big Four banks – Deutsche, Dresdner, Commerzbank, and Hypovereinsbank – have investment banking divisions, and they are major competitors of the foreign leaders: SBC Warburg, Merrill Lynch, Morgan Stanley, and Smith Barney.

The insurance sector is also highly unrestricted in Germany, with the domestic firm, Allianz, the industry leader, followed closely by Munich Re and the Italian firm, Generali, plus the French firm, AXA. German insurance law permits insurance companies to make direct loans to clients, to buy and hold equity in companies, and to hold deposits in commercial banks. Even with this degree of flexibility, insurance companies are not major lenders but, rather, are major institutional investors in medium and long-term securities, as elsewhere in the world. And with the *allfinanz* model permitted in Germany, the major banks all operate important insurance subsidiaries – up to the largest combination of the two sectors in the merged Allianz Dresdner Bank.

CHINA

The Chinese government has made large strides in changing rules on financial activity to allow for private-sector development of markets for financial services. The reality at the beginning of the twenty-first century is that many inadequacies remain to hinder private-sector banking, securities transactions, and insurance – but that all three areas now contain significant participation by foreign and domestic private-sector firms.

For example, the commercial banking industry is dominated by the four state-owned banks: Industrial and Commercial Bank of China, Bank of China, Agricultural Bank of China, and China Construction Bank. At the beginning of 2000 the four banks held about two-thirds of financial sector deposits and loans, and they operated 150,000 branches with 1.7 million employees. Foreign banks made up less than 3% of total financial assets in China at that time, and they focused primarily on servicing foreign company, foreign currency denominated financial needs. Some commercial banking needs in China were served by banks operating from Hong Kong, which has increasing access to the domestic Chinese financial market, though only for foreign-currency-denominated business.

Commercial banks in China may not engage in nonbank activities and may not own shares of stock in other companies. Foreign commercial banks may only operate in 24 designated cities, and in many instances they are set up as representative offices, which may only advise clients on financial services – with booking of loans and deposits required to be done at branches or subsidiaries elsewhere. Only 29 foreign banks were authorized to do renminbi-denominated business in China in 2000. The rest were limited to foreign-currency business.

Foreign-owned investment banks were limited in 2000 to dealing in international bond and equity issues of Chinese firms. They were required to operate as joint-venture partners with Chinese firms and were not permitted to offer domestic underwriting, trading, or advisory services. For both investment and commercial banks, the Chinese market will be forced to be more open as China accedes to the World Trade Organization.

Foreign insurance companies were allowed only to operate representative offices in China in 2000. Entrance into the World Trade Organization will force China to allow some greater access by foreign insurance firms to the domestic Chinese market, but it was not clear how significant this access would be.

ARGENTINA

Argentina's financial regulations opened up competition to domestic and foreign private-sector firms at the beginning of the 1990s. In 1991 the convertibility law fixed the peso to the US dollar at a rate of 1 to 1, and established a policy of complete dollarization in the sense that all money supply in Argentina was backed by US dollar reserves of the central bank. This dramatic policy shift ensured low inflation and interest rates for the decade of the 1990s. Unfortunately, it also eliminated the government's ability to use monetary policy to adjust the macroeconomy, and thus limited its ability to deal with economic slowdowns as at the beginning of the twenty-first century. The full-blown financial crisis that began at the end of 2001 led to elimination of the dollarization policy and a return to a flexible exchange rate – fortunately without major inflationary results, but unfortunately too late to stop the financial crisis.

Bank regulation is carried out by the Superintendencia de Entidades Financieras, a partially autonomous division of the central bank, and both foreign and domestic banks have faced similar regulation since the early 1990s. Commercial banks were required to maintain a minimum capital ratio of 11.5%, well above the Basle Accord requirement. A deposit insurance program was begun in 1995, with deposits of up to $US 30,000 guaranteed as of the year 2000. Banks are not permitted to own more than 12.5% of the shares of any nonfinancial company.

The two largest banks in the country remain the state-owned Banco de la Nacion and the Banco de la Provincia de Buenos Aires, both of which produce significant (subsidized) competition to the private-sector banks in most areas. Regulatory policy is fairly open, with no limits on the foreign exchange market or on interest rates that the banks may charge on loans or offer on deposits. By the end of 2000, foreign banks held well over half of the value of bank deposits and bank loans in Argentina. This became a moot point at the end of 2001, when a devaluation of the peso to three per dollar caused most banks to become insolvent, and the consequent financial crisis has left the banking system on unsure footing at the end of 2002.

Investment banks are largely divisions of the main commercial banks, since Argentina's law has long permitted the operation of *allfinanz* institutions. In addition, foreign investment banks have taken leading positions in securities brokerage, including Raymond James, Merrill Lynch, and J. P. Morgan from the USA. Regulation of the investment banks is carried out by the central bank and the Comision Nacional de Valores.

Insurance companies are permitted to be affiliates of the *allfinanz* institutions, but curiously the main competitors in both life insurance and property/casualty insurance are mostly global and local insurance companies. The Generali insurance company of Italy owns the leading insurers in both segments of the business, and other leaders include Mapfre of Spain and CAN of the USA in property/casualty and New York Life, Metropolitan Life, and Hartford Life in life insurance. The sector is regulated by the Superintendencia de Seguros de la Nacion, which imposed primarily a minimum capital requirement on firms authorized to operate there.

This summary of regulations and conditions in the financial markets of several countries gives a sense of the high degree of openness of these major markets and also of their convergence in regulatory and supervisory policies. While there remain many restrictions on financial institutions and activities around the world, the leading emerging markets and industrial countries have increasingly opened their borders to foreign-owned entities and to private-sector management of the financial sector. Table 4.1 sketches examples of the regulatory environment across a wide range of countries demonstrating the large degree of openness that exists today.

THE BASLE ACCORD ON CAPITAL ADEQUACY REQUIREMENTS

Since most of the major banks in the world today are global or at least multinational in their scope of activities, it is key to systemic security that prudent practices exist to avoid global financial crises. In other words, with the extensive webs of interconnections among large, international banks today, probably 15–20 of them are "too big to fail," and many others could cause major negative impacts on the global system if they were unable to meet their financial commitments. While the complete range of risks and possible causes of crisis cannot be fully known, some of the main risks are quite well known. Central bankers acting through the Bank for International Settlements in 1988 established a set of basic criteria for bank capital adequacy, toward the goal of ensuring systemic safety.

The 1988 Basle Accord[15] is an agreement among the central banks of the Group of 10 countries, calling for minimum capital to be held by banks in member countries to deal with foreseeable credit risks of their debtors. The fundamental base for the

Table 4.1   Rules on financial services sectors in selected countries, 2001

Country	Can commercial banks own investment banks?	Can commercial banks own shares in nonfinancial companies?	Can nonfinancial companies own commercial banks?	Is deposit insurance available?	Can banks set their interest rates freely?
Argentina	Yes	<12.5%	Yes	Yes	Spread
Brazil	Yes	Partial	n.a.	Yes	Ceiling
Canada	Yes	Yes	n.a.	Yes	n.a.
China[a]	Yes	No	Yes	n.a.	Yes/no
Czech Republic	Yes	No	Partial	Yes	n.a.
France	Yes	Yes[b]	Yes	Yes	Yes
Germany	Yes	Yes[b]	n.a.	Yes	Yes
Hong Kong	Yes	Yes	n.a.	Plan	Yes/no
India	Yes	Partial	Yes	Yes	Yes
Japan	Yes	Yes	Yes	Yes	Yes
Malaysia	n.a.	Yes	n.a.	Yes	Yes
Mexico	Yes	Yes	n.a.	Yes	Yes
Panama	n.a.	Very limited	n.a.	Yes	n.a.
Russia	Yes	Yes	Yes	n.a.	Yes
Switzerland	Yes	Yes	n.a.	n.a.	Yes
UK	Yes	Yes[b]	n.a.	Yes	Yes
USA	Yes	No	No	Yes	Yes

[a] In China, foreign financial services providers were largely excluded from domestic business in 2000. Their activities were mostly limited to foreign-currency business.
[b] The EU's Second Banking Directive permits banks to invest up to 15% of their regulatory capital in a firm, and up to 60% of capital in total.
Sources: Economist Intelligence Unit, *Country Finance* reports (various dates in 2001 and 2002).

determination of capital adequacy is the definition of "Tier 1 capital" as "equity capital and disclosed reserves," excluding all other forms of capital such as undisclosed (hidden) reserves, valuation adjustments, and even loan loss reserves. Additional capital in a Tier 2 category includes these various elements, but only up to a value equal to Tier 1 capital. The sum of the two categories of capital is then required to equal at least 8% of the risk assets of the bank.

Risk assets are defined as loans and other bank assets, weighted as to their riskiness. The 8% criterion is then applied to the sum of the risk-weighted assets. The risk categories are as follows:

0%:   (a) cash; (b) claims on central governments and central banks denominated in national currency and funded in that currency; (c) other claims on OECD central governments and central banks; (d) claims collateralized by cash of OECD central-government securities or guaranteed by OECD central governments.

20%:   (a) claims on multilateral development banks (IBRD, IADB, AsDB, AfDB, EIB) and claims guaranteed by, or collateralized by, securities issued by such banks; (b) claims on banks incorporated in the OECD and loans guaranteed by OECD incorporated banks; (c) claims on banks incorporated in countries outside the OECD with a residual maturity of up to one year and loans with a residual maturity of up to one year guaranteed by banks incorporated in countries outside the OECD; (d) claims on nondomestic OECD public-sector entities, excluding central government, and loans guaranteed by such entities; (e) cash items in process of collection.

50%:   (a) loans fully secured by mortgage on residential property that is or will be occupied by the borrower or that is rented[16].

100%:   (a) claims on the private sector; (b) claims on banks incorporated outside the OECD with a residual maturity of over one year; (c) claims on central governments outside the OECD (unless denominated in national currency – and funded in that currency – see above); (d) claims on commercial companies owned by the public sector; (e) premises, plant, and equipment, and other fixed assets; (f) real estate and other investments (including nonconsolidated investment participations in other companies); (g) capital instruments issued by other banks (unless deducted from capital); (h) all other assets.

There is also a scale of charges for off-balance sheet exposures through guarantees, commitments, forward claims, and so on. This requires a two-step approach whereby banks convert their off-balance-sheet positions into a credit equivalent amount through a scale of conversion factors, which then are weighted according to the counterparty's risk weighting.

By the year 1993, more than 50 countries had subscribed to the Basle Accord, and by 2000 it was the essential rule for minimum bank security globally. Because the accord ignored some kinds of risk other than counterparty (credit) risk, bankers and regulators pushed for revised rules to better fit the reality of their situations. In January 2001, the Bank for International Settlements proposed revised capital adequacy requirements, seeking to improve the security of the system through more refined rules.

The proposed revised rules call for three "pillars" of capital adequacy measurement and management:

First pillar: minimum capital requirement.
Second pillar: supervisory review process.
Third pillar: market discipline.

The first pillar follows the scope of the 1988 accord, offering much more flexibility in measuring the riskiness of bank assets. Banks will be able to use their own internal risk-measurement systems, as long as they are explained clearly and approved by regulators. The second pillar calls for national regulators to follow some specific steps to assure adequate supervision of financial institutions in their jurisdictions. And the third pillar sets out disclosure requirements and recommendations in several areas, including the way a bank calculates its capital adequacy and its risk assessment methods, so that the riskiness of banks can be evaluated accurately by the market.

By mid-2001 it was clear that the proposed rules were quite controversial, largely for reasons of incomplete definition of acceptable measures and categories of risk. Banks and national regulatory agencies had asked for postponement of the implementation of new rules and for clarifications of the proposals, such that it was expected that implementation of the new system would occur in 2005 at the earliest.

SYSTEMIC RISK – THE ARGUMENT FOR A GLOBAL LENDER OF LAST RESORT

Due to the financial crises in Mexico and Thailand in the mid-1990s, and the contagion effects of these crises on other emerging markets, the stage was set for another round of debate on the possibility of a global lender of last resort, to countries in severe financial distress. This issue has been considered before on many occasions, particularly during the Latin American debt crisis of the 1980s and in 1987 after the US stock-market crash[17].

The argument for the lender of last resort is clear: when crises arise – or even when a crisis appears to be imminent – an international lender that could bail out a troubled borrower country (temporarily) would be able to reduce the severity of the crisis and perhaps the volatility of the financial system. The IMF has this concern among its charges as a multilateral institution, but it has inadequate financial resources to provide the level of funding potentially needed. For example, the Mexican crisis resulted in a US-led bailout credit facility of more than $US 50 billion. The Asian crisis produced similar credit arrangements with the USA, Japan, and other official lenders, particularly to Thailand. The IMF alone arranged a set of three rescue packages worth almost $US 120 billion for Indonesia (42), Thailand (17), and Korea (58).

The arguments against the lender of last resort are also reasonably clear. (1) If a lender is identified and a lending amount likewise known or implied, then borrowing countries may very likely undertake imprudent policies, since they know that help is available if a crisis were to occur. Even worse, as crisis conditions began to develop, governments of the country(ies) in question would face pressure to pursue social relief policies, knowing that financial help would be forthcoming from the global lender if and when needed. (2) The decision as to which countries would obtain support under what conditions would be highly politicized and perhaps not possible to pursue on objective grounds.

The sum of these arguments makes it not at all clear whether the lender of last resort would provide a better solution to possible financial crises than the existing, *ad hoc* response mechanism. Currently, IMF lending can be mobilized to provide limited support in a financial crisis. Industrial-country support can likewise be mobilized, and in much greater amounts, but with unknown reliability in an *ex ante* sense, since it would depend on political relations with the crisis-bound country and other nonobjective conditions. Thus far since the 1930s Depression, the *ad hoc* responses have worked adequately, but with the global integration of financial markets, it is not reasonable to simply assume that such nonpolicy will work in the twenty-first century (see table 4.1).

FURTHER READING

Barth, J. R., Brumbaugh, D., and Wilcox, J. A. 2000: The repeal of Glass–Steagall and the advent of broad banking. *Journal of Economic Perspectives*, May, pp. 191–204.

Barth, James, Nolle, Daniel, and Rice, Tara 2000: Commercial banking structure, regulation, and performance: an international comparison. In Dimitri Papadimitriou (ed.), *Modernizing Financial Systems*. New York: St Martin's Press, pp. 119–251.

Black, S. W., and Moersch, M. (eds.) 1998: *Competition and Convergence in Financial Markets*. Amsterdam: North-Holland.

Bordo, Michael 1990: The lender of last resort: alternative views and historical experience. Federal Reserve Bank of Richmond *Economic Review*, January/February, pp. 18–29.

Hoschka, T. 1994: *Bancassurance in Europe*. New York: St. Martin's Press.

Lown, Cara S., Osler, Carol L., Strahan, Philip E., and Sufi, Amir 2000: The changing landscape of the financial services sector: what lies ahead. *Federal Reserve Bank of New York Economic Policy Review*, October, pp. 39–55.

Silk, Leonard 1987: Why markets are confident. *The New York Times*, March 18, Section D, p. 2.

Simmons, Beth 2001: The international politics of harmonization: the case of capital market regulation. *International Organization*, Summer, pp. 589–620.

The Economist 1987: No domino, Brazil. In "World Politics and Current Affairs," March 7, p. 12.

NOTES

Thanks to Xiaoyan Wang for her excellent research assistance in preparation of this chapter.

1 This effort has been led by the Bank for International Settlements, BIS, in Basle, Switzerland. The BIS website (http://www.bis.org) shows the current status of the negotiations on capital adequacy and risk management requirements for commercial banks.

2 This is easy for me to say, sitting in the USA. A person sitting in Argentina in 2002 would most likely have a very different opinion, as the open-market system failed Argentina miserably in that year.

3 Actually, regional expansion of branches and subsidiaries within half a dozen regions of the USA was permitted for several years before this, with full inter-state banking permission withheld until 1994. These rules existed principally to prohibit the large money center banks from New York from overwhelming the smaller, regional banks elsewhere.

4 This is the "net interest margin," as reported by the Federal Deposit Insurance Corporation.

5 See pp. 41–2 of Cara S. Lown, Carol L. Osler, Philip E. Strahan, and Amir Sufi, "The changing landscape of the financial services sector: what lies ahead," *Federal Reserve Bank of New York Economic Policy Review*, October 2000, pp. 39–55.

6 Ibid., pp. 42–3.

7 This is a very important point, which may be missed on superficial inspection. The investment banks hold very little of their clients' funds in their own securities but, rather, they pass through the funds to securities issued by other entities. So the clients' risk lies mainly in the possibility of default or other nonpayment condition of the ultimate issuers of the securities, which are thousands or millions of banks, companies, and government agencies around the world – a highly diversified risk base. The risk of dealing with the investment banks lies more in the areas of possible fraud or mismanagement of the funds entrusted to them.

8 Interestingly, banks have not been attracted to acquire life insurance companies, because the profitability of the insurers is significantly less than in banks. This results from the limited flexibility of life insurance, which is based on actuarial probabilities of benefit payouts. So the life insurers produce low profits, and banks have thus far moved to offer life insurance products through captive insurance affiliates rather than by acquiring major life insurance firms.

9 See Lown et al., op. cit.

10 In *The Big Four British Banks: Organization, Strategy and the Future* (London: Palgrave Macmillan, 1999), David Rogers argues that the Big Four UK banks have become more focused and less of *allfinanz* institutions in the 1990s, in response to competitive challenges in the various product areas. This interpretation goes against the reality of the banks' diversification into the three main areas of commercial banking, investment banking, and insurance, though the banks are focusing more within those areas; for example, in C&I lending versus retail deposit taking, or in life insurance versus property/casualty insurance, or in stockbrokerage versus underwriting.

11 In principle, US bank holding companies may own up to 25% of shares in a nonfinancial company, but in practice this is virtually never done. Banks tend to hold at most small quantities of company shares as part of their portfolios of investments.

12 HSBC does own a property management company and a shipping company, both related to its financing businesses (of real estate and trade finance).

13 Lloyd's of London is an insurance exchange with 122 member "syndicates," which are groups or individuals that take on insurance policies, typically for marine, aviation insurance, and natural disaster insurance. During 1997–9 a number of natural disasters caused losses of more than $US 1.6 billion, which shook the exchange dramatically. Many syndicates took enormous losses relative to their premiums, some left the group, and by 2001 Lloyd's was functioning profitably again.

14 This link with Zurich Financial Services came about because Credit Suisse owned 5.2% of Zurich Insurance Company. In 1998 Credit Suisse merged with Union Bank of Switzerland to form UBS, and Zurich Insurance merged with BAT Financial Services to form Zurich Financial Services.

15 Basle Committee on Banking Supervision, "International convergence of capital measurement and capital standards," Basle, July 1988.

16 0, 10, 20, or 50% (at national discretion): (a) claims on domestic public-sector entities, excluding central government, and loans guaranteed for by such entities.

17 See Leonard Silk, "Why markets are confident," *The New York Times*, March 18, 1987, Section D, p. 2; and *The Economist*, "No domino, Brazil" in "World Politics and Current Affairs," March 7, 1987, p. 12.

PART II

COMPETITIVE STRATEGIES

Contents

5 The financial landscape: organizations and *allfinanz* banking (the status quo)   73

6 Competitive strategies of international financial institutions   87

7 Competitiveness of banks from key countries (or, Why are the US banks ahead?)   105

8 Responding to the challenge of the new economy   125

5

THE FINANCIAL LANDSCAPE: ORGANIZATIONS AND *ALLFINANZ* BANKING (THE STATUS QUO)

INTRODUCTION

This chapter paints a brief picture of financial services provision in several countries, demonstrating some of the key differences in the structure of this sector across countries and identifying some of the key participants in commercial banking, investment banking, and insurance. The main universal banks or *allfinanz* organizations dominate the financial landscape in Germany, the United Kingdom, Switzerland, and Japan – and many of them are discussed in the next two chapters. The main US institutions that have major international activities are also discussed in those chapters. In the present context, the emphasis is placed on other US institutions that are far more domestic in orientation (such as Bank One, Charles Schwab, and State Farm insurance), and on other countries, namely France, Mexico, and Korea.

The financial landscape in the twenty-first century is becoming more concentrated at the global level among a group of perhaps 20 major organizations, most of which provide services in two or three of the three financial sectors (commercial banking, investment banking, and insurance). These competitors include Citigroup, Hongkong Bank, Allianz and others, as discussed in more detail in the next two chapters. At the same time, retail financial services in many countries remain in the hands of a large number of small and/or specialized providers, such as the "Mom & Pop" community banks in the USA (more than 7,000 of them). The discussion in the present chapter describes the competitors and some of their services in several countries, to give a broad perspective on the industry. It is left for the next two chapters to explore the competitive strategies of those organizations that are more active at the international level.

THE UNITED STATES

The US market for financial services has changed fairly dramatically during the past ten years. Interestingly, at the retail level there are many, many parts of the country where banking and insurance services remained largely unchanged in that time period, since the smaller retail banks and insurance companies have not disappeared at all. Small community banks continue to serve small community needs, and local independent insurance agencies continue to serve local clients in those communities. The wholesale market, on the other hand, has really gone through great upheaval, both for technical reasons (the growth of the Internet and developments in computing and telecommunications) and due to legal changes (particularly the Gramm–Leach–Bliley Act of 1999).

The banking system is characterized by literally thousands of small community banks, competing in the market alongside the major national or at least regional banks. In insurance, the picture is similar, with thousands of small players in local markets, but in this instance the small firms serve as agents of the large insurers. In 2001, there were more than 121 thousand independent insurance brokerage firms in the USA. These firms provided access to the major insurers' policies and other products, while operating as independent organizations.

The US commercial banking market is comprised not only of the relatively small firms, plus multinationals Citigroup and J. P. Morgan Chase, but also by largely domestic, regional banks such as Wells Fargo, SunTrust, and Wachovia, and the nationally located but largely noninternational Bank of America. The US investment banking market is served by the multinationals Merrill Lynch, Goldman Sachs, and Morgan Stanley, plus many regional, local, and specialized firms such as Charles Schwab, Raymond James, and Edward Jones. And, likewise, the US insurance market is served by multinationals Allianz, AXA, and Prudential, along with noninternational major firms such as State Farm, Allstate, and TIAA–CREF.

In sum, the US financial system is quite varied, by location, types of clients, and types of services. The largest *allfinanz* institutions do deal with many of the largest wholesale clients – but there are millions of additional clients served by smaller and often more specialized financial services firms. This section sketches some characteristics and strategic goals of the noninternational providers, to complement the coverage of multinational competitors elsewhere in this book.

Bank of America was once the key rival of Citibank, and the largest or second largest US bank for many years. Bank of America had branches in dozens of countries and a major international business focused on private banking and trade finance. During the 1980s this business was largely dismantled, and by the time that Bank of

America was acquired by Nations Bank, and the headquarters moved from San Francisco to Charlotte, North Carolina, in 1998, BofA had become a largely domestic bank.

Under the leadership of the new managers, BofA has been moving to expand its retail banking activities from the two coasts into the rest of the USA. International activity has not been emphasized, though some representative offices are operated overseas, and the bank does have a London branch. The bank has encountered problems with its entry into investment banking, to some extent due to the fact that NationsBank and the original Bank of America had each purchased rival investment banks in San Francisco in the 1990s, and with the merger, one of them was forced out. Also, both of these investment banks were focused extensively on the Silicon Valley and dot-com firms that dramatically declined in 2000, so that the business itself has not proven to be a strength for BofA. The bank has not taken on any activity in the insurance arena.

Bank One is a Chicago-based bank with largely Midwest activities. It was built through acquisitions from its Cleveland base in the 1970s and 1980s, until the bank finally acquired the merged National Bank of Detroit–First Chicago Bank, and moved its headquarters to Chicago in 1998. The bank has historically focused on retail banking and mid-sized corporate banking in that region. In addition, Bank One joined with Merrill Lynch in the creation of the Cash Management Account in the late 1970s, bringing in an enormous amount of business through this link. (Bank One provided the deposit structure, largely in the euromarket, to place the billions of dollars of funds "invested" in Merrill Lynch accounts.)

The bank began the 2000s in fairly weak condition after the First Chicago–NBD acquisitions. In the first few years of the new decade the bank has aggressively cut costs, restructured, and increased credit reserves to improve its balance sheet. This reversal of fortune, led by CEO Jamie Dimon, a protégé of Citigroup chief Sandy Weill, who took the reins in 2000, has fomented speculation that the company may be in line to make an acquisition, possibly of a regional rival or an investment firm.

Bank One has moved significantly into other financial services. The bank is today the third largest issuer of credit cards in the USA, and a leading investment management provider, with assets under management of $US 158 billion in 2002. On May 31, 2003, Bank One announced the acquisition of Zurich Life Insurance company[1]. So, Bank One is also becoming an *allfinanz* organization.

Charles Schwab is the largest discount stockbroker in the United States. The company grew dramatically in the 1980s, when it provided a credible alternative to Merrill Lynch, Paine Webber, and the other full-service stockbrokers. The Schwab model is to offer clients low-cost, no-frills service for buying and selling securities on major stock exchanges, primarily in the USA. Clients are mostly retail investors, who prefer to make their own purchase/sale decisions, and who just want access to the securities exchanges. This model worked particularly well during the 1990s, when millions of Americans entered the stock market and invested some of their savings in the seemingly ever-rising market.

This model clearly is open to attack by Internet-based brokers, since the low-cost goal can even more effectively be served through that medium than through other means of dealing with clients. Schwab entered the Internet brokerage business early, and has become a leader in it, rather than sacrificing its model to upstart virtual brokers or aggressive full-service brokers who have also adopted the Internet as a distribution channel. By 2002 Schwab had approximately 8 million clients, of whom more than 4.2 million had online accounts for access to Schwab products and services.

While Schwab's primary business remains making trades for investors who make their own decisions, the company also is joining the movement toward one-stop shopping for financial services. It has begun offering mortgages through its subsidiary Charles Schwab Bank. Subsidiary U.S. Trust provides wealth management, fiduciary, and private banking services for individual and institutional clients. Like its rivals, Schwab has been fighting to keep the cooling economy from chilling its revenues. After ramping up its branch and online trading operations at the end of the 1990s, the company now faces a decline in trading activity as investors shy away from stocks. The company cut expenses and reduced its workforce by about 35% between the end of 2000 and early 2003.

E*trade began as one of the country's first and largest Internet-based stockbrokers, seeking to take retail business away from the traditional brokers and from the discount brokers by competing on low costs. E*trade built up a client base of more than 3 million households by 2002. This still does not rival Merrill Lynch or Smith Barney, but it is clearly a significant part of the brokerage business.

The company did broaden its financial services scope in 2000 by purchasing the Telebanc online bank, and in 2001 by acquiring the LoansDirect online mortgage company. Now, E*Financial offers not only discount, Internet-based stockbroker service but also retail banking services.

State Farm is the largest property/casualty insurer in the USA. The firm insures about 20% of the motor vehicles in the country and is one of the main homeowner insurers as well. In recent years, State Farm has stopped writing new homeowners policies in some 15 states in an effort to improve profitability.

State Farm has seen the light of increasing competition from noninsurance firms and has itself now moved into banking. It obtained a federal savings bank charter (State Farm Financial Services) to offer deposit accounts, CDs, mortgages, auto and home equity loans by phone and on the Internet. While expanding its financial services, insurance is still the company's main source of income. Auto insurance accounts for almost 70% of the company's property and casualty premiums. Taking advantage of the currently lucrative insurance climate, State Farm has formed Bermuda-based reinsurer Da Vinci Re, together with RenaissanceRe.

American Express is a real outlier in this discussion, since it is not a bank nor a stockbroker nor an insurance company – but it offers all of these services. American Express is a financial services firm that offers travel-related services (such as tour packages and travelers' checks) as about half of its total business. The other half includes a wholesale banking business (American Express Bank) and a retail investment advisory/brokerage business (American Express Financial Services), and of course the credit card division. This multi-headed organization has survived fierce competition with Visa and MasterCard in the credit card business for decades, and it has built the world's largest travel-related service business. It is difficult to put a label on American Express, which seems to position itself as a financial services firm, but which pins so much of its activity on travel and tourism.

American Express operates its stockbroker and insurance activities as part of the AMEX Financial Services division; that is, as part of the portfolio of services offered to its investment advisory clients. This retail investment management business, similar to that of Merrill Lynch, is where American Express has pinned its growth hopes for the early twenty-first century.

These sketches of financial services providers in the United States are intended to show some of the characteristics of major players in the industry, as well as to show how really diverse the industry is today. While no sketches are given of small community banks or local independent insurance brokers, these firms make up the largest number of such service providers in the USA in the early twenty-first century. The consolidation of the industry is producing some enormous financial supermarkets such as Citigroup, but it is not eliminating the "little guys" whose clients prefer the highly personalized service that they can give. As long as the market segments served by the small firms remain too small or isolated to justify entry by the major firms, this division of the US financial system will remain. As far as global financial services in the USA are concerned, they do belong to the major firms, as examined further in the chapters below.

As far as the relative importance of the different kinds of financial service in the US economy is concerned, it is not easy to draw comparisons. Some services are asset-heavy, such as commercial banking and insurance, and others are service-heavy, and more difficult to weigh because all that is measured are returns rather than asset values. Table 5.1 compares sectors on the basis of assets, although this is a very inadequate measure of overall impact.

Interestingly, commercial banking is the largest employer among the sectors in the group, but the number of employees has been falling over recent years, and employment in this sector (now at about 2 million people) may go in the direction of the level of employment in investment banking (now at about 500,000 people). Over the past five years commercial banking employment has declined by about 10%, while investment banking employment has risen by about 20%[2]. By comparison, employment in the insurance sector was 2.2 million in 2001.

FRANCE

The French financial system shows characteristics similar to those of the systems in The Netherlands, Italy, Spain, and elsewhere in the European Union, and reasonably similar to those of Korea, China, and India. In particular, the French system is comprised of a small number of major *allfinanz* institutions that have links to major nonfinancial corporations in the country, a small number of independent commercial

Table 5.1   Relative shares of total financial intermediary assets, 1960–2001

	1960	1970	1980	1990	1995	2000	2001
Insurance companies							
Life insurance	0.1964	0.1427	0.1053	0.1115	0.1145	0.0924	0.0910
Property and casualty	0.0288	0.0252	0.0338	0.0338	0.0338	0.0242	0.0227
Pension funds							
Private	0.0366	0.0299	0.0414	0.0482	0.0517	0.0333	0.0317
Public (state and local government)	0.0351	0.0405	0.0402	0.0432	0.0383	0.0383	0.0346
Finance companies	0.0452	0.0446	0.0491	0.0463	0.0380	0.0404	0.0370
Mutual funds							
Stock and bond	0.0037	0.0047	0.0047	0.0354	0.0556	0.0522	0.0537
Money market	0.0000	0.0000	0.0115	0.0365	0.0393	0.0614	0.0674
Depository institutions (banks)							
Commercial banks	0.3714	0.3720	0.3526	0.2725	0.2539	0.2379	0.2285
Savings & loans and mutual savings	0.1938	0.1935	0.1976	0.1156	0.0659	0.0517	0.0496
Credit unions	0.0084	0.0124	0.0145	0.0164	0.0190	0.0180	0.0185
Asset-backed securities							
Federally related mortgage pools	0.0004	0.0039	0.0312	0.1002	0.1133	0.1184	0.1241
Asset-backed security issuers	0.0000	0.0000	0.0000	0.0248	0.0471	0.0762	0.0827
Other	0.0802	0.1305	0.1182	0.1154	0.1296	0.1555	0.1587
Total percentage	100%	100%	100%	100%	100%	100%	100%
Total financial sector debt ($US billion)	537.7	1,223.8	3,658.1	10,174.5	13,863.9	21,040.1	22,807.4

Source: Board of Governors of the Federal Reserve System, Flow of Funds Accounts (Total Credit Market Assets).

banks and insurance companies, and a range of foreign participants in the market. Crédit Agricole and BNP Paribas dominate the commercial banking sector, with their investment banking arms likewise the leaders in that area; and CNP Assurances (linked to banking organization Groupe Caisse des Depots) and AXA (linked to Crédit Agricole) dominate the insurance sector.

Crédit Agricole has long been the largest bank in France and one of the ten largest in the world, measured by total assets. Originally government-owned, it was privatized in 2001. The bank is the largest provider of retail financial services in France, with 16 million clients and 22,000 employees.

The group also owns two of France's largest insurance companies (Predica in life insurance and Pacifica in property/casualty insurance), along with a major asset management division (CA Asset Management and other affiliates).

Crédit Agricole acquired Crédit Lyonnais through a friendly takeover in 2003, keeping the Crédit Agricole name for the combined organization. This acquisition resulted from Banque National de Paris' hostile tender offer for Crédit Lyonnais, which was unsuccessfully carried out in 2002. To protect itself as a consequence, Crédit Lyonnais turned to Crédit Agricole, and the resulting merger was completed in 2003. Before the merger, Crédit Lyonnais was one of France's leading commercial banks, with its main activities in retail banking (including life insurance), corporate finance, and asset management. The bank had over 4 million retail clients in France at the end of 2002. Its main international activity was retail banking in France's former colonies in Africa.

Banque National de Paris (BNP) Paribas is the second largest French bank, formed from the merger of BNP and Banque Paribas in 2000. BNP Paribas is an excellent example of the French style of keiretsu or "chaebol" on the Asian model. This bank has cross-shareholdings with the insurance company AXA, that put members of each organization on the other's board, as well as ownership in other large French corporations such as St. Gobain and Vivendi. AXA, for example, has a 6% stake in BNP Paribas, while BNP Paribas has a small stake in AXA and a 22% stake in Finaxa, AXA's main investment subsidiary (which is a listed company). BNP Paribas also has a 23% stake in AXA's reinsurance subsidiary, Axa Re Finance. The two companies have a joint nonlife insurance subsidiary, Natio Assurances, they cooperate in consumer credit and leasing for small businesses, and Axa Banque, AXA's banking subsidiary, sold its securities custody and fund depository to BNP Paribas in 2001. In June 2002, BNP Paribas announced that it was selling its branchless banking subsidiary, Banque Directe, to AXA. In sum, these two organizations are tightly linked, though still traded as independent companies.

BNP Paribas has a significant presence throughout the EU, particularly in retail banking. In the USA, the bank purchased United California Bank and another smaller bank, to become the fourth largest retail bank in California by 2002.

Société Générale is the third major player in commercial banking in France and the sixth largest in the eurozone in 2002. The bank has almost 15 million clients and manages assets of about $US 300 million worldwide. Société Générale operates in all three areas of commercial banking (retail, corporate, and private banking/asset management).

In the insurance sector, most insurers now either have close links with banks or have their own banks. Of the top ten insurers, eight have direct or indirect ties to financial institutions (generally banks, but the post office in the case of CNP). AXA, AGF, and Groupama have their own banks (Axa Banque, Banque AGF, and Banque Finama). The insurer Cardif is a subsidiary of BNP Paribas, while Sogecap is a unit of Société Générale.

AXA is the world's second largest insurance company, behind ING of The Netherlands. AXA's business covers both life and property/casualty insurance, along with reinsurance and asset management. The home French market accounts for only 20% of the turnover of the internationally diversified AXA, but the company is nevertheless the country's number two provider of life and nonlife insurance. At year-end 2002, AXA had over 90,000 employees and was managing assets of more than $US

1 trillion globally. Internationally, AXA ranked number one in the property/casualty insurance business.

Asset management has become an increasingly important part of AXA's strategy. As the insurance business faces growing competition from other sectors, asset management for both internal funds and third-party funds is becoming a greater source of strength for the firm. This enables AXA to provide both insurance of the traditional kinds and "savings management" for individual and corporate clients.

CNP is France's largest life and health insurance company, with 2002 premium income of more than $US 18 billion and more than 14 million policyholders. CNP had an 18% market share in the French life/health sector in 2000, relative to AXA's 11% share and Crédit Agricole's 10% share. It is majority owned by three state-owned organizations: the Caisse des Depots et Consignations (37%), the La Caisse National des Caisses d'Epargnes (18%) national savings bank association, and the La Poste (18%) national postal service. CNP sells its policies largely through the post office and the savings banks, which provide the largest distribution network of any financial institution in France. Internationally, CNP now operates in Italy, Argentina, Brazil, and Portugal, and has decided to move into China.

MEXICO

Mexico's financial landscape changed dramatically after the Tequila Crisis of 1994–5, when the maxi devaluation of the peso caused bank clients to default and left all domestic banks with negative net worth. All of the banks had to be rescued with new capital, mainly from the government. The domestic commercial banks were sold to foreign owners almost completely, with only Banorte remaining in Mexican hands among the top ten banks in 2002. Since Mexico has allowed universal banking for many years, the main investment banks have been affiliates of the largest commercial banks – Bancomer, Banamex, and Serfin. As far as the insurance sector is concerned, the big banks own several of the main competitors of the sector. Bancomer owns BBVA Bancomer Seguros (number eight in size), Banamex owns Seguros Banamex, and Serfin owns Seguros Santander Serfin. The largest insurer, Seguros Comercial America, is owned by the Dutch bank, ING.

Banamex-Citibank is the largest overall financial services provider in Mexico since the $US 12.5 billion acquisition of Banamex by Citigroup in 2002. Citigroup chose to leave the Banamex name on its 100%-owned Mexican affiliate and to merge the much smaller Citibank-Mexico into it. Thus far, the combined bank has operated largely as a commercial banking institution, with Citi's Smith Barney investment banking division largely unrepresented in Mexico. Banamex has its own investment banking division, which continues to operate under the new organization. The overall Banamex group in Mexico thus has not yet become fully linked to the three lines of Citigroup, since the insurance groups are not linked at all, and the investment banking business is only exploring the opportunities for joint activities.

Despite these organizational growing pains, Banamex remains the number one or number two provider of most financial services in Mexico. Its 1,400 branches are comparable to those of Bancomer, and its client base is about one-fourth of the Mexican market in most services.

Bancomer–BBVA was created by the acquisition of Bancomer by the Spanish BBVA in 2000. As of December 31, 2002, Bancomer's branch network totaled 1,665 branches and 3,752 automated teller machines in Mexico, conducting a broad range of commercial and retail banking activities. The bank has branches in London and the Cayman Islands, agencies in New York and Los Angeles, and a representative office in São Paulo, Brazil. Bancomer is the second largest bank in Mexico, although trailing Banamex only marginally in most financial services categories.

Bancomer–BBVA is the part of the largest banking group in Latin America, competing closely with Spanish rival Santander in most markets. In Mexico, Bancomer is second in market share measured by assets, with 25% of total Mexican banking assets. In investment banking, the group's Casa de Bolsa BBVA Bancomer is the country's fourth largest stockbroker. In insurance, Seguros BBVA Bancomer is likewise one of the industry leaders. And Bancomer is the leading provider of pension fund management (a huge business, since government-run retirement programs have been privatized throughout the region in the past decade) in all of Latin America.

Santander Serfin, the third largest banking group in Mexico, now belongs to Spain's Banco Santander Central Hispano, which has the largest banking franchise in Latin America. Serfin held about 16% of total bank assets in Mexico in 2002, behind Banamex (26%) and Bancomer (25%).

The financial system in Mexico, as in most of Latin America, has been "sold" to foreigners, to the extent that most banking assets and deposits now are in the hands of foreign banks, and insurance companies are likewise owned by foreign investors. The investment banking business is similarly controlled by foreign firms, largely the affiliates of the same foreign banks that control commercial banking in the country. In Mexico's case this outcome resulted directly from the Tequila Crisis of 1994–5, but the tendency existed before that – and other Latin American countries have gone in the same direction without necessarily experiencing a financial crisis. Argentina's banks and brokers had largely passed into foreign hands before the financial crisis of 2001, and perhaps the recovery has been more rapid due to those deeper pockets that the foreign banks have, compared with domestic banks, to deal with such crises.

KOREA

The (South) Korean financial system was largely rebuilt after the Korean War (1950–3), and all of the main banks and brokers have been established since that time. The government has been heavily involved in the system, both as regulator of the banks and as owner of many of them. By the 1990s there were more than 2,600 financial institutions operating in the country, from local community banks to a handful of national banks. At the same time, more than a dozen major insurance companies developed. These conditions were reshaped by the financial crisis of 1997–8, when all of the banks were hit by huge loan losses, and over 600 of them were forced to close or be merged into stronger institutions.

Different from the situation in Japan, the large economic groups (chaebols in Korea) are legally prohibited from acquiring banks, and the largest banks are thus not part of any of the chaebols. The largest three banks are Kookmin Bank, Woori Bank (government-owned), and Shinhan Bank. Together, they control just under half of the credit in the banking system. Citibank, the largest foreign bank in Korea, holds less than 2% of the banking assets in the country by comparison.

Kookmin Bank is the largest commercial bank in Korea and the largest mortgage lender as well. It had 78% of outstanding mortgage loans in Korea at year-end 2002. Kookmin is also a manager of the National Housing Fund, a government fund that provides mortgage lending to low-income households and loans to construction companies to build housing for low-income households. Kookmin merged in November 2001 with HC&B Bank, another mortgage lender and commercial bank focused on retail and small and medium-sized businesses.

Woori Bank is the product of a government bail-out of several failed and failing financial institutions in 2001. The government combined Hanvit Bank (now Woori Bank), Kyongnam Bank, Kwangju Bank, Peace Bank, and Hanaro Merchant Bank into the new group, which is the second largest financial firm in Korea. Government ownership is being phased out of Woori, which still remained under government control at the end of 2002.

Shinhan Bank has become the first major *allfinanz* institution in Korea, with a stockbroker affiliate (Good Morning Shinhan Securities) and a life insurance company affiliate (Shinhan Life Insurance).

Korea's investment banking business has been mostly operated by affiliates of the major chaebols over the past half-century, but since 1998 foreign firms have been allowed to enter the market, and now Morgan Stanley, Goldman Sachs, and Merrill Lynch are major players along with the two largest local investment banks – LG Investment & Securities and Samsung Securities. Given the government's stated intent to create Korean global competitors in universal banking, it can be expected that more chaebol-related investment banks will now develop.

In the insurance sector, Korea has strict rules dividing life insurance business from nonlife insurance. Even so, both types of business may be operated under one holding company, and in fact the largest firm in both segments of the insurance market is Samsung. The other major insurers are largely affiliated with chaebols as well, including leading names such as Korea Life, SK Life, Samsung Fire & Marine, Hyundai Fire & Marine, and LG Fire & Marine.

Overall, the Korean financial system was restructured after the Korean War to follow much of the US system, although the Korean government participated much more actively in the sector than the US government has done. Just as in the USA,

Korea has moved to allow all three financial services to be offered within one financial group at the end of the 1990s, so that *allfinanz* institutions are likely to dominate the industry in the years ahead.

MANAGING THE *ALLFINANZ* INSTITUTION

An interesting concern that has arisen as a result of the convergence among major international financial services providers toward the *allfinanz* model is: How do you manage such a beast? It is easy to talk about harmonizing cultures, or maintaining independent divisions (the two extremes of organizing such firms), but all of these entities want to take advantage of economies of scale and transferable skills and knowledge, while continuing to motivate people in the different divisions. That is, all of the organizations want both kinds of benefits at the same time as they want to avoid the problems associated with differences in style, compensation, risks, and even offices among the three business segments.

The commercial banking business has to be limited to some extent to comply with government-imposed rules on minimum capital, prudent management, and even acceptable ownership. Clients of such banks then receive services that are sometimes guaranteed by the government (e.g., through deposit insurance) and always overseen by the central bank. Contrast this with the investment banking business, in which government protections seldom exist, and where stock-market investments may go up or down – in comparison with bank deposits that pay interest but do not risk principal. And on the corporate side, investment banks do underwriting of securities, which they do not fund themselves; rather, they take on the risky task of finding adequate investors in the market to buy clients' issues of stocks, bonds, and so on. This contrasts with bank lending, in which a commercial bank will evaluate the creditworthiness of the client, charge an interest rate that reflects this condition, and make a loan of the bank's own funds accordingly.

Each of these characteristics compares with the highly standardized provision of insurance contracts, such as life, health, homeowners, and auto policies. Such insurance carries risks that are extremely well known, and is priced very competitively as a result. The contrast with the other two sectors is really striking. Still, there are insurance categories that appear much more like investment banking in the risks that they cover and the skills needed to define the risks and design the policies. These are risks such as earthquake or hurricane damage, or the risk of loss of ability to perform for athletes, musicians, actors, and so on. These nonstandardized risks, among many others, make some parts of the insurance business quite complicated, and thus quite risky. Even within insurance companies it is sometimes difficult to manage the divisions that deal with the more standardized and the more unusual risks in the same organization.

The net result of this trichotomy of businesses is that we see regularly in the press statements about the difficulties involved in managing combined organizations. Citigroup has sold off the Travelers property/casualty business, keeping only the life insurance, which is arguably more of a bank-like product. Allianz has encountered continuing difficulties with managing the investment banking business of Dresdner Bank, to the point at which it has been repeatedly rumored that the Dresdner Kleinwort Wasserstein investment banking division may be sold off. Goldman Sachs and Morgan Stanley have stayed carefully away from commercial banking – though rumors persist that one or both may be considering a commercial banking link-up of some kind.

For regulatory reasons, it is essentially necessary to manage an *allfinanz* institution as three separate divisions, whether organized under a holding company or with one of the operating divisions owning the others. Even so, the key decisions of how to allocate available funds and what kinds of risks to take are necessarily made at the top – where commercial bankers, investment bankers, and insurers will have different points of view. The risk-reducing benefit of running an organization that is spread across the three sectors is seen readily in the case of Citigroup, whose profits have held up well during 1998–2002, despite commercial banking lagging far behind investment banking in the first two years of this period, and then investment banking dropping off dramatically with the crash of the dot-coms in 2000. The less-diversified investment banking firms such as Merrill Lynch and Goldman Sachs have been far more affected by the stock-market downturn, just as the more narrowly focused commercial banks such as Bank of America and Bank One trailed further back in the late 1990s.

WHERE ARE FINANCIAL SERVICES ORGANIZATIONS GOING?

One thing that may be the clearest about the direction of financial services in the new century is that we cannot see very far as to where they are going. Consolidation among the largest providers seems to be a given for this decade. As a result of the EU's Second Banking Directive, banks in Europe can enter each other's markets, and so cross-border mergers and acquisitions in that region are starting to occur. But nothing in Europe compares with the massive sell-off of local institutions in Latin America. And in Asia, the big economic groups continue to control many of the leading banking institutions, although in Japan, due to the ongoing financial weakness, the consolidations have now gone beyond the keiretsu and have produced mega-banks with ties to more than one keiretsu.

In countries such as the USA and Germany, there does seem to be room for the community banks that provide very personalized, if limited, services to their clients. These local institutions fill niches that do not attract the large financial groups, but the numbers of small clients are enormous in total, so the community banks play an important part in the overall financial system.

Governments have gotten out of the commercial banking business in most industrial countries, and increasingly also in emerging markets. The public policy structure has moved greatly toward aiming at better supervision of banks and other institutions, while leaving the business decisions and ownership risks to the (private-sector) managers of those financial institutions. Calls for greater regulation as part of the general backlash against globalization have not produced any major steps backward in financial regulation.

The insurance sector shows signs of greater consolidation across borders, with the increasing acquisitiveness of firms such as Allianz and AXA. In addition, as insurers are merged into commercial banks, these combined organizations are likely to be the main insurance providers in the years ahead.

NOTES

1   *Financial Times*, May 31, 2003, p. 8.
2   See US Department of Labor, *Employment, Hours, and Earnings, United States, 1990–95* (Washington, DC: Bureau of Labor Statistics, September 1995).

6

COMPETITIVE STRATEGIES OF INTERNATIONAL FINANCIAL INSTITUTIONS

INTRODUCTION

The early stages of the twenty-first century are proving to be cataclysmic for the world's banks and other financial institutions. The dual processes of deregulation and technological advance have created a vastly different playing field for financial services provision compared to what existed just a decade ago. The response of leading financial institutions must be to develop strategies that enable them to establish dominant positions in the key services that they choose to emphasize, from retail banking to insurance/risk management to securities underwriting. While niche strategies will continue to serve the thousands of smaller institutions that fill roles in almost every category of financial service in most countries, the leaders will need to build broader-based capabilities. What will work in this context?

The analysis below considers key elements of the current strategies of ten of the world's largest and most successful financial institutions. Based on their successes and difficulties in the new environment, we can identify a number of features that are associated with greater (or lesser) success. The bulk of the discussion here is used to describe the strategies of these institutions. Generalizations and key strategic building blocks are then drawn from these accounts.

One of the building blocks of a successful strategy is the development of areas in which the institution can achieve superior performance relative to its rivals. These key activities, or core competencies, range from superior quality of service in some financial activity such as money management, to superior geographic distribution of services. For example, Citigroup and Hongkong Bank (HSBC) have much more extensive networks of retail affiliates than any other financial institutions worldwide. These networks allow the two institutions to provide superior point-of-sale dealings with clients worldwide, or at least in many of the important markets around the world. The services that require direct contact with clients are better provided by an institution with a wider extension of affiliates, and these two possess more than twice the number of office locations than their nearest competitors. In the retail banking business in particular, this is a huge advantage. In other services such as underwriting of securities, on the other hand, this may not be an advantage at all.

Another area of competitive advantage is the ability to provide a broad scope of financial services to clients. Given the global convergence on an *allfinanz* or *bancassurance* model, grouping commercial banking, investment banking, and insurance under one roof, the institutions that can really be financial supermarkets – or actually full-service financial providers – will have an advantage over rivals. Clearly, Citigroup has accomplished this positioning in the United States, though equally clearly the firm has not yet done so in the rest of the world. Similarly, the German insurance company Allianz became an *allfinanz* institution when it consolidated its holding in Dresdner Bank, merging the two entities in 2001. Allianz has a more extensive international extension of its combined banking and insurance services than Citigroup, though it is not the market leader outside of the insurance business in any country. The Dutch firm ING has likewise become a full-fledged *allfinanz* institution, with its world-leading life insurance business (including Aetna in the USA), its major international investment banking business (including the acquired business of Barings), and its commercial bank.

One more source of competitive advantage, that may enable an institution to beat out rivals in the market, is the ability to provide superior service to corporate clients. This service, however, may be defined as corporate banking, as securities underwriting, as risk management, as advising on mergers and acquisitions, or as a combination of all of these items. In fact, the ability of an institution to be the leading provider of corporate financial services probably will produce more than one viable model in which an institution can gain supremacy. At present, it could be argued that Goldman Sachs, as well as Citibank with Smith Barney, along with a small number of others, have built core competencies in this field in the USA and Europe. There are two questions to be pursued: Are these competencies sustainable? And if so, what are the building blocks needed to create the competencies?

These core competencies are only suggestive of the kinds of bases on which international financial services providers can build sustainable strategies in the twenty-first century. Using a review of what ten of the leading firms are doing today, it may be possible to extract some lessons for them and their key competitors. It may be helpful to consider the competitive directions of the ten selected institutions in a broad way, before looking at each of them individually. In terms of the functional scope of their activities, they line up as shown in table 6.1.

From this account, it is clear that the institutions in question have a fairly wide variety of distribution of their activities, with most focusing on investment and

Table 6.1 The activities of the ten selected institutions

Institution	Insurance as % of total business	Investment banking as % of total business (includes stockbrokerage)	Commercial banking as % of total business
Citigroup	9	10	Global consumer – 50, corporate – 31
HSBC	–	Corporate, investment banking – 39	Commercial banking – 23, personal financial services – 34, private banking – 4
Allianz Dresdner (1)	61	–	39
Mizuho Group	–	69	31
UBS	–	52	48
Merrill Lynch (4)	–	99	1
Deutsche Bank (2)	20	33	47
Fidelity Investments	1	99	–
ING Group	54	10	36
Goldman Sachs	0	100	0

Sources: Investex, plus:
(1) Crédit Lyonnais Securities – Allianz report.
(2) BHF Bank Report – Deutsche Bank.
(3) Prudential Financial, company report.
(4) Global Access company report: interest and dividend accounted for 52% of 2002 revenues; asset management and portfolio services fees, 14%; commissions, 14%; principal transactions, 10%; investment banking, 9%; and other, 1%.

commercial banking. The two traditional insurance companies are moving toward that model, although insurance still dominates their total portfolios. The question still remains: Which model(s) are viable? And the answer requires a more careful examination of the businesses of each institution.

Looking at the institutions from another perspective, how extensive are their operations geographically? Table 6.2 shows this distribution.

The distribution shows clearly that these institutions are largely domestic in terms of their market-leading activity, except for the investment banking area, in which the leaders in the USA and Europe are largely the same institutions. Table 6.2 somewhat overstates the noninternational scope of these firms, since major investment banking activities, such as underwriting of securities, tend to be concentrated in New York, London, and Frankfurt – so that a small number of overseas affiliates does not necessarily mean a limited amount of international activity.

Table 6.2   The number of branches or offices in 2003

Institution	Total	Home	Abroad				
			USA	Europe	Japan	Other Asia	Elsewhere
Citigroup	4,511	981	Home	566	899	79	1,986
HSBC	8,711	1,765	946	2,916	6	952	2,186
Allianz Dresdner	1,506						
Mizuho Group	737	675	8	5	Home	27	4
Deutsche Bank	1,418	389	148	771	5	79	26
UBS	422	319	40	61	2	–	–
Merrill Lynch	750	693	Home	26	6	18	7
ING Group (Netherlands)	436	40	69	182	7	93	45
Goldman Sachs	43	16	Home	10	1	7	9
Fidelity Investments	135	88	Home	21	1	18	7

Sources: company websites; analyst reports. Disaggregation was not available for Allianz Dresdner.

THE BROAD STRATEGIC DIRECTIONS OF THE TEN INSTITUTIONS

Citigroup

Citigroup was named the world's best bank, the world's best foreign exchange bank, and the world's best global bank in emerging markets for the year 2001 by *Euromoney*[1]. This *allfinanz* group ranked first globally by market capitalization and also for the strongest Tier 1 capital, while remaining second only to Mizuho Financial in terms of total assets[2]. Its investment bank Salomon Smith Barney ranked third in efficient underwriting of sovereign bonds in emerging markets, according to a survey of the issuers conducted by *The Banker* in August 2001[3]. The company was also named first in several regional markets for its performance in that year.

Since the merger with the Travelers' Insurance and Salomon Smith Barney in 1998, Citigroup's expansion policy has been aggressive, ranging from major industrialized markets to emerging markets. The expansion mostly has been limited to retail banking and credit card business through mergers and acquisitions. The institution's global corporate division is presently paving the way for major expansion in corporate banking and insurance business as well. The group sees a need to further develop brand consciousness and its image, especially among the growing younger population in all its markets worldwide. To avoid multiple branding, the names of its affiliates now begin with "Citi." The company has also decided to drop "Salomon" from the name of its investment bank wing, which has been called Smith Barney since 2002. A century-old name will slowly be phased out to become Citigroup Corporate & Investment Bank in the future.

Citigroup has the highest market share in the credit card business, with assets totaling over $US 70 billion. A major step in this business was Citibank's acquisition of AT&T credit cards in 1999. The company has acquired $US 1.6 billion of credit card receivables from Korea Exchange Bank. It also purchased the United Kingdom credit card receivables of about $US 426 million at a price of $US 526 million from People's Bank (USA).

For Citigroup to demonstrate success as a leader in *allfinanz*, but particularly in universal banking, and to sustain its long-term reputation, it will have to emerge from the crisis of confidence in 2002. The bank was hit with a number of accusations of conflict of interest between investment bankers and research analysts, with helping Enron to set up shell corporations that enriched individuals at the corporation's expense, and with a handful of other criticisms that hurt the credibility of the institution[4].

Hongkong and Shanghai Banking Corporation (HSBC)

HSBC Holdings plc is the second largest banking and financial services organization in the world[5], with its headquarters in London. It received several top rankings for the year 2001, such as the best bank of Western Europe, from leading analysts[6]. The group has been commended for its efficient risk management and treasury management[7].

The group's international network comprises about 6,500 offices in 78 countries and territories in Europe, the Asia-Pacific region, the Americas, the Middle East and Africa. HSBC is the brand name for all of its financial services, which include personal, commercial, corporate, investment, and private banking; trade services; cash management; treasury and capital markets services; insurance, consumer, and business finance; pension and investment fund management; trustee services; and securities and custody services[8]. The global network was formed from organic growth in Asia, plus major acquisitions in the other regions, including Midland Bank in the UK, the Republic, Marine Midland, and Safra Banks in the USA (along with Household Finance Corporation in 2003), Bamerindus in Brazil, Banco Edwards in Argentina, and Grupo Financiero Bital in Mexico.

HSBC is a truly global bank not simply because of its heavy presence in Asia, the Middle East, the UK, and the USA, but because of its commitment to emerging markets and less developed countries. The bank has about half its $US 569 billion in assets in the developing world, making it particularly vulnerable to the emerging market crises that have shaken financial markets since Mexico's 1995 peso crisis[9]. The bank has aggressively moved from traditional commercial banking into dynamic areas of wealth management and consumer finance.

The bank's strategic planning has a 50-year long-term view of the needs of the emerging markets and expansion of financial services, and the goals are made clear to the current stockholders. The bank's management bears a unique culture, which distinguishes from its competitors in all of the financial services industry, thrift being an important aspect in all managerial practices, including executive compensation and other perquisites. For example, the group's chairman received a compensation of about $US 2.6 million for the year 2000, compared to $US 20 million received by the chief executive of Citigroup[10].

The bank remains a leader in Hong Kong based dollar business, but to cope up with the fierce competition in Asia, the bank has reorganized its investment banking and increased its participation in non-Hong Kong currencies, and also in equity capital markets, securitization, and acquisition finance. The group formed an ambitious joint venture with Merrill Lynch to offer online banking and brokerage services to all its clients in private banking, especially to accommodate the changing risk profile of its younger clients in Asia. This Internet-based service is expected to be implemented in stages in other key markets.

HSBC's leadership and trend setting in mergers were adequately demonstrated in the first ever acquisition of a French bank by a foreign institution, and the whole process is considered a textbook example for avoiding the pitfalls that threaten cross-border transactions in general and banking takeovers, in particular. Crédit Commercial de France was acquired for $US 10.6 billion in 2000.

Allianz Dresdner

The Allianz Group, known as Allianz Dresdner from January 2002, has been recognized as the best property insurer[11] for the year 2001[12]. The company presently operates in over 70 countries, mainly through subsidiary companies, with the corporate head-quarters in Munich, Germany. Its clientele exceeds 60 million people and firms, including more than half of the Fortune 500 companies. More than 57% of its revenues come from abroad and more than two-thirds of its employees are in its foreign offices. The company ranks 25th among the largest companies of the world and is also the word's second largest insurer[13]. The size of the company is apparent from its $US 1.38 trillion in total assets and $US 708 billion of assets under management as of December 31, 2001. The group's core business stems through three distinct dimensions of protection (property and casualty insurance), provision (life and health insurance, and also private pension), and performance (asset management). The strength of the group rests on these three pillars, which are known as the three P's.

When the proposed merger plans between Deutsche Bank and Dresdner Bank (Germany's number one and number three banks) were not fruitful, Allianz agreed to purchase Dresdner. It already owned 20% of the Dresdner shares. The merger deal was structured in an innovative and tax-efficient way, such that Allianz did not have to raise any additional capital[14]. By purchasing the remaining 80% interest it did not already own in Dresdner Bank for $US 20.6 billion, it became a financial conglomerate in insurance, asset management, and banking as the combination of the world's second largest insurer and Germany's third largest bank[15]. The group also became the world's fourth largest financial services supermarket[16]. The deal also helped Allianz to give up cross-shareholding. The mutual swaps of shares between Munich Re and Allianz for those of Dresdner and HypoVereinsbank have ironically resulted in another *allfinanz* institution between those other two partners.

Allfinanz was the motivating factor for Allianz to acquire Dresdner, since the firm believes that its insurance clientele of 17 million in Germany alone will not be satisfied with existing services. Increasingly, German nationals are keenly interested in buying financial assets such as stocks, rather than staying with traditional savings and insurance policies[17]. Allianz's goal is to be always in the top five of the financial services firms worldwide. The firm has had cooperative distribution agreements with several banks to distribute insurance in the past and has experienced stiff competition from the same banks in selling asset management products. Therefore, it has accepted the notion that success in *allfinanz* depends on owning the channels of distribution[18]. Commerzbank's already prevailing link with Generali, an Italian insurance company, and Deutsche Bank's possible alliance with France's AXA, have also established the need for Allianz to be an *allfinanz* institution just to stay abreast of its domestic competitors.

Allianz has traditionally focused on the retail sector and on institutional lending and insuring. By acquiring Dresdner Bank, the combined group has taken on the wholesale investment banking business, which appears to extend the firm into an area of less capability and interest. For this reason, it may not be surprising to see Allianz spin off or otherwise dispose of the Dresdner Kleinwort Wasserstein investment banking division in the future[19]. A retail stockbrokerage division would fit well into the Allianz model, but securities underwriting and M&A do not appear to be a good fit.

Merrill Lynch

Merrill Lynch is the largest US-based stockbroker firm, and it ranks as one of the top three in most areas of investment banking, from underwriting corporate bonds to corporate finance. Merrill has over 700 offices in the USA, and another handful overseas. The firm employs about 56,000 people (as compared with Morgan Stanley's 60,000 and Goldman Sachs' 16,000), the largest group of whom are retail financial advisers. Merrill has approximately 14,000 advisors in the USA and 2,000 overseas.

Merrill has built its business combining retail stockbrokerage with corporate investment banking in almost equal measures. While the vast majority of employees work in retail brokerage, Merrill's earnings are split 46%/45% between the retail and corporate businesses (with investment management that serves both segments making up the other 9%). The firm's strategic intent is to become the world's leading wealth management company, managing assets for both retail and institutional clients.

Merrill's weakness in competing at the top level of investment banking is, just as for Goldman Sachs, its lack of a large balance sheet; that is, its lack of a lending business, which would enable the firm to partly finance its investment banking clients' needs. This issue has become a real challenge to top investment banks in the 1990s and early 2000s, and was certainly part of the reasoning behind the mergers of Travelers with Citibank and of J. P. Morgan with Chase. The logical solution to this problem would be a merger or acquisition with some firm such as HSBC, which has excellent global reach and a large lending business – or with Bank of America or Bank One, that have likewise large balance sheets, though virtually no global reach[20].

The company recognizes that it must compete based on its ability to serve distinct client segments. For clients with portfolios of less than $US 100,000, Merrill offers a Financial Advisory Center (similar to that of Charles Schwab), in which clients can call to speak with representatives and also trade on line. For clients with portfolios above this minimum and up to $US 10 million, Merrill offers the services of its traditional advisers, now called Financial Advisers. And for clients with portfolios of more than $US 10 million, the company offers Private Wealth Advisers with a full range of private banking capabilities. Notice that in each instance, Merrill has moved away from an emphasis on transactions (securities trading) and toward an emphasis on wealth management.

The new focus on wealth management means that Merrill Lynch has to offer clients advice about investments, risks, allocation of their assets (and their liabilities), etc. By arguing that "advice is the name of the game," Merrill is putting a new and major training effort on its advisers, to enable them to deliver advice and manage complex situations ranging from tax minimization to estate planning to banking and insurance needs. It is this last point that reemphasizes the logical direction that Merrill needs to find a commercial banking partner or acquiree to provide the range of *allfinanz* services that are envisioned. Merrill Lynch has cut back its non-US presence in Japan as well as in Europe, so the current US focus would be very well supplemented by a partner with major non-US strength.

Mizuho Holdings

Mizuho Holdings Financial Group (MHFG) became a bank holding company by combining the Dai-Ichi Kangyo Bank, the Fuji Bank, and the Industrial Bank of Japan in September 2000. The name Mizuho means "new, bountiful and rich harvest of rice." The three-way merger invited the terms of reference *godzilla* and *dinosaur* to describe the new institution, because of its size, measured by assets valued at $US 1.3 trillion[21]. The business model of the world's largest financial institution describes its trust, securities, consumer banking, and corporate banking divisions as its four pillars. In October 2000, the three banks announced consolidation of their respective securities subsidiaries into Mizuho Securities, and of their trust subsidiaries into Mizuho Trust & Banking. The group is also in the process of realigning the banking divisions of the three former banks into two entities. The Mizuho Bank will deal in the consumer and customer banking business segments, and Mizuho Corporate Bank will specialize in corporate banking business. The group began to manage them as legally separate subsidiaries from spring 2002.

Like other Japanese banks, Mizuho will have to concentrate on strengthening its domestic operations before launching a renewed international offensive. Such a policy will imply scaling down its current international presence and creating strategies for forming strategic alliances with foreign partners in international banking[22]. The formation of Mizuho reflects the process of realignment in the Japanese banking industry, as three other such alliances are also taking shape, in Bank of Tokyo-Mitsubishi,

Sumitomo Mitsui, and UFJ (United Financial of Japan). All four institutions could be global firms on the basis of their size. But their ability to compete with their European and US counterparts remains suspect, due to the problem of the enormous amounts of nonperforming loans that each one faces[23].

The main challenges for the Mizuho group to remain competitive (beyond the systemic bad-debt problem in Japan) are in the integration of the three existing information systems and introduction of risk management and risk-adjusted capital allocation as used by its Western counterparts. Mizuho's commitment to spend about $US 1.2 billion over the next few years to become a leader in information technology and financial technology shows that the largest financial institution is certainly committed to create the new brand it aspires to build. It will identify the most efficient system among the three former individual banks and implement the same throughout the new entity under a centralized system[24], the essential purpose being consolidation and reorganization of the information technology activities. Again, the key to achieving this goal may lie more in systemic revitalization than in Mizuho's own strategy.

United Bank of Switzerland (UBS)

UBS is the world's leading provider of private banking services and one of the largest asset managers globally. The UBS Group was formed in 1998 through the merger on equal terms of two of the largest Swiss banks, Union Bank of Switzerland and Swiss Bank Corporation. UBS is present in all major financial centers worldwide, with 1,500 offices in 50 countries employing 77,201 people, 41% of whom are in Switzerland and 39% in the Americas. UBS manages $US 1.47 trillion of invested assets for clients worldwide.

UBS operates four core businesses. UBS Wealth Management and Business Banking consists of the world's largest private banking business and also Switzerland's largest corporate banking business. UBS Global Asset Management is a leading institutional asset manager and mutual fund provider, with invested assets of $US 403 billion, offering a broad range of asset management services and products to institutional and retail clients across the world. UBS Warburg operates globally as a major securities and investment banking firm. And finally, UBS Paine Webber, one of the top US wealth managers, became part of the UBS Group in November 2000. Its distribution network of 8,535 financial advisors manages over $US 464 billion of invested assets, providing sophisticated wealth management services to affluent clients[25].

UBS's current key strategic initiatives include European wealth management, implemented through an increased onshore presence in Germany, Spain, France, the UK, and Italy, to achieve 80% of European wealth. The focus is on core affluent clients (euro > 500,000). Other strategic initiatives include investment banking in the USA. UBS intends to leverage existing UBS Warburg strength and UBS Paine Webber distribution capabilities. Their strategy is to hire top talent to optimize sector coverage and obtain market share gains in primary and secondary US-equity business[26].

Deutsche Bank

Deutsche Bank was historically the largest commercial bank in Europe, until the 1990s. When HSBC moved its headquarters to London from Hong Kong, it surpassed Deutsche in assets and other measures of size. Deutsche has been involved in all areas of commercial and investment banking and, through the related Munich Re, has also been heavily involved in insurance. As a result of the deregulation in Germany and in Europe, competition has grown much more intense, and Deutsche Bank has decided to move into a more focused profile, emphasizing investment banking and corporate commercial banking.

This has meant an effort to put all of its retail branches into a joint venture with Dresdner Bank. The so-called Deutsche Bank 24 was going to be a combination of these banks' retail and Internet businesses to expand through Europe. When the Deutsche–Dresdner merger was called off in 2001, the retail strategy likewise was derailed.

On a separate front, the three main German banks have spun off their mortgage lending businesses into a new firm, Eurohypo AG. This venture is 30% owned by Deutsche, but it is no longer a consolidated subsidiary of the group. This retail business thus has been separated from the core activities of Deutsche.

The Corporate and Investment Bank group division has focused on fixed income securities (generating around 60% of their revenues)[27], tailored derivatives and structured products, as well as on foreign exchange. However, the fact that their commercial and/or personal banking segments remain unprofitable and with unattractive rates, given their high cost to income ratios (above 90%), still remains a concern.

The acquisition of Bankers Trust in 1999 gave them a credible, domestic US equities franchise, with established reputation in a number of sectors, especially high yield and equity underwriting. (Bankers Trust had merged with the well-established Alex Brown two years before). This was a more stable business strategy than relying on hiring individuals and hoping they bring business with them, or hiring a team and allowing it virtual autonomy for the rest of the organization[28].

In September 2001, Deutsche reached an agreement with the Zurich group on the acquisition of Scudder Investments (ZSI), an American asset management company, as a way to grow in asset management. Their successful acquisition is yet a challenge, given that Deutsche has inherited a rather unprofitable franchise, with a first half 2001 cost to income ratio of 106%[29]. This agreement was ratified three months later, by Definitive Agreements specifying that Deutsche Bank would acquire 100% of US-based asset manager Zurich Scudder Investments, excluding Scudder's UK operations (Threadneedle Investments) from Zurich for the equivalent of $US 2.5 billion[30].

Internationale Nederlanden Group

Internationale Nederlanden Group (ING) is the world's largest life insurer, as well as a major commercial bank and asset manager. The firm is headquartered in The

Netherlands, though – as with most Dutch multinationals – well over half of ING's business is outside of the home market. The insurance business outside of Holland is led by the US affiliates, which were primarily the acquisitions of Aetna Life Insurance and Reliastar Insurance. ING has 50 million private, corporate, and institutional clients in 65 countries, and a staff of over 110,000 people. The group was formed from the merger of Nationale-Nederlanden insurance company and NMB Postbank Groep in 1991.

ING has a core competency in building life insurance operations in emerging markets. Including the ventures begun in China and India in 2001, ING has operated 16 such start-ups worldwide. Given that this kind of insurance is new to many emerging markets consumers, the opportunities for growth are very large. ING is currently the largest life insurance company in Latin America (due largely to the acquisition of Aetna), with major affiliates in Mexico, Brazil, and Chile.

A key strategic element at ING is its distribution philosophy: "click–call–face." This is a flexible mix of Internet, call centers, intermediaries, and branches with which ING can deliver client services toward the goal of achieving easy access and convenience, immediate and accurate execution, personal advice, custom solutions, and competitive rates.

Goldman Sachs

Goldman Sachs is the largest investment banking organization that is not affiliated with a commercial bank or other nonbank entity such as a retail stockbrokerage. The firm is frequently listed as a global leader in investment bank rankings, particularly as the Best Investment Bank in M&A and the Best Investment Bank in equity issue[31]. While not located extensively throughout the world, Goldman does have a major presence in London and Frankfurt, as well as in Tokyo and Hong Kong. The firm has 45 offices in 20 countries worldwide, with approximately 23,000 employees worldwide, of which over 90% work in the USA.

Goldman's strategy remains focused on advising and seeking financing for large corporations, as well as investing in businesses that it believes can be resold for large profits. It is organizationally divided into two groups: Global Capital Markets and Asset Management and Securities Services. The Global Capital Markets division offers the traditional investment banking services of corporate financing, mergers and acquisitions, and underwriting of securities issues. It also provides securities trading services, from advice and creation of derivatives to market making in stocks and bonds. The Asset Management division provides direct management of investment portfolios for clients, as well as advising clients on their own investment strategies. This division provides a securities trading service as well, mostly at the wholesale level for stocks and bonds.

The firm is also competing with commercial banks in the personal trust business, based upon its brand recognition and global reach. Its wealthy clientele accounts for more than 40% of the Forbes 400 richest Americans[32].

Fidelity Investments

Fidelity is a privately held company (Fidelity Management and Research, FMR) that began as a mutual fund manager in 1946. Today, Fidelity is the world's largest mutual fund management company, with over $US 900 billion under management. The firm offers more than 300 funds and has over 17 million customers. It is also the largest provider of 401(k) retirement accounts in the USA. Fidelity has offices in 70 US cities and in 20 other countries.

During its entire history, Fidelity has used telecommunications as a core distribution channel for its services. This began with the telephone and with management of enormous databases of account information, and continued with Internet-based services and information management. In the past few years, Fidelity has made a strong move into discount securities brokerage, currently placing the firm second to Charles Schwab in this market segment in the USA. The Internet is Fidelity's principal distribution channel for this business. And Fidelity's 17 million mutual fund investors are a captive audience for this additional service.

Fidelity's boldest strategy is its push to spin new businesses out from its technology backbone. The most successful of these is employee benefits services, an outgrowth of Fidelity's giant 401(k) business, which runs back-office administrative processing for plan sponsor companies. In 1995, Fidelity began handling defined benefit plans and health and welfare services. In 1998 it expanded into payroll processing, and in 2001 it added employee stock plan services and Workplace 529 Savings Plans (for college expenses). Today, Fidelity provides outsourced benefits services to more than 200 companies with 1.6 million participants, a figure that has more than doubled since 1999.

Although Fidelity does not have to announce its financial results because it is privately held, the firm did announce that in 2001 the employee benefits services business generated one-fourth of total revenues (and much more of earnings, since the mutual fund investments had very weak performance along with the overall stock market).

SOME LESSONS FROM THESE FINANCIAL SERVICES STRATEGIES

The sketches presented here are far too limited to offer a very clear picture of either the industry's future look or of any individual firm's overall strategy. Surely each of the firms will take advantage of opportunities that arise unexpectedly, and may lurch into or out of insurance products, for example. Or one or another of the institutions will decide to build a much larger foreign presence. In any event, opportunistic behavior will shift the panorama probably as much as the main contextual drivers – deregulation and technological advances.

One of the most notable lessons to draw from the foregoing commentary on ten major financial services providers is that essentially none of them is truly global in the year 2002. Citigroup is quite widely spread with its commercial banking activities, but is very weak in Asia and in some parts of Europe, not to speak of most emerging markets. Likewise, HSBC is quite strong in Asia but is relatively weak in the USA and the Americas in general. And both of these groups are extensive with their commercial banking businesses, while relatively limited in their investment banking and insurance activities outside of the home market and a small number of others. The largest investment bank (Goldman Sachs) is essentially a US phenomenon, with very little foreign presence outside of London. The leading insurers (Allianz and ING) are, like Citigroup and HSBC, strong in their domestic markets and a few others, but generally fairly weak at the global level. In sum, there is plenty of room for globalization of this industry.

It appears that the leading model for the large financial services providers is based on a commercial banking organization with insurance and investment banking appendages. While Goldman Sachs remains an outlier from this model, the rest of the organizations are building in this direction[33]. The insurance companies in particular have moved away from pure insurance to offer commercial banking services and to build asset management businesses beyond just the management of policyholders' wealth (in the case of life insurers). In fact, it appears that the property/casualty or life/health insurance segments will not be viable alone for the large providers: in order to stay competitive, they will have to follow the ING and Allianz models to build major commercial banking businesses, or perhaps major asset management businesses. Insurance products are too narrow as financial services, so the major competitors will not be able to pursue such a limited market segment[34].

When looking at the strategies of the leading institutions as described by their leaders, it is apparent that none of them does, or intends to, base its strategy on cost leadership. This is probably not surprising, but it means that the firms must look for other ways to differentiate their services from each other. Typically, in the services sector, key points of differentiation are high-quality services and availability of services. These certainly are targets of the firms described here. Proprietary skills are a logical source of competitive advantage for providing high-quality service, but that alone is not likely to be adequate as a basis for competing for any of these major firms. In sum, given that financial services have historically been highly regulated and largely domestic, the challenge is clear to all that (1) in the deregulated market, *better service* is needed to create a viable image or brand, and (2) cross-border business will grow greatly, and thus major competitors will need a strategy(ies) for extending their services more globally. The question is how to accomplish this.

The main competencies that the firms appear to be developing and promoting are: management of broad-scope services, including all three branches of financial services; offerings of broad distribution geographically, with offices in many locations and use of the Internet to reach clients in the "any time, any place" context; differentiated quality of service, which seems to be based on the people skills of key personnel; and perhaps the capability to manage the process of growth through acquisition. These are not the only core competencies in the industry, but they are almost all found in every one of the key competitors today. A sketch of the core competencies of each of the ten firms is shown in table 6.3.

Table 6.3 The core competencies of ten global financial services providers

Institution	Core competency	Geographic context (presence of $US 1 billion or more)	Key competitors
Citigroup	Global retail distribution; world leader in foreign exchange, project finance, cash management; offers full array of *allfinanz* products	USA, UK, rest of Europe, Asia, and Mexico	Bank of America, HSBC, Santander, Deutsche Bank, J. P. Morgan Chase, Merrill Lynch
HSBC	Global retail distribution; leader in securities underwriting in Asia	UK, rest of Europe, USA, Asia, and China	Citigroup, Santander, Barclays, Citigroup, Lloyds TSB
Allianz Dresdner	Leader in property insurance	Germany, rest of Europe, USA, Latin America, and Asia	Bayerische Landesbank, Commerzbank AG, Deutsche Bank
Mizuho Group	Leading lender in Japan	Japan, Europe, Asia, and USA	Bank of Tokyo-Mitsubishi, Mitsubishi Tokyo Financial, Sumitomo Mitsui, UFJ Holdings
UBS	Equity underwriting; leader in Europe	Switzerland, rest of Europe, USA, and Asia	Credit Suisse, Citigroup, Deutsche Bank
Merrill Lynch	Largest US retail stockbroker network	USA, Europe, Japan, and other Asia	Goldman Sachs, Citigroup, Morgan Stanley
Deutsche Bank	Leader in bank lending and bond issue in Europe; world leader in risk management	Germany, other Europe, USA, and Asia	Allianz Dresdner, Citigroup, Credit Suisse
Fidelity Investments	World leader in mutual fund management	USA	Templeton, Magellan, Charles Schwab, Merrill Lynch, Vanguard Group

Table 6.3   (cont'd)

Institution	Core competency	Geographic context (presence of $US 1 billion or more)	Key competitors
ING Group	Leader in life and health insurance policies	Netherlands, Belgium, EU, USA, and Asia	Allianz, AXA, Citigroup
Goldman Sachs	Top-ranked underwriter globally for stocks and bonds; world leader in M&A	USA, UK, and Asia	Morgan Stanley, Merrill Lynch, CSFB

Notes:
1 Top three competitors as identified by Hoovers in the company profiles.
2 For Mizuho Group – the competitors listed are for Mizuho Holdings, Inc.
3 Methodology: Hoover's list of competitors is not computer-generated, based on SIC codes. Instead, their editors handpick companies that are pursuing the same customers.

Interestingly, a main conclusion that may be drawn from the table and the descriptions of the ten financial services providers is that they are in many ways "noncompeting groups." That is, they compete with each other in one business or another, but each has a core business or two in which the other major competitors are not present. HSBC has an extensive retail branch network through Asia, which is not even subject to competition from most of these rivals. Mizuho's commercial banking franchise in Japan is hardly touched by the others. ING's life and health insurance business is not significantly opposed by any of the other firms here; nor is Allianz's property/casualty insurance business. None of these business segments is a monopoly – in every case local competitors actively challenge these leaders for clients and market share. But the ability to be a global (or at least large, international) competitor in financial services seems to depend on the ability to carve out a unique market segment from those supplied by the international rivals.

At the same time, it should not be ignored that the firms are competing for the business of multinational companies, which seek out funding, insurance, and other financial services wherever it is most convenient. With this group of clients, the ten major financial services providers are competing to some extent around the world – though even in this context the competition tends to be limited in locations, mostly occurring in London, New York, Frankfurt, Hong Kong, and Tokyo.

There is no doubt that, as long as business cycles do not converge completely across the globe, interregional diversification of activities will provide stability to the firms able to build such business. This opportunity is one that all ten firms are

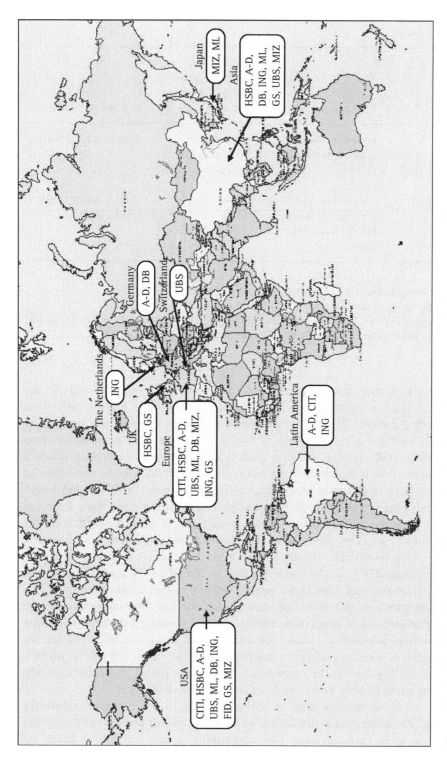

Figure 6.1 The international presence of the ten major financial services providers. A-D, Allianz Dresdner; CITI, Citibank; DB, Deutsche Bank; FID, Fidelity Investments; GS, Goldman Sachs; HSBC, Hongkong and Shanghai Banking Corporation; ING, Internationale Nederland Group; MIZ, Mizuho Holdings; ML, Merrill Lynch; UBS, United Bank of Switzerland.

seeking, mostly through aggressive strategies of acquisition in other regions. HSBC, Allianz, Deutsche Bank, ING, and UBS all have taken significant stakes in the US market, with only Mizuho trailing in that group. On the other hand, all of the US firms have been building major European bases (other than Fidelity), although Merrill Lynch and Goldman Sachs are much more active in London than elsewhere outside of the USA. Figure 6.1 gives some idea of this degree of international presence of the firms.

Note that Citibank and HSBC are the most widely spread leaders in (mostly retail) financial services around the world. Other providers such as Fidelity and Mizuho are very small competitors outside of their home countries. It is somewhat misleading to see how most of the firms do have a significant presence in Asia; but for some this means Japan only, and for others a concentration in Hong Kong. And likewise, it appears that the firms are all active in Europe; but within Europe it is clear that the banks and insurance companies emphasize distinct markets segments and countries.

There is plenty of opportunity for these firms to expand their horizons, and perhaps the key lesson is that expansion across geography presents fewer severe challenges to their core competencies than attempts to expand across financial services.

NOTES

This chapter is coauthored with Kumar Venkataramany of Ashland University. Thanks to Sangit Rawlley, Marie Gant, and Carrie Wheeler for their research assistance on this project.

1   Antony Currie, Chris Cockerill, and Jennifer Morris, writing in *Euromoney*, July 2001, pp. 55–6, 59, and 67.
2   Stephen Timewell, "Top 1000 world banks," *The Banker*, 15(905), July 2001, pp. 130–7.
3   *The Banker*, August 2001.
4   Anthony Bianco and Heather Timmons, "Crisis at Citi," *BusinessWeek*, September 9, 2002.
5   See note 1.
6   Timewell, "Top 1000 world banks."
7   Anja Helk, "Awards for excellence: emerging Europe," *Euromoney*, July 2001, pp. 77–8.
8   Source: the group's website.
9   John Barham, "The thinking banker's thinking banker," *Latin Finance*, September 2001, pp. 10–12. HSBC acquired Bital, the fifth largest Mexican bank, in 2002 for just over $US 1 billion.
10 The company's executives fly economy class on business travel and their chairman takes the subway (metro transit) to work every day.
11 Lloyds of London, the Ace Group, and the American Insurance Group (AIG) have been recognized for personal and political risks, liability insurance, and environmental risks, respectively, by Global Finance in its first ever list of rankings of insurance companies.
12 Paula, L. Green and Adrian Leonard, "World's best insurance companies of 2001," *Global Finance*, 15(12), November 2001, pp. 45–51.
13 *Fortune*, July 23, 2001.
14 Stephen Driscoll, Theodor Stuth, John Rieger, and Shigeaki Kobayashi, "Mergers and acquisitions," *International Tax Review*, July 2001, pp. 15–25.

15   Gordon Platt, "Europe: Allianz agrees to buy Dresdner," *Global Finance*, 15(5), May 2001, p. 10.
16   Andrew Capon, "After Allianz," *Institutional Investor*, 35(5), May 2001, pp. 93–5.
17   Anonymous, "Finance and economics: let the revolution begin," *The Economist*, April 7, 2001, pp. 77–8.
18   Capon, "After Allianz."
19   See, for example, Lina Saigol, "Allianz mulls future of Dresdner unit," *Financial Times*, July 16, 2002, p. 14.
20   The bank/brokerage combinations are once again coming under scrutiny in the early 2000s, as the stock market has fallen and a number of large financial institutions are facing major losses on their credits to firms such as Enron and WorldCom.
21   Kevin Rafferty, "Big, bold but . . . ," *Euromoney*, no. 380, December 2000, pp. 30–5.
22   Anthony Rowley, "Sure signs of a comeback," *Banker*, 150(898), December 2000, p. 57.
23   Anonymous, "Consolidation into four big groups," *Focus Japan*, 28(3), April 2001, pp. 3–6.
24   Anonymous, "A jumbo from Japan: Mizuho Holdings," *Global Finance*, 15(7), Summer 2001, pp. 48–9.
25   http://www.ubs.com/e/index.html
26   http://www.ubs.com/e/index/investors/presentations/seminar.newdialog.0011.Upload1.pdf/ubswconf.pdf
27   Ibid., p. 5.
28   Anthony Currie, "Tribal warfare in North America," *Euromoney*, March 2000, issue 371.
29   Timewell, "Top 1000 world banks."
30   Company press release, "Deutsche Bank and Zurich Financial Services sign definitive agreements," Frankfurt am Main and Zurich, December 4, 2001.
31   Peter List, Gordon Platt, and Adam Rombel, "World's best investment banks 2000," *Global Finance*, 14(11), November 2000, pp. 52–9. See also Bank of America Securities, "The Goldman Sachs Group," *Equity Research*, January 23, 2003, pp. 1–5. http://pdf.galegroup.com/getPDF?repNum=7165077&appUI=itweb&date=1044315578&digest=33064A9290177246316D3A5401B76122
32   Cheryl Winokur, "With hire of J. P. Morgan exec, Goldman is the latest trespasser on Banks' Trust turf," *American Banker*, 165(88), May 8, 2000, p. 1.
33   Merrill Lynch in mid-2002 was another exception, but this author expects to see Merrill linked up with a major commercial bank within the next year or two.
34   This will not preclude the smaller niche players or "boutiques" from surviving by offering specialized services to their limited numbers of clients.

7

COMPETITIVENESS OF BANKS FROM KEY COUNTRIES (OR, WHY ARE THE US BANKS AHEAD?)

During the mid-1980s, banks based in the United States were forced out of the leadership role among international banks (in asset size and profitability) by their Japanese and some of their European brethren. The reason for this apparent abrupt decline in US banking leadership had to do with a weak US economy and with exchange rates, but still the pecking order appears to have changed about 15 years ago. We demonstrate that the demise of the US banks is greatly exaggerated[1], and that rather they are leading the world's banks in many measures of performance at the beginning of the twenty-first century. We also suggest reasons for the successes of the US banks.

The Euromoney 500 listing of the world's largest banks (based on market capitalization) given in table 7.1 shows the members of the top 25 for the period since 1981.

If we look simultaneously at the variations of the US dollar during this time period, it is clear that much of the growth of the non-US banks arises from the great devaluation of the dollar from 1985 to 1990. The USA had six banks in the top 25 in 1981 and 1985, dropping to only one in 1990, but then returning to four in 1995 and seven by the year 2000. These variations in leadership based on shareholders' equity closely parallel the dollar's decline and revival over the past decade and a half.

On a different note, US banks have been and once again are leaders in many measures of performance. If we switch from size to profitability, the largest US banks clearly dominate their European and Asian counterparts after 1991, and they were among the most competitive before the crises[2] of the 1980s. Likewise, if we measure the efficiency of the banks, again the American banks are at the top of the list during the 1990s[3]. Table 7.2 shows a comparison of three of the largest US banks and three

Table 7.1 Euromoney 500 rankings (the top 25 banks ranked by value of shareholders' equity)

No.	1981	1985	1990	1995	2000
1	Crédit Agricole Group	Citibank	Union Bank of Switzerland	Sumitomo Bank	Citigroup
2	Barclays	Crédit Agricole Group	Sumitomo Bank	Hongkong Bank	Bank of America
3	Citibank	Barclays	Barclays	Dai-Ichi Kangyo Bank	HSBC Holdings
4	National Westminster Group	Banco do Brasil	Dai-Ichi Kangyo Bank	Sanwa Bank	Crédit Agricole Group
5	Banco do Brasil	National Westminster Group	National Westminster Group	Fuji Bank	Chase Manhattan
6	Bank of America	J. P. Morgan	Fuji Bank	Bank of America	Bank of Tokyo-Mitsubishi
7	Lloyds	Fuji Bank	Sanwa Bank	Sakura Bank	Deutsche Bank
8	Union Bank of Switzerland	Deutsche Bank	Industrial & Commercial Bank of China	Citibank	BNP Paribas
9	Deutsche Bank	Union Bank of Switzerland	Deutsche Bank	Crédit Agricole Group	Wells Fargo
10	Dai-Ichi Kangyo Bank	Sumitomo Bank	Mitsubishi Bank	Mitsubishi Bank	UBS
11	Midland Bank	Bank of America	Citibank	Deutsche Bank	Industrial & Commercial Bank of China
12	Swiss Bank Corp.	Mitsubishi Bank	Mitsui Taiyo Kobe	Industrial & Commercial Bank of China	Credit Suisse Group
13	Fuji Bank	Chase Manhattan	Swiss Bank Corp.	Industrial Bank of Japan	Dai-Ichi Kangyo Bank
14	Chase Manhattan	Dai-Ichi Kangyo Bank	Caisse d'Epargne Ecu.	Union Bank of Switzerland	Bank One
15	Credit Suisse	Swiss Bank Corp.	Crédit Lyonnais	Barclays	Fuji Bank
16	Hongkong Bank	Lloyds TSB Bank	Industrial Bank of Japan	ABN Amro Holding	Sakura Bank
17	Mitsubishi Bank	Sanwa Bank	Banque Nationale de Paris	Westdeutsche Landesbank	Banco Bilbao Vizcaya Argentaria
18	Sumitomo Bank	Industrial Bank of Japan	Bank of China	Nations Bank	Sanwa Bank
19	J. P. Morgan	Manufacturers Hanover	ABN Amro Bank	Swiss Bank Corp.	Bank of China
20	Sanwa Bank	Hong Kong Bank	Caisse Depots Con.	Long-Term Credit Bank of Japan	Banco Santander Central Hispano
21	Royal Bank of Canada	Cassa de Risp.	Rabobank	Tokai Bank	First Union
22	Standard Chartered Bank	Credit Suisse	Dresdner Bank	Chemical Bank Corp.	Agricultural Bank of China
23	Rabobank	Midland Bank	Hongkong Bank	Bank of Tokyo	Fleet Boston Financial
24	Manufacturers Hanover	Rabobank	Tokai Bank	C E Prevoyance	Rabobank Nederland
25	Dresdner Bank	Chemical Bank	Long-Term Credit Bank of Japan	Bank of China	Sumitomo Bank

Source: Euromoney, various issues.

Table 7.2 Performance data for international banks

Bank and year	ROE	ROA	Efficiency ratio	Loan loss provisions/ total assets	Tier 1 capital[a]
Chase Manhattan					
1992–8	14.97	0.94	62.7	0.78	8.12
1998 only	18.42	1.27	57.7	0.37	8.33
Citibank					
1992–8	12.21	0.85	67.1	1.52	8.51
1998 only	13.95	0.79	69.3	0.41	8.68
J. P. Morgan					
1992–8	15.66	0.87	70.6	0.03	8.00
1998 only	8.66	0.75	89.0	0.14	8.00
Barclays					
1992–8	12.18	0.47	66.2	1.38	7.35
1998 only	17.62	0.57	66.3	0.22	7.40
Lloyds TSB					
1992–8	24.09	1.03	58.6	0.95	8.30
1998 only	32.90	1.51	46.5	0.33	8.70
National Westminster					
1992–8	11.04	0.49	69.0	0.84	7.75
1998 only	21.53	1.04	68.5	0.27	8.30
Commerzbank					
1992–8	8.69	0.26	66.8	0.49	6.15
1998 only	10.40	0.34	63.0	0.27	6.30
Deutsche Bank					
1992–8	7.96	0.29	73.3	0.35	5.20
1998 only	10.30	0.32	78.1	0.13	5.20
Dresdner Bank					
1992–8	9.53	0.28	68.4	0.36	5.85
1998 only	9.83	0.27	79.5	0.31	6.00
Bank of Tokyo-Mitsubishi					
1992–8	0.55	0.09	65.9	0.62	4.75
1998 only	−12.94	−0.42	n.a.	1.24	5.23
Dai-Ichi Kangyo					
1992–8	1.68	0.32	100.8	0.42	5.23
1998 only	−0.19	−0.01	104.5	0.78	5.86
Sanwa Bank					
1992–8	−3.91	−0.10	109.4	0.30	5.43
1998 only	−22.60	−0.93	166.5	1.71	6.05
Credit Suisse					
1992–8	4.59	0.41	63.8	0.43	11.45
1998 only	11.70	0.48	74.4	0.49	12.00

Table 7.2   (cont'd)

Bank and year	ROE	ROA	Efficiency ratio	Loan loss provisions/ total assets	Tier 1 capital[a]
Swiss Bank Corp.					
1992–8	6.67	0.50	63.1	0.91	7.50
1998 only	10.30	0.49	[b]	[b]	8.30
Union Bank of Switzerland					
1992–8	6.09	0.49	63.9	0.51	9.60
1998 only	10.30	0.32	78.4	0.10	9.80

[a] 1997 and 1998 average only.
[b] Swiss Bank Corp. merged into UBS in 1998.
J. P. Morgan and Chase Manhattan merged in 2000, but that does not affect the data here.

of the largest banks from each of the United Kingdom, Germany, Japan, and Switzerland on several performance dimensions other than asset size or equity value, measured during the 1990s.

What are the causes of these conditions? It is clear that restrictions on nationwide banking in the United States contributed to the US banks' inability to achieve the very large size of the Japanese and European banks. As these restrictions have decreased, the US banks have regained much of the lost size leadership, though they are still smaller than a handful of global powerhouses such as Bank of Tokyo-Mitsubishi and United Bank of Switzerland[4]. But with respect to performance, how were the US banks able to maintain notably superior results relative to the top banks of the key competitor countries during the 1990s? Hopefully, the answer to this question will also apply to the competitive conditions in the early twenty-first century.

Some of the answer is easy to understand. With the economic downturn and continued recession in Japan since 1991, bank performance as well as business performance in general has been weak. Similarly, in Germany, the reunification of East with West Germany caused a major economic slowdown beginning in 1991, and, while the huge shock of the first few years' reintegration is over, the rebuilding of the eastern part of the country continues to drag the economy somewhat. Switzerland also suffered from near-recession conditions for much of the 1990s, due to a domestic real estate crisis, the depressing influence of neighboring Germany's downturn, and the continuing overvaluation of the Swiss franc. In fact, overall economic conditions do play an important part in the broad picture. Figure 7.1 depicts the economic growth rates of the five countries whose banks are compared.

US aggregate economic performance was truly outstanding compared to the main industrial-country rivals, and especially compared to Japan and Switzerland, during the 1990s.

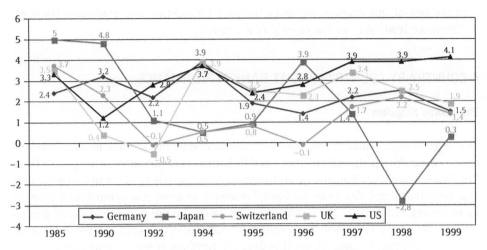

Figure 7.1   Real GDP growth rates of banks' home countries (annual percentage growth rate of real GDP).
Source: OECD, *Historical Statistics*, 1997 edn. (Washington, DC: OECD, 1997); World Bank *Country Data* (2000).

Another major factor contributing to the relative superiority of US bank performance in the 1990s is the fact that banks from Germany, Japan[5], and Switzerland were permitted to hold equity investments in other companies – and these investments were held at book value, thus depressing bank earnings when capital gains were not realized. Certainly for the German banks, "hidden reserves" of this type accounted for a very important part of the banks' asset portfolios, and thus contributed to lower earnings than would otherwise have been reported. Since 1996, this information has been made available to the public, and the banks' performance can thus be inferred, even though the holdings of equity remain at book value. In Japan much the same situation has existed, with estimates of hidden reserves even now unavailable.

The third factor to which US bank performance may be attributed is management quality. Because US banks have been subject to the discipline of the open market during the entire period, this reality has meant that they have had to respond to demands for quarterly earnings, high return ratios (return on equity, ROE; return on assets, ROA), and efficient operations (i.e., *low* efficiency ratios, since the ratio is noninterest expense divided by net income). Japanese banks, by contrast, generally have been part of large Japanese industrial groups, or keiretsu, and their goals have been broader than just maximizing shareholder returns. German banks similarly have had stakes in industrial companies, and have taken supportive positions that have not always served the goals of maximizing returns to shareholders. But more importantly in Germany, the labor laws have denied the banks the opportunity to rationalize their personnel structures, so they are greatly overstaffed relative to British and American rivals.

In the rest of this chapter, we make the case for existing and continued US bank performance leadership in the twenty-first century.

A COUNTRY-BY-COUNTRY LOOK AT BANK PERFORMANCE

The United Kingdom

The three British banks in our sample[6] demonstrated the second highest level of performance during the 1990s after the US banks. This outcome stems partly from Britain's relatively solid economic performance in the period (relative to European and Japanese rivals), and also from the banks' attention to good cost controls as measured by efficiency ratios. Also, the fact that British banks are not part of industrial groups enables the banks to pursue shareholder interests directly. They do not hold low-return investments in equities, so this drag on earnings is not present either.

Barclays Bank is the largest UK-based bank in our sample. Its business is quite diversified, though Barclays has exited the mortgage lending and the European equity/investment banking businesses. Also, Barclays' insurance business is quite limited relative to the rest of the bank's activities. Barclays is extremely active in worldwide international banking (e.g., trade finance and cross-border lending) and in global asset management. With the acquisition of Wells Fargo Nikko Asset Management, Barclays became one of the five largest asset managers in the world, with $US 425 billion under management. Table 7.3 shows the distribution of financial services activities at Barclays and the other banks that are analyzed here.

Note that Barclays has an extensive retail network in the UK, and that UK activities account for about 78% of the bank's global business, including about two-thirds of the profits.

National Westminster (NatWest) participates in all aspects of investment and commercial banking, asset management, and insurance, but is considered a second-tier player in many of these activities. Both Barclays and NatWest have withdrawn from their retail banking activities in the USA, though they remain number one and number two in the UK retail market. NatWest has built up its asset management and investment banking business with acquisitions of Gleacher & Co. (a US M&A boutique), J. O. Hambro Magan & Co. (a European M&A firm), Greenwich Capital Markets (US fixed income), and Gartmore (an asset manager). During 1999, NatWest received hostile takeover bids from both the Royal Bank of Scotland and the Bank of Scotland, and was ultimately acquired by the Royal Bank of Scotland. The combined bank will be an even more significant player in the European market.

Lloyds TSB Bank is primarily a retail bank that emphasizes mortgage lending and that has outstanding cost controls and profitability ratios (an efficiency ratio of 56% and a ROE of 25%, the best in this study). The mortgage emphasis grew dramatically with Lloyds' acquisition of the TSB Savings Bank in 1995. Insurance revenue is more important at Lloyds TSB than at any other bank in the group; Lloyds TSB has the third largest share of new life insurance business in the UK and the largest share

Table 7.3 Activities as a part of total bank business, year-end 1998

Bank	C&I lending (assets) ($US billions)	Number of branches	Asset management (Y/N)	Insurance (Y/N)	Mortgage lending (assets) ($US billions)	Investment banking (Y/N)
Citibank	115.4	3,000	Y	Y	60.2	Y
Chase Manhattan	57.8	600	Y	N	36.6	Y
J. P. Morgan	13.89	No retail*	Y	N	None	Y
Barclays	51.9	2,006	Y	Y	N/A	Y
Lloyds	N/A	2,900	Y	Y	69.4	Y
National Westminster	21.8	2,000+	Y	Y	24.9	Y
Deutsche Bank	131.1	2,310	Y	Y	1.67	Y
Dresdner Bank	112.5	1,500	Y	Y	45.5	Y
Commerzbank	51.1	1,044	Y	Y	33.3	Y
Credit Suisse	74.63	417	Y	Y	50.8	Y
UBS	60.72	409	Y	Y	49.8	Y
Swiss Bank Corp.	44.42	400	Y	Y	52.1	Y
Bank of Tokyo-Mitsubishi	221.4	327	Y	N	46.1	Y
Dai-Ichi Kangyo	10.24	339	Y	N	233.6	Y
Sanwa Bank	7.11	290	Y	N	266.6	Y

Prior to the merger with Chase Manhattan, J. P. Morgan had about 40 branches throughout the world.
1998 exchange rates: $US/£ = 1.66; DM/$US = 1.67; SF/$US = 1.38; yen/$US = 115.6.

among commercial banks. Lloyds TSB acquired a second insurance company in 1999, which should help boost fee income, making it the dominant commercial bank in the insurance market.

In the UK retail market, Lloyds TSB has the largest share of checking accounts and personal loans, as well as the leading share in sterling advances and deposits among the Clearing Banks. Lloyds TSB is second in the UK in credit cards issued, and third in share of outstanding mortgages. Lloyds TSB is a minor player in investment banking and has the smallest amount of international banking of the institutions in our study.

Germany

The German banks are all active worldwide in wholesale commercial and investment banking, as well as in private banking to high net worth individuals. Whereas credit cards represent a significant source of income at US and UK banks, they are currently unimportant in retail domestic banking in Germany. German banks have expanded relatively rapidly in Asian wholesale banking over the past few years, compared to their British and American counterparts, so they have suffered more from the Asian crisis.

Deutsche Bank is the largest German bank and the paragon *allfinanz* bank, offering wholesale banking services throughout the world and retail banking throughout Germany, Italy, and Spain. Executive management has announced an interest in expanding their retail banking franchise into both France and Switzerland via an acquisition of available branches or an entire bank. The acquisition of Bankers Trust in the United States has cemented the German bank's position as the largest bank in the world, measured by asset size. Following the merger, Deutsche Bank has significantly enhanced its wholesale and investment banking clout in the USA[7] and Europe, as well as its role in worldwide asset management.

The bank offers investment banking and asset management services through Deutsche Morgan Grenfell (DMG) and other smaller subsidiaries such as CJ Lawrence in the USA. Deutsche Bank offers a full range of insurance products and services as well. Thirty-one percent of Deutsche Bank's revenues come from fee income, and the bank is a major player in money management, where it has over DM 350 billion under management.

Deutsche Bank is the prime example of the impact of hidden reserves on a bank's financial ratios. The bank's ROE is much lower than those of its US and UK counterparts – however, if the "paper profits" on the stock portfolio were included in earnings, returns would improve to a level more similar to those of the other competitors. The German banks hold equity securities in their portfolios at book value, because realization of capital gains would be subject to a tax of 57%. If Deutsche Bank were to sell its portfolio of equities and invest the funds in additional loans similar to its existing portfolio, then ROE would increase by about 25%. Alternatively, if the capital gains were realized each year, returns would jump considerably. However,

ROE would still be below the US and UK banks. A planned merger between the Deutsche and Dresdner banks failed to materialize when the executive management of Deutsche Bank decided not to include in their post-merger plans Kleinwort Benson, the investment banking unit of Dresdner Bank.

Dresdner Bank, which was fully acquired in 2001 by Allianz (Germany's largest insurance company), is also an *allfinanz* bank, with activities across the board from retail banking to asset management. Dresdner acquired Kleinwort Benson, the British merchant bank, in 1996, and also expanded its investment banking activities in the USA with the acquisition of Wasserstein Perella. The bank is expanding its private banking business throughout continental Europe and selected parts of Asia. Early in 2000, Dresdner acquired the Channel Islands based Orbis Trust Group and Lombardkasse, a Frankfurt-based financial services firm. Dresdner had about DM 330 billion under management before considering the impact of the Allianz acquisition.

Commerzbank, the third largest bank in Germany (before the merger of Bayerische Vereinsbank and Hypobank), likewise provides a full range of financial services. The bank had a better cost/income ratio than its larger German counterparts for 1991–8, as well as superior profitability measures. Commerzbank has not acquired an investment bank, and is growing its investment banking business internally. The bank did acquire a small US asset manager, and had about DM 120 billion under management in 1999.

Switzerland

The Swiss banks are well known for their global private banking and worldwide asset management businesses. The long-lasting economic downturn in Switzerland has led to extremely large levels of nonperforming loans in the Swiss banks' domestic portfolios. Consequently, this has required substantial increases in loan loss provisioning. Poor asset quality is the major reason for the low ROE ratios among the Swiss banks.

UBS/SBC, or **United Bank of Switzerland**, became the world's second largest bank by merging the Union Bank of Switzerland and the Swiss Bank Corporation (SBC). While the post-merger bank has the dominant market share of domestic loans and deposits, United Bank of Switzerland is more dependent on fee income (from trading, investment banking, and asset management) and global banking than its European and US competitors. The combined United Bank of Switzerland is the largest asset manager in the world, with $US 913 billion under management[8]. The United Bank of Switzerland has sold its 25% stake in Swiss Life, Switzerland's number one life insurer, to institutional investors, as it focuses on more profitable businesses.

Before the merger, Union Bank of Switzerland generated 52% of its revenue from fee income. Trading income produced 20% of total revenues and asset management 16%, while brokerage and investment banking fees generated 16%. The bank had also established a life insurance company and a leading position in equity derivatives. Union Bank had also established a joint venture to build a strong private equity business, in which the bank would temporarily acquire equity interests in companies, with a view to reselling them at a later date. During the first half of 2000, UBS agreed to purchase Paine Webber, a large US investment banking, brokerage, and asset manager, for about $US 16 billion.

Before the merger, SBC was also a major player in worldwide asset management. SBC owned SG Warburg in the UK and Dillon Read in the USA, both leading investment banks. It also acquired a large US asset manager, Brinson Associates, and a Chicago-based derivatives boutique, O'Connor Associates. These acquisitions positioned SBC as a leading global investment banking firm by 1995. In a strategic alliance with Zurich Insurance, SBC arranged to sell insurance products through its extensive branch network. Private banking produced 39% of gross profits in 1996.

Credit Suisse owns First Boston Corporation, a major investment banking firm, and the European equity and investment banking unit of Barclays de Zoete Wedd (BZW), which was recently purchased from Barclays Bank. As with United Bank of Switzerland, a major activity for Credit Suisse is private banking, due to the long tradition of Swiss banking secrecy and safety. In 1997, Credit Suisse acquired Winterhur, the third largest Swiss insurance company. By 1997, Credit Suisse was the fourth largest global asset manager, with $US 476 billion under management. With its acquisition of the money management business of Pincus Warburg, Credit Suisse has further enhanced its stature as one of the world's largest money managers. In addition, Credit Suisse purchased Donaldson, Lufkin, and Jenrette (DLJ), another large US investment banking firm with sizeable retail brokerage and asset management businesses.

Japan

All of the Japanese banks have suffered enormous losses and continuing depressed profits during the 1990s. This is due largely to the overall economic recession in Japan, and surely also to the structure of the Japanese financial system, in which the banks are linked heavily to industrial groups, whose fortunes have declined. Historically, the Japanese banks have been less involved in asset management activities than their European counterparts, due to Glass–Steagall-type restrictions under Japan's analogous banking law. Insurance involvement was forbidden to Japanese banks until the Big Bang of April 1, 1998. Under the new law, full universal banking was permitted in Japan by the end of 1999.

Bank of Tokyo-Mitsubishi was the largest Japanese bank, with $US 675 billion in total assets as of March 31, 1997. It is a member of the Mitsubishi keiretsu, along with 27 other corporations. The bank was the exception among Japanese city banks, almost all of which experienced losses in fiscal years 1995 and/or 1996. The two merged banks' combined accounts for those years show small profits, due mainly to the significant and growing income from overseas activities, especially those of Bank of Tokyo. Domestic (Japanese) earnings for both years were negative.

Bank of Tokyo-Mitsubishi is a full-service commercial and investment bank, with 326 branches in Japan and offices in 43 other countries. The bank earned 91% of its gross revenue from commercial banking activity in fiscal year 1997, and 9% from investment banking activities. The bank is a national leader in commercial and industrial lending, as well as consumer credit. The bank is also active in providing custody service and offering cash management and money transfer services. Directly or through affiliates, Bank of Tokyo-Mitsubishi offers credit cards, leasing, factoring, venture capital, mortgage loans, and advisory services. It is not involved in the insurance sector. With mid-1990s changes in the financial services legislation in Japan, BTM is now involved in asset management, but its participation is small on a worldwide scale.

Dai-Ichi Kangyo Bank, previously the largest Japanese bank, was surpassed when its two rivals (Bank of Tokyo and Mitsubishi Bank) merged in 1996. Dai-Ichi suffered much the same fate as the other large Japanese banks in the 1990s, with low profitability and occasional outright losses. DKB is a full-service, universal bank, with divisions in investment management, mergers and acquisitions, and other financial services, as well as commercial banking.

Dai-Ichi Kangyo Bank has set a goal of being Japan's "Best Commercial Bank" as part of its overall corporate vision. The bank is *not* part of any of the large Japanese keiretsu or company groups, different from several of its key rivals. The bank's 339 branches give it the third largest network in Japan (after Sakura Bank and Asahi Bank). Because the bank's major shareholders include almost a dozen insurance companies, the results of the Japanese financial Big Bang should be to consolidate the insurance business along with Dai-Ichi's commercial and investment banking businesses.

Dai-Ichi Kangyo Bank underwent dramatic top management change in 1997, when a federal judicial prosecution convicted the bank of mafia-related lending and subsequent crimes in trying to hide the activity. The entire management committee of the bank was replaced, and a new strategic direction and more transparent management practices were implemented. In mid-1999, Dai-Ichi announced a merger with Fuji Bank and Industrial Bank of Japan, under the name Mizuho Financial Group. This combination has vaulted Dai-Ichi, or rather Mizuho, again to the top of the Japanese size rankings, and indeed into the position of being the world's largest bank, with assets of about $US 1.3 trillion.

Sanwa Bank was the third largest Japanese bank at the end of the 1990s. The bank is a member of three industrial groupings, which include, among others, Orix, Sharp, Kyocera, Suntory, Hitachi, and Nissho Iwai, as well as the Hankyu group. In financial services, Sanwa is linked with Toyo Trust and Banking (in which Sanwa bought the controlling interest in 1999). Also in 1999, Sanwa formed a large financial network with alliance partners Koa Fire and Marine Insurance, Taiyo Life Insurance, Daido Life Insurance, and Universal Securities Company. Nippon Fire and Marine Insurance joined the group in late 1999. Sanwa Bank was founded in 1933 as a merger of three Osaka-based banks, the largest of which was Konoike Bank.

As one would imagine, Sanwa Bank has a large corporate banking business, especially linked to the members of its industrial groupings. This business includes money and capital markets products, and interest rate and exchange rate hedging products, as well as credit derivatives. On the investment banking side, Sanwa has recently built a major presence, with acquisitions of Universal Securities and Dai-Ichi Securities in 1999.

Sanwa Bank has an extensive consumer banking business, with 44% of its loans going to individuals and small and medium-sized firms. The bank has 335 branches throughout Japan and 53 overseas. When the Japanese government deregulated the financial services sector in 1993, allowing commercial banks to enter into securities underwriting and trading, and allowing investment banks the reverse, Sanwa immediately (in 1994) established Sanwa Securities Company and an investment management company to deal with investment banking activities. In the later 1990s, Sanwa built up its investment banking business with the acquisition of Towa Securities, and in 1999 with the acquisitions of Universal Securities and Dai-Ichi Securities. This combination makes Sanwa the sixth largest asset manager in Japan.

In March 2000, Sanwa announced plans to merge with Asahi Bank and Tokai Bank, making the combination the third largest financial institution in Japan, after the Bank of Tokyo-Mitsubishi and Dai-Ichi–Fuji–IBJ groups. The new group including Sanwa began operation under a single holding company in April 2001.

Along with these mergers, Sumitomo Bank and Sakura Bank have announced a broad alliance that could eventually lead to their merger as well. Sumitomo Bank has already formed a holding company in 1998 that includes one of Japan's largest brokers, Daiwa Securities. Sakura is a product of a merger itself, between Tokyo-Kobe Bank and Mitsui Bank in 1996.

This consolidation is being driven by a sweeping deregulation of Japan's financial sector and moves by banks to finally deal with a mountain of bad loans from the decline of the country's economy and financial markets that began in 1990. The deregulation effort has been garnering momentum, knocking down walls between various financial businesses, and exposing banks to new competition, while opening up new opportunities in areas such as brokerage, mutual fund sales, and asset management.

The United States

The US banks have been the most successful in terms of profitability ratios during the past eight years among our sample group of large banks in five countries. This was not the case during the 1980s and early 1990s, when most of the money center banks suffered huge losses in emerging market loans and in domestic real estate and LBO lending, following a series of rolling regional recessions in the United States. The US banks have been the leaders in bank merger and acquisition (M&A) activity. The mergers of NationsBank with Bank of America and of Citicorp with Travelers

Group, as well as a host of mergers among super-regional banks in the USA, appear to have acted as a catalyst for worldwide bank M&A activity.

Citicorp is the only US bank that could be classified as an *allfinanz* institution, which is involved in commercial banking, investment banking, and insurance on a global basis. Citicorp has a global presence in retail banking, with consumer banking services available in most major countries. Citicorp is seeking a global brand image similar to that of Coca-Cola in retail banking. It is also the largest bank credit card company in the world, with more than 60 million card holders and about $US 70 billion in receivables around the world. Two-thirds of Citicorp's loan portfolio is consumer-oriented, while one-third is commercial and industrial loans. Citicorp is one of the few US money center banks that offers insurance products to its domestic retail clients. Citicorp has had a ROE of more than 20% per year in the past few years, similar to that of the leading UK banks and well ahead of other global rivals.

Citicorp is clearly divided into two franchises: the global corporate bank and the full-service consumer bank. The corporate bank provides both commercial and investment banking services to corporate customers around the world, from loans to underwriting securities, to cash management. The consumer bank likewise offers a wide range of financial services – from loans to deposits to insurance – to retail clients in many countries. Each of the two client categories produces about half of the bank's profits, and geographically the bank is greatly diversified between industrial and emerging markets. In the 1990s, Citicorp was active in purchasing financial institutions in emerging markets, as legal restrictions declined in many countries.

The 1998 merger with Travelers Group to form Citigroup classified the company as a huge and powerful *allfinanz* global financial services institution. The combination of Citicorp's investment banking operation with that of Salomon Smith Barney in Travelers has placed Citigroup at the forefront of universal banking. In January 2000, Citicorp's Salomon Smith Barney unit announced that it will buy the global investment banking division of London-based merchant bank Schroders, doubling Citigroup's investment banking platform in Europe.

Chase Manhattan became the largest US bank in 1997, after its merger with Chemical Bank. However, Chase slipped to third place in asset size following the mergers of NationsBank with Bank America and that of Travelers with Citicorp. Then, with its merger with J. P. Morgan in 2000, Chase regained the top spot among US commercial banks. Immediately prior to the merger, Chase had a global presence in investment banking and in wholesale lending, but it did not offer insurance or retail branch banking on a global basis. The bank's two main businesses were global corporate banking and nationwide consumer banking in the USA. In retail banking, Chase had relationships with 25 million individuals and households, including credit cards, auto finance, consumer lending, and mortgage banking. In corporate banking, Chase was the number one relationship bank to corporate America, number one in global loan syndication, number one foreign exchange bank in New York and London, number one provider of risk management and advisory services, number one in interest rate swaps and advisory agreements, number one in dollar clearing, number one in global custody, number one provider of treasury management services to large companies, number one in clearing-house payment volume in CHIPS, CHAPS, and Fedwire, and a leader in several other categories of financial service.

J. P. Morgan had been far more focused than Chase or Citicorp in the global wholesale banking area. Morgan has traditionally not offered retail banking services, except for private banking for wealthy clients. Its emphasis has been on investment banking and corporate advisory services, domestically and worldwide. Morgan's trading revenue was greater than its net interest income for 1996. J. P. Morgan has had much higher efficiency ratios than its US counterparts – hence the quest for a merger partner, since executive management were not pleased with the ROE and ROA, despite the company's gradual transformation into an investment bank. J. P. Morgan ranked very high as a global asset manager, with $US 234 billion under management at year-end 1998. In September 2000, Morgan announced that it would be acquired by Chase Manhattan, making the combined bank an even greater power-house in investment banking and wholesale commercial banking in the USA.

A STATISTICAL LOOK AT RELATIVE PERFORMANCE

Moving from the descriptive account of affairs above, we can also examine the relative performance of banks from the five countries on a statistical basis. Toward this end, data were collected for all 15 banks for the period 1991–8. For this period, we were able to obtain essentially complete information on all of the banks, even though we had to drop the last year or two of banks that have been merged (such as SBC, that merged with Union Bank of Switzerland in 1998).

The issue to be explained was profitability, our measure of performance. We alternatively used return on equity and return on assets, but ROE always produced superior statistical results. Thus, only ROE results are presented in table 7.4. Other performance measures could be efficiency, which we used as an explanatory variable to help explain profitability, or bank capital, which we likewise used as one of the factors that helps explain profitability.

On the explanatory variable side, we began with the efficiency of each bank, as defined by the ratio of the bank's noninterest expense to total revenue (efficiency ratio). A higher ratio implies a worse efficiency of bank operation. Second, we considered the risk of the banks as measured by Tier 1 capital – the lower the Tier 1 capital ratio, the riskier the bank. Third, we included the bad loans of each bank, measured alternatively as nonperforming assets and as loan loss provisions. It turned out that loan loss provisions produced a superior statistical result, so we only present that information in table 7.4. Higher loan loss provisions presumably mean a lower-quality loan portfolio. Fourth, the size of the bank was included, measured as total asset value. This was not hypothesized to produce differences, especially since all of the banks are among the largest 50 in the world. Fifth, we included home-country GDP in dollars, hypothesizing that higher-growth countries would have better-performing banks. And finally, we expected that a higher corporate tax burden would hurt bank profits, and thus that taxes paid would correlate negatively with profitability.

Table 7.4 Statistical tests of performance by banks from five countries

	Model 1		Model 2	
Determinants of bank performance	Estimated coefficient	t-statistic	Estimated coefficient	t-statistic
Constant	−46.05	(−2.04)**	−37.16	(−1.48)
Total assets	−3.6e-5	(−4.44)***	−3.5e-5	(−4.04)***
Efficiency ratio	−18.50	(−2.79)***	−19.06	(−2.86)***
Tier 1 capital ratio	−2.67	(−4.14)***	−2.68	(−3.76)***
Loan loss provisions	−390.14	(−2.59)**	−348.57	(−2.23)**
Noninterest earnings	358.15	(2.82)***	351.85	(2.73)***
Home-country GDP in dollars	0.93	(3.72)***	0.84	(3.23)***
Corporate income tax rate	–	–	−1.35	(−0.14)
Number of observations	88		86	
R^2	0.51		0.51	

* = Significant at 90% confidence level; ** = significant at 95% confidence level; *** =   significant at 99% confidence level.

Hence the model to explain the banks' relative return on equity[9] was as follows:

$$\text{ROE} = \alpha + \beta_1(\text{total assets}) + \beta_2(\text{efficiency ratio}) + \beta_3(\text{Tier 1 capital})$$
$$+ \beta_4(\text{loan loss provisions}) + \beta_5(\text{noninterest income})$$
$$+ \beta_6(\text{home-country GDP}) + \beta_7(\text{corporate income tax paid})$$

The model test results are shown in table 7.4. Separate regressions were run for the full model with all factors. We then eliminated the one variable (taxes) that proved insignificant and ran the model again, as shown.

The statistical results are quite interesting, with all of the variables producing significant coefficients in line with expectations as described above. Larger banks were less profitable than smaller ones in the sample, perhaps leading to the conclusion that the largest Japanese and continental banks were overextended in terms of their internal resources for managing their assets. The smaller, US-based banks (small such as Citibank!) were more successful during the 1990s in building up their ROE.

MORE ON COMPARATIVE PROFITABILITY RATIOS

Why do the profitability and other performance measures differ so clearly across the world's largest banks, and particularly between the US and UK banks versus those from the other European countries and Japan? According to the data just analyzed, the between-country differences were large in terms of the stage in the economic cycle – that is, the GDP growth rate (which also affects loan loss reserves and provisions) – and efficiency ratios[10]. In addition, bank strategies such as a focus or lack of focus on investor performance in the short run, diversification into areas beyond commercial banking (such as investment banking and insurance) and quality of management, are likely additional factors that play a role here. More specifically, in Germany, Switzerland, and Japan, the weak economies in the 1990s led to high levels of unemployment and nonperforming loans, which in turn led to higher levels of loan loss provisions. This then led to lower profits and high (poor) efficiency ratios in all three countries. Low income was also the result of Japanese and German banks holding large stock portfolios at book value, so that annual returns failed to reflect stock appreciation in the market. In Switzerland, the banks also suffered from a weak economy and high levels of nonperforming assets in 1996 (primarily in the domestic real estate sector), which consequently led to large loan loss provisions[11]. With the exception of that year, the Swiss banks were fairly similar in performance to the US and UK banks in efficiency ratios. However, Swiss bank profitability ratios have still lagged behind those of US and UK banks.

We would like to be able to measure the quality of bank management in some additional manner, such as speed and flexibility of decision-making, or ability to manage more diversified portfolios of activities. The problem here is that our outcome of profitability should already reflect management quality, so trying to measure it separately may not be a useful venture.

The degree of diversification into additional financial services was a logical place to look for inter-bank differences, but the available data did not enable us to draw useful categories among the banks. Table 7.3 does identify some possible directions for comparing the banks' relative focus on different financial services, but we were unable to obtain data for all years for everything from number of branches to existence of insurance or asset management businesses. Since these data are not reported in a standard way across banks or countries, we were unable to obtain an adequate set of information across the years for our modeling.

SUMMARY

All of the banks are making great efforts to increase efficiency, whether through branch closings, layoffs, or eliminating other redundancies. Banks throughout the world have improved their technology, information systems, and alternative delivery systems in order to reduce costs and spur additional sales. Banks have also learned that in-market and adjacent-market mergers must be followed by extensive cost-cutting to make the acquisitions nondilutive in their impact.

The Swiss banks were similar in scope to the big German banks, but they are less dependent on their domestic retail banking business for profits than the large German banks. The Swiss banks generate a much larger percentage of total income from international lending, private banking, and asset management than the German banks. They also have much lower (better) efficiency ratios than the German banks.

The strategies, goals and objectives, and sources and uses of funds among the banks differ. Most banks now offer investment banking (except Lloyds TSB); many banks either sell insurance or own insurance companies (except J. P. Morgan and Chase – now merged – and the Japanese banks); all considered asset management and private banking to be vital functions; and mortgage lending was important at most banks (except J. P. Morgan and Barclays). All of the banks were highly dependent on their foreign operations to provide a large proportion of their customer base and income (except Lloyds TSB). Credit cards were important revenue producers for the UK banks, Citicorp, and Chase, less so for the Japanese banks, and of little importance or not even issued by the German and Swiss banks and J. P. Morgan. The only institution in the group not to offer standard retail banking services for customers, at least in the home market, was J. P. Morgan. (This, of course, has now changed with the merger of J. P. Morgan into Chase.)

On average, the UK and US banks had lower noninterest expense-to-income ratios and higher profitability ratios during the 1990s as compared with their German, Swiss, and Japanese counterparts. This can be partially explained by the better economic conditions in the UK and the USA during the period, higher taxes in Germany, differences in accounting treatments, and an absence of concern at the executive management level for shareholder returns at the biggest German, Swiss, and Japanese banks – at least until recently. It is interesting to note executive management changes at the CEO level at all six German and Swiss banks during 1995-7, when bank performance was especially weak in both countries. Another reason for the lower ROE ratios among the German and Japanese banks is their investment philosophy of holding large positions in equity securities at book value. Only dividend payouts contribute to current profitability.

Even with the Big Bang in Japan in 1998, and with the recent changes in German and Swiss bank managements and strategies, it appears that the global competitiveness of the banks will continue to favor the US and UK banks in the early twenty-first century.

FURTHER READING

Allen, Linda, and Rai, Annop 1996: Operational efficiency in banking: an international comparison. *Journal of Banking and Finance*, 20, pp. 655–72.

Brimmer, Andrew 1998: Competition and the integration of the markets for banking and financial services. *North American Journal of Economics and Finance*, 9, pp. 187–202.

Gart, Alan 1994: *Regulation, Deregulation, Reregulation*. New York: John Wiley.

Goldberg, Lawrence, and Hanweck, Gerald 1991: The growth of the world's 300 largest banking organizations by country. *Journal of Banking and Finance*, 15, pp. 207–23.

Grosse, Robert 1997: The future of the global financial services industry. *The International Executive*, Fall, pp. 599–617.

Kim, Seung, and Singer, Robert 1997: US and Japanese banks: a comparative and evaluative analysis. *The Bankers Magazine*, March–April, pp. 56–61.

Levinson, M. E. 1995: Why banking isn't declining. *Federal Reserve Bank of San Francisco Weekly Letter*, San Francisco, January 20, pp. 1–3.

Sanford, Charles 1994: Financial markets in 2020. *Economic Review*, Kansas City: Federal Reserve Bank of Kansas City (First Quarter), pp. 19–28.
Spiegel, John, Gart, Alan and Gart, Steven 1996: *Banking Redefined*. Chicago: Irwin.

NOTES

This chapter is coauthored with Alan Gart, of the Indiana University of Pennsylvania. The authors would like to thank Shreyas Chari and Pari Thirunavukkarasu for their excellent research assistance on this project and Professor Taeho Kim for his valuable comments on an earlier version of this study.

1   One paper, Seung Kim and Robert Singer, "US and Japanese banks: a comparative and evaluative analysis," *The Bankers Magazine*, March–April, 1997, pp. 56–61, even asserts that the US banks have lost their competitive edge in the 1990s. This is a wholly inaccurate statement, since their information comes mainly from the 1980s, and their basis of measuring competitive edge is asset value, rather than market value of the bank, or profitability, or efficiency.

2   The major crises include: first, the LDC debt crisis, in which the large American banks had more than the total value of shareholders' equity loaned to LDC nonperforming borrowers; second, the savings and loan (S&L) crisis, which hurt many financial institutions in the commercial banking sector as well; and third, the real estate crisis, in which major commercial banks encountered large numbers of mortgage borrowers unable to meet their loan payments.

3   Yet another measure of banking activity is the participation of banks in innovative and rapidly growing segments of the market such as derivatives. The US banks really dominate this segment – but it does not appear in size measures, since the derivatives are typically "off-balance-sheet."

4   The merger between Citicorp and Travelers Group vaulted Citi back into the one of the largest global financial services companies, with market value of about $US 135 billion and assets of just under $US 700 billion. The new company is called Citigroup, and is a prominent player in commercial banking, investment banking, asset management, and insurance. Deutsche Bank is still larger, especially after its acquisition of Bankers Trust. The merger of Bank of America with NationsBank has moved this additional US bank back into a global leadership position. The Japanese banks trumped all of these mergers with the combination of Dai-Ichi Kangyo, Fuji, and Industrial Bank of Japan into the Mizuho Group, with assets of about $US 1.3 trillion, in 1999.

5   In the Japanese case, equity ownership is limited to at most 5% of the outstanding shares of another company.

6   The largest "British" bank today is the Hongkong Bank (HSBC), which moved its world headquarters from Hong Kong in anticipation of the 1997 return of the colony to Chinese rule. The largest part of HSBC's business is in Asia, but with its acquisitions of Midland Bank in the UK and Marine Midland and Republic Bank in the USA, HSBC is fully a global player.

7   In the acquisition, Deutsche Bank gained Alex Brown company, a major US underwriter of corporate equity, as well as the Bankers Trust relationships with big US companies and a large trust management business.

8   During 1996, UBS turned down an offer from Credit Suisse to merge. However, following a year of huge losses in 1996, plus domestic branch overcapacity, a bleak domestic

outlook, and minimal return on investment, UBS agreed to merge with SBC to form one of the largest banks in Europe and in the world with assets of close to $US 600 billion. The new bank, called United Bank of Switzerland, should be able to generate a ROE of between 15 and 20% within a few years, following the completion of expense cuts and consolidation of operations.

9   The same analysis was done using ROA as the dependent variable, producing results that are similar but slightly less significant statistically.

10   The German banks were penalized by substantially higher national and local corporate income tax rates, as can be seen in the following table:

Country	National corporate tax rate (%)	Local corporate tax rate (%)
Germany	45	20.48
Switzerland	7.83	
UK	31	
USA	34	Various
Japan	37.5	7.76

11   The ROE of the Swiss banks during 1996 was lowered substantially by large loan loss provisions and restructuring charges. The following table shows ROE ratios before and after these provisions and charges:

Bank	Before/After
SBC	10.10%/-14.90%
CS Group	9.60%/-15.20%
UBS	8.90%/-1.50%

8

RESPONDING TO THE CHALLENGE OF THE NEW ECONOMY

INTRODUCTION

The enormous changes in the financial environment that have occurred during the 1990s and are occurring in the 2000s demand new strategies from the financial institutions that intend to survive into the next decade. Tremendous pressure exists for banks to grow larger, so that they can use their internal resources to fund major lending opportunities. This pressure underlies much of the consolidation of the investment banking sector, as those firms choose to be acquired by large banks and thus to expand their balance sheets. At the same time, opposing pressure exists for banks to focus on narrow ranges of products in which they are excellent, rather than to become financial supermarkets, since this strategy consistently failed during the 1980s and 1990s. And these two pressures are only a couple of the ones currently bombarding financial institutions in the newly deregulated environment of global competition.

A means of responding to the pressures that are striking the financial services sector in the early twenty-first century is through the concept of Transformational Management[1]. Using this tool, financial institutions can better position themselves and move to create sustainable competitive bases. In addition, they can explore the process of incorporating the Internet into internal operations and into client services through this perspective.

THE FOUR-PHASE SEQUENCE OF TRANSFORMATIONAL MANAGEMENT

Transformational Management is the process of corporate strategy determination that calls for a firm to project its domain of business activity into the future, to identify

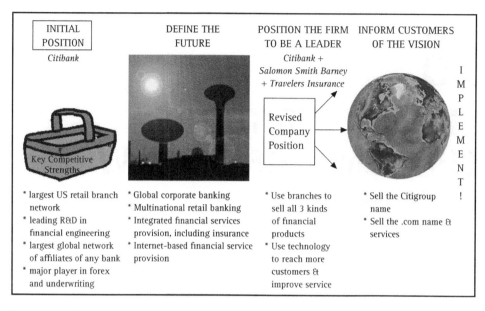

Figure 8.1 Citibank's Transformational Management process.

mechanisms for competing successfully in that context, and to educate the market about that future and about the company's ability to provide the services/products that will be needed in that future. It requires an active effort to define the technological and regulatory environments that will prevail in the future, as well as to anticipate the competitors who will populate the market. And finally, it requires a clear and timely implementation plan to take advantage of rapidly moving opportunities and to focus the firm's efforts on completing the cycle from identification of the strategy to its realization. The process is sketched in figure 8.1 for the example of Citibank, which is elaborated below, along with two other examples.

The firm must first assess its core strengths, which enable it to exist profitably. Without some competitive strengths, or the possibility of developing them, there would be no basis for projecting a future competitive position. This requires not only identification of competitive strengths, but also evaluation of who the key competitors are. This exercise in establishing the firm's *Initial Position* is really backwardlooking, since it only evaluates the firm's situation up to the present time.

The first step in transforming the organization and the strategy is to *Envision the Future*. Depending on the competitive context (e.g., a country, a particular market segment, a global broad market, etc.) selected as the firm's target, the relevant competitors may well be different from those encountered to date. This requires a process of futurism. The firm's leaders must envision the technological and regulatory environments that will characterize the market(s) in which the firm wants to operate in the near-term future (say, the next 3–5 years). This does not have to be "high-tech," necessarily, but just forward-looking.

In the financial services sector, this is particularly important, with the global deregulation trend and Internet-based changes that are ongoing. Even though the details of the future cannot be known, it is actually easy to see many of the relevant elements. For example, by the mid-1990s in the United States, it was clear that nationwide banking was in the process of becoming a reality legally, and that *allfinanz* service provision was occurring through the blurring of limits between financial services sectors, even before the Gramm–Leach–Bliley Act of 1999 (to eliminate barriers among commercial and investment banking and insurance). It was also obvious that the Internet would demand new positioning of services to take advantage of that medium, even though the precise mechanisms to do this were and are unclear.

Once the target context is defined, the firm must decide on the kinds of business activity that it wants to pursue in this environment, positioning itself to take maximum advantage of the new reality. This is to *Design a Strategy to Meet that Future*. The strategy does not need to follow just on the existing competitive strengths of the firm but, rather, it requires building/acquiring additional strengths that may be required to succeed in the new context.

Third, the customers and potential customers have to be informed of this vision and of the firm's capabilities to provide the market-leading products and services. This step requires not only an external effort to *Sell That Future*, but also an internal effort to convey the direction and requirements to the firm's own managers and staff members.

The final step is to *Implement the Plan*. This final step is easy to downplay in the efforts to pursue the first three parts of the sequence, but obviously all is lost if the implementation is not carefully considered and carried out. As in any strategic planning process, the goals need to be identified clearly and measurably, and implementation has to be evaluated according to the degree of success in achieving those goals.

A PRIOR CONDITION: THE FIRM'S *INITIAL POSITION*

Take the **Citibank** case. In the mid-1990s, Bank of America was the largest US commercial bank, with Citibank close behind, followed by NationsBank and Chase Manhattan. The Citibank leaders saw that commercial banking was going to continue to lose ground to investment banks in terms of extending credit to corporate clients (through securities issuance, rather than deposit/loan intermediation), and even in terms of capturing savings – in mutual funds rather than bank deposits. They also saw the possibility of expanding activities in other financial sectors such as insurance and, even more attractively, asset management.

But prior to moving to the stage of defining a way forward, the bank needed to identify its competitive strengths relative to the relevant competitors. Citibank defined its geographic target as global rather than national. Any goals would be pursued in competition with financial services firms at the worldwide level, rather than just within the United States. This perspective did not mean that Citibank would follow an identical strategy in each country, but that the target market was consumers, corporate clients, and governments around the world – and that competitors were definitely not just other US banks.

The strengths (the *Initial Position*) that the bank was able to define were numerous. The fact that Citibank possessed the largest US retail branch network at the time gave it an advantage over both (domestic and foreign) commercial banks and other financial services providers in terms of access to retail customers in the United States. This situation was almost exactly the opposite in most other countries, where Citibank had a marginal retail presence, focusing mostly on corporate business and private banking. A second major competitive advantage was Citibank's role as the preeminent source of financial innovation in the world. Citibank had been first or among the leaders in introducing all kinds of financial and technological innovations, from automatic tellers to currency forward contracts and options, from telephone banking to global cash management. This advantage was truly global in scope, relative to competitors almost everywhere. A third key advantage was Citibank's possession of the largest global network of affiliates of any bank. Since most of the non-US affiliates were involved principally in wholesale business activities, Citibank was able to offer the most extensive distribution of corporate banking services to multinational companies and other wholesale clients worldwide. These are only a few of the strengths that Citibank brought to the table as it undertook the process of Transformational Management in the mid-1990s (see figure 8.1).

As another example, consider the German insurance company, **Allianz**. In the mid-1990s, Allianz was Germany's largest insurance company and the third largest in the world, with major businesses in both property/casualty and life insurance. Under the German legal system, Allianz was permitted to have major shareholdings in other financial and industrial companies. At that time it had key holdings of shares in Deutsche Bank (5% of the bank's equity) and in Dresdner Bank (22% of that bank's equity), in addition to investments in numerous other financial and industrial firms.

Allianz viewed the strengths of its *Initial Position* as residing in four areas in the mid-1990s. First, the firm was one of the acknowledged world leaders in insurance products, in both life and property/casualty segments. Second, it had better distribution than almost all competitors. Only AXA had a larger network of offices around the world. Third, Allianz had complementary businesses in its portfolio of holdings, due to Germany's allowance of cross-shareholdings. The major stakes in Deutsche Bank and Dresdner were only part of the total portfolio. And finally, Allianz was one of the world's top ten asset management companies, with about $US 400 billion under management in 1998. This capability in asset management derived directly from the need to invest insurance premiums in long-term investments, to provide for future policy payouts.

As with Citibank, Allianz defined its market to be global, though with a European foundation. While Allianz wanted to provide a wide scope of financial services, it limited itself largely to the insurance policies, annuities, and asset management activities of that sector, and left retail and wholesale commercial and investment banking to its alliance partners (particularly the two largest German banks).

As a final example, **Hongkong and Shanghai Banking Corporation** (Hongkong Bank, or HSBC) was the long-time leader in commercial banking in Asia, and particularly in Hong Kong. In the late 1980s it was obvious that major changes in the Hong Kong business environment would likely take place upon reversion of the colony to Chinese control on July 1, 1997. In 1990 the bank moved its headquarters from Hong Kong to London, largely as a defensive strategy against the political risk. As part of this process, HSBC undertook a Transformational Management process beyond the geographic diversification.

Maintaining the same time frame as for Citibank and Allianz, we can see that for the *Initial Position* in 1995 the key strengths of HSBC were its possession of the largest network of retail affiliates of any bank in Asia, its leadership as well in the wholesale banking business in Asia, and its large global network of affiliates (including Midland Bank in the UK and Union Bank and Marine Midland Bank in the USA). In the Asian region, HSBC was the clear leader in provision of international services, particularly trade finance and foreign exchange.

STEP 1: *ENVISION THE FUTURE*

In the context of US deregulation and global market integration, Citibank saw a future competitive environment that would require broad-scope financial services providers to be able to offer their services to retail clients throughout the country with physical facilities, as well as electronically. On the wholesale level, it was clear that these services would have to include traditionally investment banking products, such as securities underwriting and trading, as well as asset management. And at the global level opportunities were arising to establish full-service operations in many countries, where previously only limited, and typically international, services had been permitted to foreign banks.

Citibank looked for US options that would give the bank a major presence in investment banking and asset management, as well as in the retail insurance sector, and that would fit nicely into the retail branch network. The initial growth of the Internet also provided a challenge to see how this channel of distribution could be fitted into the bank's portfolio of services.

Allianz was pursuing a strategy of globalization, with affiliates throughout Europe and in Asia and the Americas at that time. Looking at the global financial services industry, it was clear to Allianz that its insurance market was being invaded by other financial services providers, and that its core asset management business was likewise subject to incursion from noninsurance competitors. Allianz saw that to survive and prosper it had to be a truly global provider of not only insurance services, but at least asset management as well. And with the evident consolidation in financial services in general, it was obvious that Allianz would also have to consider becoming directly involved in banking.

Allianz defined the future of its intended business as requiring a global presence in a coordinated set of financial services activities including insurance and asset management, but also potentially extending to other, particularly retail, financial services. It did not see an existing or future core strength in securities underwriting or trading; that is, in investment banking.

HSBC's leaders saw the future competitive terrain that they wanted to serve as global corporate banking, multinational[2] retail banking, and the provision of integrated financial services. With the geographic coverage that the bank had already achieved by the mid-1990s, the challenge was to integrate these affiliates and to provide clients with truly global services. The traditional trade financing and international services would continue to be focal areas but, additionally, HSBC wanted to build domestic retail business in its key markets (the UK, the USA, and China). And the bank wanted to continue to build its regional dominance in commercial banking services throughout Asia.

STEP 2: *DESIGN A STRATEGY TO MEET THAT FUTURE*

Once the broad outline of the firm's intended competitive domain and the key challenges in that domain have been sketched, the firm must design a set of steps to position itself as a leader. These steps include both restructuring of the organization and investing in R&D to enable the firm to produce the new products or services that will be demanded in the unfolding environment.

Citibank took a huge step in the process of Transformational Management in the late 1990s, when it agreed to merge with Travelers Group and to become a universal bank, or really an *allfinanz* institution – even before the US legislators had approved rules permitting such activity. (In 1998 Citigroup, as the merged entity was called, was given a period of about two years to begin the integration of the two firms, after which key businesses such as insurance would have to be divested if US law and/or Federal Reserve rules had not changed to permit banking and insurance businesses under the same holding company.) Citibank's leaders took the risk of entering into a complex set of financial businesses, because they foresaw the convergence of commercial and investment banking and insurance in the USA, just as it was already a reality in most of the other industrial countries. By betting in such a huge way on the US regulatory reform, the newly named Citigroup[3] positioned itself to enter rapidly into the full-service financial market and also to take maximum advantage of the electronic services that are possible.

The stated intent of the merger was to position Citigroup as the country's leader in integrated financial services, operating at the retail level largely through Citibank branches countrywide and at the wholesale level through New York based underwriting, asset management, and other service provision for corporate and institutional clients. The important steps to (1) sell all three kinds of products (e.g., bank deposits and loans, stocks and bonds, and insurance policies and asset management) through the branch network and (2) use technology to reach more clients and improve service were both begun at the time, but even three years later were not complete. Happily for the group, the US Congress did approve legislation to permit

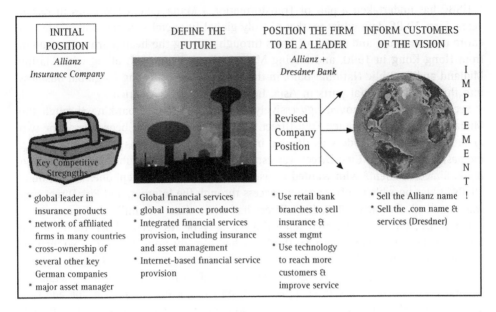

Figure 8.2   Allianz's Transformational Management process.

allfinanz institutions, so the insurance business was not lost to the previous regulatory prohibition.

The strategy pursued by Allianz took several years to unfold, in terms of its interest to build a major branch network for retail sales of financial services in Germany. The firm looked to build on its alliances with both Dresdner Bank and Deutsche Bank, which attempted to merge in the year 2000. Allianz had intended to utilize the Deutsche Bank 24 network of branches and automatic tellers to sell its retail insurance products along with the two banks' products. However, this attempted merger broke down, and both banks ended up with dissatisfied shareholders and a continuing commitment to link up with another institution to expand their scope.

In early 2001, Allianz agreed to take full ownership of Dresdner Bank, and to divest its holding in Deutsche Bank. This gave Allianz a nationwide network of branches in Germany through which to sell not only bank deposits, loans, and other services, but also its own insurance products and asset management services. Given Allianz's major focus on retail financial services (e.g., personal and homeowners' insurance policies), this major bet on Dresdner's retail banking arm may prove successful.

Allianz's Transformational Management process is described in figure 8.2.

For Allianz, more than the other two firms discussed here, the need to expand into additional financial services (i.e., beyond insurance) was a pressing priority. With the elimination of barriers to entry in insurance in the United States, and with global financial services integration, the *raison d'être* of insurers is more and more in doubt. The strategy of Allianz confronted this challenge head on.

HSBC has undertaken a pair of Transformational Management processes in recent years. First, HSBC defined its market as truly global financial services, and created an entire new structure and set of affiliates through moving the headquarters to London from Hong Kong in 1990, and buying Midland Bank in the UK, along with Marine Midland and Republic National Bank in the United States, to bring its global business into three roughly equal parts in Asia, Europe, and North America.

Second, HSBC has moved aggressively into Internet-based banking through the Midland Bank division called First Direct. This Internet bank has been one of the two or three most active leaders worldwide in developing this means of banking during the past several years. First Direct was established in 1989 as a subsidiary of Midland Bank, aimed at clients who wanted to use their accounts via telephone. By the mid-1990s, it was possible to offer account access through the Internet, and FirstDirect.com was launched. By early 2000, First Direct had more than one million clients.

For HSBC, the organizational repositioning may be less of a shock than for the other two examples here, because the bank had already gone through a wrenching transformation in the 1980s, to prepare for Hong Kong's return to Chinese control in 1997. Given that HSBC already had reconfigured its business into three segments of the world, and had moved headquarters from Hong Kong to London, the addition of the Internet-based banking division has probably been felt as less of a threat than at the other institutions.

STEP 3: *SELL THAT FUTURE*

With the firm's own direction clearly defined, the task remains to educate the public about the conditions that are coming and the way in which the firm's products or services offer superior qualities in that future. Citibank is probably the most advanced in this regard, having regularly innovated with new products and services over many years. Thus, for Citibank to present to clients and potential clients the idea that its banking services are available on line and will be supplemented with stock-market products and insurance products should likely produce a positive response, since Citibank is regularly the leading innovator in the financial markets. Likewise, moving stockbroker clients of Smith Barney into the use of a wider range of Citigroup services should be relatively easy, given the Citi name and innovative record.

Even in Citigroup, getting customers to understand the vision requires instilling this vision into its own diverse internal marketplace. This implies a lengthy process of integrating two enormous institutions and corporate cultures – perhaps three, if we consider Smith Barney as separate from Travelers Insurance Group. It also requires investing in research and development into new financial products and structures that take greatest advantage of the full range of combined financial services that the group can provide. In particular, it requires a continuing effort to develop services to be offered through the Internet, to build on existing customer relationships and to develop new ones. One key technology that is being developed is that needed to operate an electronic financial center, so that clients can deal with Citigroup for deposits and loans, stock and bond, and other investment management transactions, and insurance products, in a single location (virtual or real).

In the case of Allianz, this requires the development of additional financial services beyond its traditional insurance policies and asset management business. Even though Allianz was a major shareholder in both Deutsche Bank and Dresdner Bank, the firm still did not have its own direct access to the clients of those banks. By buying Dresdner Bank, Allianz has gained the owned banking arm that may allow it to sell a much broader portfolio of financial services, and do so through electronic means as well as through branches and insurance agents. It remains to be seen how successfully this new model can be presented to the public.

The other side of the story is that Allianz has established a leadership position worldwide in insurance products, and has educated the public about the benefits of its portfolio of those products. However, it has not demonstrated any presence in the banking market, other than through its ownership of shares in banking institutions. In the asset management business, Allianz has accomplished the goal of educating clients about its capabilities, but this still leaves both investment banking (possibly to be divested) and commercial banking as new areas for the firm. Allianz needs to complete the steps of internalizing commercial banking activity, and then conveying the message to the market.

Some major steps still remain to be taken in this process, even before seeing how technology and market conditions develop in the years ahead. Allianz is still seen as an insurance company, in a world in which integrated financial services will be the only viable model for large competitors[4]. Whether the provision of an integrated portfolio of products comes from the acquisition of new affiliates or the development of the previously announced Deutsche Bank 24 (presumably now "Allianz Dresdner Bank 24"), Allianz must implement this stage of the process before going further.

Hongkong Bank (HSBC) has the most advanced strategy of the three institutions as far as virtualization is concerned. HSBC does not have a fully integrated set of financial services available either through First Direct or any of its traditional banking branch networks, so that implementation remains to be accomplished. Given that such integration has only been permitted in the USA for a couple of years, it is not surprising that the process is incomplete. Still, in a competitive environment that really does move in Internet time, HSBC will have to move rapidly to implement the service integration now.

Probably the key difficulty for HSBC is to sell the company name to clients in a way that will convey the image of an institution with global reach, with world-leading distribution capabilities through its affiliate network, and with a full *allfinanz* portfolio of products. In 1998, the bank launched a campaign to convert its various commercial bank acquisitions to the HSBC name, dropping Midland, Republic, and so on. This informing of the public has been done successfully in Asia, but is still in progress in the United States; and is only partially completed in Europe, with the conversion of Midland Bank to HSBC. It is easy to see why many analysts argue that

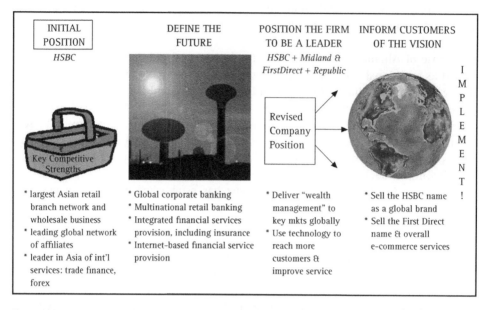

INITIAL POSITION	DEFINE THE FUTURE	POSITION THE FIRM TO BE A LEADER	INFORM CUSTOMERS OF THE VISION
HSBC		HSBC + Midland & FirstDirect + Republic	
Key Competitive Strengths		Revised Company Position	
* largest Asian retail branch network and wholesale business * leading global network of affiliates * leader in Asia of int'l services: trade finance, forex	* Global corporate banking * Multinational retail banking * Integrated financial services provision, including insurance * Internet-based financial service provision	* Deliver "wealth management" to key mkts globally * Use technology to reach more customers & improve service	* Sell the HSBC name as a global brand * Sell the First Direct name & overall e-commerce services

I M P L E M E N T !

Figure 8.3   Hongkong Bank's Transformational Management process.

HSBC should ally with Merrill Lynch, to gain both additional US distribution and also a brand name that conveys a more global image.

Figure 8.3 depicts HSBC's Transformational Management process.

Note that the transformation of the bank began about two decades ago, with the process of relocating its headquarters and building business in North America and Europe. On the basis of its fundamental competitive advantages, which may center on the bank's knowledge of Asian markets and possession of Asian clients, HSBC is attempting to put together the structure for selling universal banking products globally.

The crucial next step is for the firm to commit to pursuing the R&D and other expenses needed to achieve the competitive position envisioned in the new business environment.

STEP 4: *IMPLEMENT THE PLAN*

As much as may be said for the analytical part of the process, the *implementation* of the chosen strategy may be the hardest step to take. In the case of Citibank, this has meant giving up a lot of the firm's autonomy to (the former) Travelers in the new organization, and really "betting the company" on the universal banking model. This was ultimately accomplished by the fact that Travelers' leader Sandy Weill wrested sole leadership of the combined firm from his co-equal colleague from Citibank, John Reed. Once Weill had gained control, the universal banking model was cemented into the core of Citigroup's strategy, and the implementation then shifted to expanding the group's presence in more markets and to finding ways to cross-sell products between divisions and to streamline the provision of services.

For Allianz, the implementation problem is perhaps even more complex than at Citigroup, since the base of the organization in insurance products is narrower than in commercial banking. Perhaps a kind of "reverse takeover" of management may occur, with the universal banking model put into place at the combined Allianz Dresdner Bank, and the repositioning of insurance as one (key) financial product in the portfolio. This would better position the firm to sell the broad range of financial services. Another part of implementation is the global expansion of the firm to lead in financial services, and Allianz has taken numerous steps to build its global insurance business, through acquisitions of large insurers in several countries.

In the case of Hongkong Bank (HSBC), the implementation of its transformational process has proceeded quite far, with very extensive expansion in all three Triad regions of the world. The attempt to build a leading role in wealth management does not seem to have produced results thus far, but perhaps the acquisition of a leading asset management firm may catapult HSBC into a much stronger position in this area. The group's virtualization strategy appears to be unfolding relatively peacefully, and First Direct is becoming a globally known and respected brand name. The competitive environment for Internet-based banking services is, of course, still far from settled.

CONCLUSIONS

Transformational Management is a process of strategic management that enables a firm to position itself to serve the future market(s) that it selects and to present a coherent picture to internal and external audiences about that future and about the firm's capabilities. The fascinating aspect of this process in the current context is that all three institutions whose transformations are ongoing have largely defined their turf as being the same: the provision of truly global financial services to a worldwide client base. All three have histories of extensive retail sales networks, and yet all three have built industry-leading businesses in corporate financial services as well.

Their turf is, however, far from identical. Allianz is far more focused on insurance and related products than the other two; Citibank has much greater activity in investment banking than the other two; and HSBC has by far the largest franchise in Asia. Despite these differences, and the likelihood that each institution will lead the others in these sectors, an unquestionable convergence is occurring. Each competitor will have to redefine its relevant markets and positioning as technological and competitive conditions evolve. The Transformational Management framework provides a comprehensive basis for elaborating strategy in this complex and dynamic environment.

NOTES

Sincere thanks to Francis Nzeuton for his excellent research assistance on this project and on the Transformational Management program overall.

1   This concept is developed further in Robert Grosse, "Transformational Management," chapter 2 in R. Grosse (ed.), *Thunderbird on Global Business Strategy* (New York: John Wiley, 2000).
2   The retail business is called "multinational" rather than global, to distinguish that it is largely local in each country, whereas investment banking and corporate banking are more globalized.
3   This commentary overstates the vision of Citibank, since in fact the transformation process was co-equally led by Travelers Group, and particularly by its leader, Sandy Weill. Thus, the Transformational Management of Citigroup unquestionably comes from both the vision of the bank and the vision of the stockbroker/insurance company. Indeed, the whole process could be viewed as a transformation of Travelers, which saw the need to move into full-service financial business.
4   This point is certainly debatable, since one or more large insurance company(s) may survive for several more years. However, the logic is very compelling that insurance companies need a wider range of financial products to offer customers – or to focus on narrow niche products, or to offer global risk management services (see chapter 9) – to survive.

PART III

WHERE THE SECTOR IS HEADING

Contents

9	Why insurance won't survive	139
10	Investment banking at the crossroads	153
11	Financial instruments and financial structures	167
12	The generation of long-term investment to support bond and stock-market growth	179
13	International financial centers	191
14	Surviving the twenty-first century	201

9

WHY INSURANCE WON'T SURVIVE

INTRODUCTION

The insurance sector in the United States is in the same position in the early 2000s as the savings and loan (S&L) sector was in the mid-1980s. Until this time, state governments provided varied rules and regulations governing the ownership and operation of insurance companies, so that local consumers of insurance services would be protected against risks of unfair pricing, deceptive practices, and possible failure of insurance providers. As far as ownership is concerned, commercial and investment banks were prohibited from entering the insurance business to own insurance companies. As far as prudential practices are concerned, insurance providers were and still are required to meet minimum capitalization requirements, to hold minimum assets against possible claims, and to meet other financial criteria to ensure the viability of the insurers.

The government protection with respect to ownership in this sector was greatly reduced under the Financial Services Modernization Act of 1999, and now banks, stockbrokers, and other firms can freely enter the insurance business[1]. This change means that banks and other kinds of firms may now enter the insurance sector, both cherry-picking the attractive pieces of the business (such as sale of annuities, and underwriting of insurance policies) and competing in full-service insurance activities. Given that the insurance sector has no particular competitive barriers to entry (other than perhaps firm size), now that the regulatory protection has been dropped, new entrants are systematically eating away at the insurers' profitable business activities. The new entry is coming through the acquisition of existing insurers by banks and brokers, as well as through banks simply adding insurance products to their existing lines of business. In either case, the insurers are very hard pressed to defend their turf.

In this context of greatly heightened competition, the fundamental question is: What can insurance companies do to survive? Surely they need revised business models to confront the new competitors. Also, they need to respond to the threat of the Internet as a service provider – though, as in commercial banking, the Internet will probably be more of a key channel of distribution, rather than the source of new "virtual" competitors. This chapter describes competitive conditions in the USA and several other countries in the insurance sector, and pieces together some ideas on how insurance companies can build strategies to survive in the twenty-first century.

THE US INSURANCE SECTOR

Not that much of the business was all that attractive in the first place. Life insurance is an extremely stable business, based on policy writing for provision of death benefits to the policyholder's survivors. The average life expectancy is known to a very close approximation of current reality, and one company cannot charge higher fees than another company for the same benefits (except perhaps for slightly higher charges when the quality of service can be differentiated). So, given competition, life insurance has low margins, and is not particularly attractive as a stand-alone business. Table 9.1 shows the low but stable profitability of the sector during the 1990s, when life insurance firms in the USA earned about 5.3% per year return on equity, compared to an S&P 500 average of about 17.3% per year.

Table 9.1   US property/casualty and life insurance premiums, and claims, 1990–9 ($US billions)

Year	Property/casualty premium income	Life premium income[a]	Property/casualty insured losses	Life insurance benefit payout	Property/ casualty net income[b]	Life insurance net income[b]
1990	217.8	76.7	−21.7	24.6	11.2	4.02
1991	223.0	79.3	−20.5	25.4	13.8	4.11
1992	227.5	83.9	−36.3	27.2	−2.5	4.27
1993	241.6	94.4	−18.1	28.8	14.5	4.66
1994	250.6	98.9	−22.1	32.6	11.6	4.93
1995	259.7	102.8	−17.4	34.5	19.5	5.28
1996	268.6	107.6	−17.2	36.3	20.8	5.61
1997	276.4	115.0	−6.0	37.5	35.5	6.11
1998	281.5	119.9	−17.7	40.1	23.2	6.63
1999	287.0	120.3	−25.5	41.4	14.3	7.27
% change, 1990–9	31.8%	56.8%	−17.7%	68.3%	27.7%	81%

[a] Life insurance premium values do *not* include health insurance data or annuity income. When health policy and annuity income are included, life and P/C incomes are approximately equal through the 1990s.

[b] Net income includes policy net income plus income from investments (and for life insurance, includes annuity income).

Sources: A. M. Best & Co.; *Best's Review* Property & Casualty Industry Survey January 11, 2001; Life & Health Industry Survey April 19, 2001; American Council of Life Insurers.

However, the same logic shows why life insurance is so easy for banks to copy and simply add to their portfolios of other financial products. Why is an insurance agency needed to sell a life insurance policy, when a bank office could do the same, and even arrange direct deductions from the client's checking account to pay the premiums? The answer is that it isn't – except if the insurance agency can offer some additional service(s), such as the sale of annuities and/or the management of a client's assets. But annuities are just one more investment product that banks can sell just as easily as insurance companies, so this possible point of differentiation is not a viable one either. In sum, the life insurance business is extremely difficult to defend against broad-scope financial services providers, since its products (services) are so standardized. The main concern of regulators is to ensure that the policyholders will be treated fairly, and that benefits will be paid as contracted; that is, that the insurers remain in business so that future benefits are paid as agreed. Banks can comply with these concerns just as well as insurance companies.

With respect to health insurance, also defined as part of the life/health subsector, the degree of standardization of coverages and other policy characteristics is lower. The health insurance business is growing rapidly as the average life expectancy increases in the USA and elsewhere, making doctor and hospital treatments more frequent and thus insurance more important to guaranteeing access to services. While some of this segment has fairly standardized policy aspects, such as corporate policy provision for large numbers of participants, other aspects of it are quite new or fragmented, making simple policy design difficult. Within the USA, the debate about public versus private social security provision fuels the debate on the health insurance business today.

The situation is certainly different for property/casualty insurance, where the risks are not as simple to define and price. Auto insurance, which constitutes just under half of all property risks insured, is generally quite stable, with actuarial calculations of benefit payouts showing very steady streams over time. In this way, auto insurance does not differ dramatically from life insurance. With respect to home insurance, however, the possibility of a natural disaster such as a hurricane or an earthquake can cause claims for literally thousands of homes and other buildings at one time, thus imposing an enormous cost on the property insurers (on an infrequent basis). Thus, property insurance can have very spectacular payouts and very volatile payout frequencies, as shown in figure 9.1, making it a much more complex instrument than life or auto insurance.

The possibility for banks to copy this product without extensive knowledge of the sector is much lower than for the previously mentioned products[2].

Another issue that should be considered in the insurance context is the area of *reinsurance*, in which insurance companies buy their own insurance, essentially passing the risk on to third parties – for a price that constitutes the third parties' revenue for running the risk. This is a logical step from the initial underwriting of insurance policies. The insurer may become exposed to very large risks in a particular type of insurance or geographic location, or with respect to a specific client. Other insurers or speculators may be willing to buy some of that exposure, in return for a

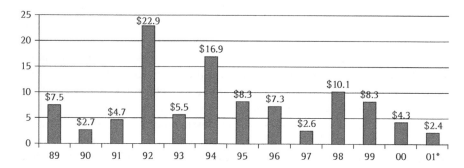

Figure 9.1   US insured catastrophe losses (in $US billions). Note that the estimate for the first half of 2001 (see asterisk) is as follows: first quarter, $US 705 million; second quarter, $US 1.7 billion.

Source: Property Claims Service, Insurance Information Institute.

premium paid by the originating insurance company. So, reinsurance can be accomplished with contractual arrangements similar to banks' loan syndication, in which multiple banks agree to share the financing (and risks) of extending a large credit to a borrower(s).

An alternative mechanism for passing insurance risk on to third parties is the securitization of that risk. This arrangement functions similarly to the process of securitization in banking. The initial insurer (lender) sells off part of the portfolio of insurance risk (loans) to third-party investors, in exchange for a yield paid to the buyer. The reinsurer (the purchaser of the securitized debt) holds the insurance policy risk (loan default risk) in exchange for the interest payments by the originator, which are largely covered by the insurance premiums. As with the traditional reinsurance, legal recourse for claimants under the original insurance policies remains with the original insurer. The original insurer then must exercise the bond provision that essentially passes the loss on to the bondholders. This form of securitization has proven very popular in the USA since the disasters of Hurricane Andrew in 1992 and the Northridge earthquake in 1994. By 1997 more than $US 1 billion of catastrophe insurance bonds had been issued[3], and other forms of insurance policy-backed bonds were beginning to take off in the market as well.

The reinsurance business is not necessarily different from initial insurance in concept, but it is another function that may allow insurers to exist if banks do not choose to enter into this segment. Once again, however, there is no particular reason why banks and other investors would not enter this business, assuming that the risks and rewards are sufficiently attractive. For reinsurance risks that are not well known (such as some property/casualty risks), there may be specialized knowledge of the business that makes it difficult for a bank or other noninsurer to enter this business, and may thus require specialized investors.

Another area of specialization by insurance companies is *asset management*. Given the relationship between initial, periodic premiums paid by insurance policyholders, and later (or never) disbursements by the insurance companies to meet claims, there is a huge amount of money to be invested during the intervening period.

The investment management carried out by insurance companies is both internal and provided to clients for their own separate investments. The policy premiums that must be invested to provide funding of future claims and income to the insurance company owners constitute the main part of the internal funds to be invested and managed. Policyholder investments in various financial instruments, such as annuities and mutual funds, are the principal external asset management concern of insurance companies.

As part of life insurance policies, insurers have historically sold investment instruments, particularly annuities, to their policyholders. The annuities are periodic (typically fixed-value) payments that pay out a specific sum at maturity. A ten-year annuity with a maturity value of $US 1,000 and a guaranteed return of 5% per year would require a semiannual investment of $39.06 by the investor (policyholder). This kind of instrument is simply one more type of deposit/investment structure that banks or other suppliers can offer just as well, such that insurance companies have no particular advantage in offering annuities relative to competitors. This reality once again points to the difficulty that insurance companies now face in defending their turf without the earlier legal barriers to entry.

Insurance companies are among the largest institutional investors in the world's capital markets. Table 9.2 shows a comparison of major US insurance companies and other major institutional investors.

It is obvious from table 9.2 that the insurance companies have lost their leadership as asset managers in the USA to more broadly diversified financial services providers during the past 25 years. By 2001, insurance companies in the USA as a group managed $US 4.2 trillion in assets, or 11.6% of a total US capital asset market of $US 36.3 trillion.

The situation in the 1970s could have led to a competitive advantage in asset management for insurance companies over their rival financial services providers, except that there is nothing proprietary about the insurance companies' ability to manage funds for their clients or for their own portfolios. The key advantage that the large insurance companies had was large size; however, if the size of insurance companies is stacked against the size of commercial banks, mutual funds, and even large pension funds today, the insurers are clearly smaller and thus less able to realize economies of scale or specialization. This reality is reflected in the 1999 ranking of asset managers, which shows AXA Financial as the only insurance company in the top ten US asset managers. Even if we move to the top 50 asset managers, insurance companies comprised only seven of the top 50 in 1999.

A final important issue in the United States and in some other countries such as the United Kingdom is *demutualization*. As insurance companies find the need to build up their financial services activities beyond policy underwriting, they are discovering the need to have additional financial resources available. Access to capital markets is difficult under the mutual company structure, since the firm's shareholders are its policyholders, and their investment is limited to policy premiums[4].

Table 9.2 Assets under management of leading US institutions

1975 Ranking	$US billions	1989 Ranking	$US billions	1999 Ranking	$US billions
Metropolitan Life Insurance	20.2	American Express	159.4	Fidelity Investments	956.0
Prudential Insurance of America	18.1	Prudential Insurance of America	144.3	Barclays Global Investors	782.6
Morgan Guaranty Trust	17.8	Aetna Life & Casualty	110.4	State Street Global Investors	672.4
First National City Bank	15.0	Equitable Investment Corp.	91.9	Capital Group Companies	424.2
Equitable Life Assurance Society	10.1	Bankers Trust	89.6	Merrill Lynch Asset Management	557.3
New York Life Insurance	8.7	Fidelity Investments	83.2	Mellon Bank Corp.	463.6
U.S. Trust	8.6	Metropolitan Life	79.3	AXA Financial	462.7
California Employees Retirement	8.2	Merrill Lynch Asset Management	76.8	Morgan Stanley Dean Witter	419.9
John Hancock Mutual Life Insurance	7.6	Wells Fargo	72.0	Citigroup	419.2
Aetna Life & Casualty	7.3	J. P. Morgan	68.4	Putnam Investments	391.3

Source: *Institutional Investor*, July 1999, pp. 75–106; and July 2000, pp. 97–8.

The change to a joint stock company permits insurers to issue securities in the open market, and thus to raise new capital through stock share or bond issues.

Demutualization brings with it a dependence on the financial markets, since investors in the insurance companies will include nonpolicyholders. This dependence will make the insurers less likely to defend the interests of policyholders and more likely to pursue the interests of shareholders, as in any joint stock company. This change in perspective for the insurance companies has made the process of demutualization a rocky one in many instances, as policyholder groups seek to maintain their treatment under the mutual company structure.

OTHER INSURANCE MARKETS OUTSIDE OF THE USA

Insurance companies in the rest of the world are less segregated from other financial services than in the USA for the most part, as *allfinanz* models have permitted insurers to belong to larger financial groups for many years. Even so, the consolidation of the financial services sector in recent years has seen major mergers and acquisitions involving insurance companies in many countries.

The United Kingdom

In the UK, the largest insurers are parts of the *allfinanz* banking institutions. While Prudential remains largely focused on the insurance sector, its Internet bank, Egg, is the European leader in this financial service, and Prudential is also a leading asset manager at the global level, with $US 220 billion under management at year-end 2000. This firm and another four of the largest British insurers are briefly described below.

Prudential plc has over £220 billion insurance and investment funds under management, over 22,000 employees worldwide. In the UK, Prudential is the leading life insurer, the biggest pension provider and one of the largest institutional investors. Egg is the UK's leading financial services e-commerce provider, with over 940,000 customers and deposit funds of £7.6 billion. Following the acquisition of M&G in April 1999, the Prudential group is the UK's leading unit trust provider. In Asia, Prudential is one of the largest insurers, with operations in ten countries. In the USA, Prudential owns Jackson National Life, one of the top life insurance companies. In Europe, Prudential has partnership agreements with CNP Assurances in France and Signal Iduna in Germany.

CGNU was formed by the 1998 merger of Commercial Union and General Accident, with the addition of Norwich Union to the mix in 2000. The London-based company is the UK's top multi-line insurance company and one of the six largest insurers in the world. CGNU's general insurance products include auto, fire, and health coverage. It also offers life insurance, personal pensions, annuities, and unit trusts, as well as such financial services as investment management (CGNU is the second largest fund manager in the UK) and stockbrokerage. The company operates in more than 50 countries worldwide, focusing on the European market.

One of the UK's largest banks, **Abbey plc** (formerly Abbey National) offers retail, wholesale, and business-to-business banking services through a network of some 750 branches. Abbey also provides wealth management services and consumer loans. Other offerings include life and general insurance, primarily through subsidiaries Scottish Mutual and Abbey Life. Abbey plans to expand its presence in the insurance marketplace with its purchase of mutual life insurer Scottish Provident.

The main business of London-based **Alliance & Leicester** is writing mortgages and taking deposits, but the firm also sells life insurance (through its Alliance & Leicester Life Assurance subsidiary) and offers personal investment products. Its commercial banking activities include asset financing, cash management, commercial lending, and debit and credit card clearing. Alliance & Leicester has some 310 branches and nearly 1,000 ATMs in the UK, and also offers telephone, Internet, and postal banking.

AXA UK (formerly Sun Life and Provincial Holdings) offers general, health, and life insurance, as well as asset management, primarily through its AXA Insurance, AXA Ireland (also operating in Northern Ireland), PPP healthcare, AXA Sun Life, AXA Investment Managers UK, and other subsidiaries. The London-based group sells life, commercial vehicle, private auto, health, home, and personal insurance, as well as pensions and other investment products. AXA UK's asset management activities are concentrated primarily on managing subsidiaries' funds. AXA UK is a wholly owned subsidiary of the French AXA, the world's largest insurance company.

Germany

In Germany, **Allianz** continues to lead the insurance pack, and is the second largest insurance company in the world. In 2001, Allianz took full ownership of the previously partially owned Dresdner Bank, thus becoming immediately a major global competitor in *allfinanz* services.

The Stamford, Connecticut, based holding company **General Cologne** is a subsidiary of Warren Buffet's holding company, Berkshire Hathaway, and it commands a global presence in some 150 countries. Business is divided into four primary regiments: North American property/casualty reinsurance, international property/casualty reinsurance, life and health reinsurance, and financial services. The company's main subsidiary, General Reinsurance, is one of the biggest property/casualty reinsurers in the USA. Its second largest operating company is Kölnische Rückversicherungs-Gesellschaft (Cologne Re) of Germany, the world's oldest reinsurer and a major force in international reinsurance. The company controls almost 90% of Cologne Re. GeneralCologne Re also owns General Re–New England Asset Management, which provides asset management services for other insurers. Other company units provide derivative products, insurance brokerage, and real estate management.

The Hanover Rückversicherungs company, based in Hanover, Germany, and better known as **Hanover Re**, is that country's second largest reinsurer behind Münchener Rückversicherungs-Gesellschaft (Munich Re) and the fifth largest worldwide. The property/casualty unit of the ever-diversifying Hanover Re accounts for some 40% of all premiums and is geared toward markets in the USA, Germany, and Japan. Its life/health business is marketed through subsidiary Hanover Life Re and focuses on treaty (groups of risks) rather than facultative (individual risk) policies. Financial reinsurance is provided through Hanover Re Advanced Solutions, a Dublin-based consortium managed jointly with HDI Reinsurance (Ireland); both Hanover Re and HDI Reinsurance (Ireland) are subsidiaries of HDI Haftpflichtverband der Deutschen Industrie. Hanover Re's business program (through Clarendon Insurance Group) focuses on hard-to-place risks and niche insurance markets in the USA. HDI owns 75% of Hanover Re. This group is the exception among the German insurers, with activities only in the insurance sector.

Münchener Rückversicherungs-Gesellschaft (**Munich Re**) provides back-stop coverage for insurers worldwide. Coverage includes fire, life, auto, liability, and other types on both facultative (individual risks) and treaty (groups of risks) bases. Europe is its biggest market (about 75% of premiums) and the company plans expansion through acquisitions there. Its American Re subsidiary is a leading property/casualty reinsurer in the USA. As insurance clients seek less expensive ways to manage risk, reinsurance markets have stagnated. In response, Munich Re has moved into direct insurance. Its

92%-owned ERGO subsidiary, number two in Germany behind Allianz, sells life, health, and property/casualty insurance throughout Europe. Continuing its expansion, ERGO has acquired Alte Leipziger Europa and Italian life insurer Bayerische Vita. In a quest to become a financial services firm, Munich Re has also entered the asset management game, forming MEAG Munich ERGO AssetManagement, a joint venture with ERGO.

Japan

In Japan, the main insurance companies are all parts of the dozen largest keiretsu, the widely diversified business groups that include Mitsui and Mitsubishi, among others.

Osaka-based **Nippon Life Insurance**, the world's fourth largest insurer, leads the Japanese market. A door-to-door sales corps peddles its plain-vanilla products, including individual and group life and annuity products. Deregulation has allowed the company to move into such areas as corporate and residential lending. Other activities include real estate development and management, and a variety of educational and philanthropic projects. The majority of the company's overseas activities focus on providing coverage to Japanese companies and citizens abroad. Nippon Life is also partnering with such firms as Deutsche Bank and Sakura Bank (now part of Sumitomo Mitsui Banking Corporation) to offer investment trusts, personal lending, and other services. Nippon Life is part of the Sanwa keiretsu.

Dai-ichi Mutual Life Insurance is Japan's number two insurer (behind Nippon Life Insurance). Founded in 1902, the firm sells individual and group life insurance, as well as individual and group pension products. Like other Japanese insurance firms, Dai-ichi Mutual faces the Big Bang of deregulation and concomitant competition from foreign companies previously barred from the Japanese market. The company has become the first of Japan's life insurance firms to set its own premium rates. Dai-ichi Mutual Life operates overseas through a handful of subsidiaries and offices. It is part of the Mizuho Group.

One of Japan's largest life insurance firms, **Asahi Mutual Life Insurance** sells life and health policies to individuals and groups. Its specialized policies include ones that pay victims of cancer, stroke, and heart attack. Asahi Mutual is a member of Insurope, a global network that offers insurance to Japanese companies abroad and to foreign companies in Japan. The firm has formed an asset management joint venture with the USA's Metropolitan Life Insurance and is also setting up an Internet unit. Increased competition from industry deregulation and Japan's economic woes have hurt the firm, which plans to demutualize and join a partnership with Tokio Marine and Fire and Nichido Fire & Marine. Asahi Mutual is part of the Dai-Ichi Kangyo (Mizuho) Group.

Part of the Mitsubishi Group, **Meiji Life Insurance** is one of Japan's largest life insurers. It offers individual life and annuities; group life and pensions; and investment products. It formed subsidiary Meiji General Insurance in response to a 1996

Japanese law allowing firms to sell both life and nonlife insurance products. Meiji Life operates in Asia, Australia, Europe, and North America. The insurer has alliances with Dresdner Bank and Allianz AG, and has plans to enter a joint venture with Tokio Marine & Fire to sell insurance to Bank of Tokyo-Mitsubishi's clients.

These commentaries on key firms in several of the world's largest national insurance markets illustrate the growing consolidation of the sector, into *allfinanz* institutions more than into simply larger insurance companies. Indeed, there is no leading insurer left in the group that is not part of a financial services group that includes a major asset management company along with the insurance business, and most of them also include commercial banking activities as well. At this point, it may be useful to reconsider the point made at the outset: How can insurance firms position themselves to survive in the deregulated and globalized environment of the 2000s?

COMPETITIVE STRATEGY

Given these various conditions, it is an inescapable conclusion that independent insurance companies, without extensive additional financial services, will not be able to keep up in the open competition of the twenty-first century. Insurers that become banks – as State Farm, Allstate, and several others have begun to do – or that acquire banks – as Travelers and Allianz have done – will be able to pursue the strategies of broad financial services providers, just like other banks.

Look at the situation in the USA today. The largest insurance companies are shown in table 9.3.

From the group shown in the table, none of the pure life insurance companies has formed or acquired a commercial bank. (Prudential and Nationwide operate in both kinds of insurance, and both have banks.) On the property/casualty side, all but Berkshire Hathaway, CAN, and Farmers have formed financial groups offering

Table 9.3   The largest US insurance companies

Property/casualty company	1999 revenues (in $US billions)	Life/health company	1999 revenues (in $US billions)
State Farm	44.6	Prudential of America	26.6
American International Group	40.7	Metropolitan Life	25.4
Allstate	27.0	New York Life	21.7
Berkshire Hathaway	24.0	Nationwide Life	15.1
Loews (CNA)	21.0	Northwestern Mutual	14.1
Travelers Group	10.6	The Hartford	13.5
Nationwide	9.2	Equitable Life	12.7
TIAA–CREF	39.4	Farmers	3.27

commercial banking services and asset management, along with insurance policies. CNA is part of Loews Group, which owns Loews Hotels, Lorillard Tobacco, and Diamond offshore oil drilling. Berkshire Hathaway also owns substantial investments in a wide range of industrial and commercial companies (such as Dexter Shoes, Benjamin Moore Paints, Dairy Queen, and several jewelry chains) – but not in commercial banking.

The challenge is that banks that enter the insurance market will be able to draw away clients by offering a broader array of services and/or easier access to the insurance services than pure insurance companies. The insurers that enter banking will need also to buy banking expertise to deal with the much wider array of financial services, beyond dealing simply with insurance-related financing.

Considering the situation from a classic competitive advantage perspective, the key competitive advantages in this sector must be identified. Insurance companies presumably possess knowledge of their business that is not possessed by banks. The specialized knowledge should enable insurers to protect their business through withholding the knowledge from the market. This is a logical expectation, but one that can be resolved by the banks if they hire away experienced insurance managers from the insurance companies. And it is much easier to develop knowledge of a very limited number of products/services in insurance than it is for insurers to go in the other direction and develop knowledge of a wide range of banking products and services.

Distribution channels are another potential source of competitive advantage in the sector. Certainly, State Farm and Allstate have many more points of sale at local insurance agencies than any commercial bank in the USA. At the end of 2000, State Farm had 16,000 agents and Allstate had 13,000, located in all 50 states. These numbers far exceed the number of branches of any bank. On the other hand, if automatic teller machines are considered as points of sale of a number of bank services, then thousands of banks have even more locations than any insurance company – through the ATM networks that use MasterCard, Visa, and other electronic consortia for bank service provision.

On the basis of discussions with insurance industry executives, a number of key competitive advantages in this sector are shown in table 9.4.

Table 9.4 Key competitive advantages in the insurance sector

Advantages	Disadvantages
Knowledge of the customers/customer relationships	Heavily people-based production and sale of services (costly)
Knowledge of the risks, products, and other aspects of the sector	Relatively standardized services
Extensive distribution channels (local agencies or independent agents)	Highly regulated → highly noninnovative
Brand name recognized for reliability and service	

The ability of an insurance company to defend itself is based on its ability to maintain these competitive advantages relative to potential entrants into the business. As with many other service providers, the insurance companies rely heavily on the knowledge and skills of their employees and contract agents to provide competitive advantages. As competition builds in the era of deregulated competition in major insurance markets, the competitive advantages of the insurers seem to be outweighed by broad-scope financial services providers that are able to offer more services and greater flexibility to their clients. Also, the banks are increasingly able to offer national and even global access to account information and to their services, easily exceeding the capabilities of the insurers.

How will insurance firms be able to develop competitive advantages and defend them successfully in the future? It is clear that the main strategy will require diversification into other financial services. It is just too difficult to beat broad-scope firms on price or on availability of services.

An alternative direction may be to develop broader risk-management services, such as the provision of futures and options contracts and other risk derivatives, which would enable users to select among a portfolio of alternatives from a single company. Today, commercial banks offer more of these risk management tools, but there is no reason why insurance companies could not broaden their offerings – assuming that knowledge of risks and risk management techniques really is a competitive advantage of the insurance companies over outsiders to the sector.

A simple example of this kind of reasoning is that a property/casualty company could respond to the threat of losing clients to self-insurance (which is becoming more popular among large firms) by offering catastrophe insurance just for devastating losses, giving up premium income but preserving and perhaps even gaining clients due to the lower cost and more narrowly defined policies. In addition, the insurer may find that clients are willing to purchase additional hedging tools for managing smaller risks. And clients may even be willing to buy risk management advising as a service from the insurers.

At the same time as these pressures are squeezing the largest insurance companies, just as with commercial banks, there very likely will remain a variety of niche markets for insurance products that will allow small firms to survive. The analogy would be the "Mom & Pop" retail community banks. Such small retail insurance providers could survive by providing more personalized service to families and small-business clients, just as in commercial banking. For the major competitors, however, the world will look more and more like Citigroup and Allianz.

NOTES

I would like to thank Sangit Rawlley and Marie Gant for their excellent research assistance on this project.

1   Each state still retains the right to impose prudential rules on insurance providers, to ensure the financial viability of the insurers and to protect policyholders' rights. The 1999

Federal rules disallow the individual states from keeping banks out of the insurance business.

2   Even so, the diversification possibilities are still available. So, if a bank or other owner of an insurance business can provide property insurance policies to a wide range of geographically dispersed clients, the impact of large and infrequent disasters that trigger policy payouts can be reduced in the overall portfolio. Still, disasters such as Hurricane Andrew in 1992 would have affected any insurer's overall profitability for that year, given the more than 60,000 homes destroyed and $US 15.5 billion in insured losses.

3   See, for example, *The Economist*, "An earthquake in insurance," February 28, 1998, pp. 73–5.

4   This is exactly analogous to the S&L industry, where the owners are the depositors, who hold "membership" in the S&L, rather than stock shares. Just as with the S&L associations, the insurers are undercapitalized relative to bank competitors, and in order to compete more successfully they are looking to enter the financial markets via stock issue – in other words, demutualization.

10

INVESTMENT BANKING AT THE CROSSROADS

INTRODUCTION

Investment banking is probably the least understood of the various areas of financial services discussed here. The reason is primarily that the scope of investment banking is seldom identified clearly. For example, investment banking includes not only underwriting of securities issues and arrangement of mergers and acquisitions, but the creation of derivatives, financial advising, and numerous other activities as well. And if we include stockbrokerage in the mix – since it is indeed part of investment banking – we can see that the number of people involved in the sector is actually quite large, and not just a handful of very high-priced deal-makers on Wall Street.

The net result of the discussion in this chapter will be to conclude that investment banks that provide only a narrow range of deal-making and advisory services will be unable to compete in the big leagues of the sector, and they will have to join forces with commercial bankers, retail stockbrokers, and/or wealth management providers. This is somewhat similar to the logic in our discussion of the insurance sector. It will be possible for smaller niche players to operate in investment banking, just as in insurance, but the major firms will need to offer a greater range of services. And in investment banking in particular, these additional services include funding (lending) to clients, not just offering advice and guidance on how to secure such financing[1]. Despite these pressures, investment banking success in the largest firms is largely dependent on people skills, rather than on funding or some kind of economies of scale. As long as investment banks can maintain leadership in the skills required for underwriting, advising on mergers and acquisitions, and some other functions, it is not likely that they will be beaten out by commercial banks with deeper pockets or by other intermediaries.

Returning to the question of definitions, investment banking includes at least the following activities:

- Underwriting corporate stock, bond, and other securities issues.
- Arranging, evaluating, and advising on corporate merger and acquisition (M&A) activities.
- Arranging financing for corporations through nonloan vehicles such as commercial paper, financing facilities, and securitization of accounts receivable.
- Providing risk management services through the creation/issuance of derivative instruments such as futures and options.
- Providing buy-and-sell opportunities in a secondary market for existing securities (brokerage).

One study defines the set of activities comprising investment banking, as shown in figure 10.1. As one can readily see from the two lists, there are quite a few different investment banking services, which are quite varied in their nature, their clientele, and their value. For example, retail stockbroker services are quite small in their impact per transaction – but the firm can carry out thousands of trades every day, and thus generate interesting, actually very large, income. At the other extreme, major mergers or acquisitions between companies are far, far fewer in number, but may involve values of billions of dollars per transaction. And likewise with respect to staffing needs: the investment bank may employ thousands of retail stockbrokers to deal with millions of individual clients, while at the other extreme the M&A staff may be numbered in dozens of people, dealing with a likewise limited number of clients and deals.

The ultimate question of interest here is as follows: How can an investment bank succeed as a major player in more than just a niche market of this total panorama? There will not be one right answer: firms could focus on a variety of strategies – from being the provider of the highest-quality services to being the provider of greatest accessibility through possession of the best distribution network. The most useful way to arrive at some answers will be to describe the existing and expected competition that exists in major parts of the investment banking spectrum, and then to try to draw out some lessons that will serve in the evolving environment.

WHO ARE THE MAJOR PLAYERS?

For the most part, major players in investment banking are large, *allfinanz*, and universal banking institutions[2]. In its annual survey of investment banks, ranking along seven types of activity, *Institutional Investor* magazine in 2001 found the results shown in table 10.1.

As noted earlier, most of the top 25 investment banks in every category are institutions that provide commercial banking services along with underwriting, deal-making, and so on. The exceptions are Merrill Lynch, Goldman Sachs, Morgan Stanley, Lehman Brothers, Bear Stearns, Rothschild, Lazard, and Greenhill[3].

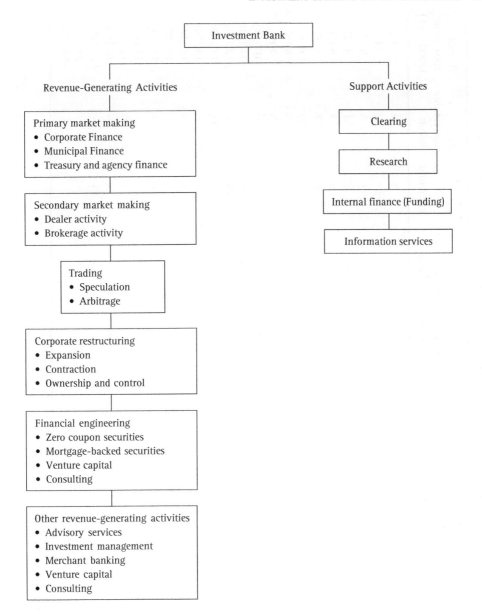

Figure 10.1   Investment banking activities.
Source: John Marshall and M. E. Ellis, *Investment Banking and Brokerage* (New York: McGraw-Hill, 1994), p. 5.

Table 10.1 Investment banking: top firms (2001 rankings/league tables; January 1, 2001 to May 30, 2001)

Firm	Global merger volume	US investment-grade debt	US high-yield debt	Global equity volume	Asset-backed securities	Eurobond	US convertible bonds	Overall 2001 rank (2000 rank)
Credit Suisse First Boston	4	5	1	4	1	3	4	1 (4)
Goldman Sachs	1	8	3	1	11	12	2	2 (1)
Morgan Stanley	2	7	4	2	6	7	5	3 (2)
Merrill Lynch	3	2	9	3	12	8	1	4 (3)
Citigroup	8	1	2	5	2	5	3	5 (5)
UBS Warburg	5	9	11	6	–	4	7	6 (8)
Deutsche Bank Alex Brown	10	10	6	9	4	1	10	7 (7)
Lehman Brothers	11	4	7	8	6	14	6	8 (9)
J. P. Morgan Chase	6	3	5	15	3	6	9	9 (6)
Dresdner Kleinwort Wasserstein	7	–	–	10	–	9	–	10 (11)
Bank of America	–	6	8	11	5	–	–	11 (13)
Société Générale	15	–	–	7	17	19	–	12 (15)
Bear Stearns	19	11	10	–	7	–	11	13 (10)
Rothschild	9	–	–	–	–	–	–	14 (16)
Barclays Capital Group	–	15	–	–	16	2	–	15 (17)
Lazard	12	–	–	–	–	–	–	16 (14)
Greenhill & Co.	13	–	–	–	–	–	–	17 (23)
First Union	–	12	15	–	9	–	–	18 (20)
BNP Paribas	–	14	–	–	–	–	8	19 (18)
ABN Amro	–	19	–	18	–	10	–	20 (12)
HSBC	–	18	–	–	15	13	–	21 (19)
Bank One	–	13	–	–	–	–	–	22 (22)
CIBC Oppenheimer	–	–	14	–	–	–	–	23 (21)

Source: Institutional Investor, February 2002.

The first nine of the banks are generally considered to be the "bulge bracket," firms that provide industry-leading (top ten), broad-range services in investment banking. It is primarily this group that is the target of discussion in the analysis, in which the goal is to uncover strategies that may be sustainable for banks that want to be more than niche players. To get an idea of the activity focus of different members of the investment banking community, table 10.1 shows clearly that UBS Warburg is not active in designing and selling asset-backed securities, J. P. Morgan Chase is weak in Global Equity issuance, and Lehman Brothers is weak in eurobond issuance. Otherwise, the bulge bracket firms are highly competitive in all areas of investment banking, as defined by the league table.

These results can be contrasted with the standings of other banks in the table. Specialists in mergers and acquisitions include Dresdner Kleinwort Wasserstein (which may be considered to be in the bulge bracket, despite its weaknesses in several areas), Lazard, and Rothschild, while these firms are weak or not even present in US securities issuance. Specialists in US issues that do not participate importantly in international markets include Bank of America and First Union (Wachovia). And in contrast, specialists in euromarkets, with very little participation in the US domestic market, include Société Générale and Hongkong Bank (HSBC).

At all levels of the table, the most hotly contested investment banking activity is issuance of US investment grade debt. This is because many kinds of investors, such as pension funds, are limited to placing their funds into investment-grade securities, so that this is by far the largest segment of the bond market.

AN EXAMPLE: DRESDNER KLEINWORT WASSERSTEIN

At the very edge of the bulge bracket is the German *allfinanz* institution, Dresdner Kleinwort Wasserstein (DrKW). This is a wholly owned part of Dresdner Bank, which in turn is part of the Allianz group, with its origination in the insurance sector. Through acquisition of US investment banking boutiques, Dresdner obtained the experience in acquiring companies in the process of privatizations outside of the United States, and expertise in fund management of Kleinwort Benson, the London-based group. Dresdner obtained the M&A experience and expertise, the leading US restructuring practice, and a top-three ranked US high-yield business by acquiring Wasserstein Perrella, a US-based group. Dresdner Bank had earlier been involved directly in investment banking in Germany, but had decided that to be an important player globally, it needed to add some significant skill and customers through these acquisitions.

The strategy to become a bulge bracket investment bank has put Dresdner/DrKW at the edge of the group, but the profitability of these activities has been inadequate to please the shareholders of the bank (and the insurance company parent). In 2002, Allianz Dresdner was reconsidering the fit of DrKW into the overall organization, toward the possible end of spinning off the investment bank to shareholders or finding some other exit from the business.

A SECOND EXAMPLE: BANK OF AMERICA

As a counterpoint to the situation of DrKW, Bank of America (BofA) has a very large domestic US franchise, with retail business in most states and a significant share of domestic underwriting and good market positions in most of the major instruments. Where BofA is absent is the euromarket, and also in mergers and acquisitions. The failure of BofA to join the bulge bracket of investment banks could easily be remedied through the acquisition of a key M&A player such as Greenhill or Lazard.

BofA did make a major foray into investment banking with the 1997 acquisition of Robertson Stephens, a large San Francisco based stockbroker company. Robertson Stephens was an expert in advising and underwriting for high-tech (Silicon Valley) firms, as well as being the major retail broker in California. At the same time, NationsBank, which acquired BofA in September of 1998, had acquired the San Francisco rival, Montgomery Securities, which also specialized in dealing with high-tech firms, in 1997. This was actually a very conflictive situation, since several partners of both investment banks had been members of the same firm earlier, and were bitter rivals in San Francisco. Given that NationsBank was the acquirer in the "merger" with Bank of America, it was no surprise that its investment banking group would win out afterward. Thus, in August 1998, the Robertson Stephens investment banking business was sold to BankBoston[4]. The net result left Bank of America with an investment banking arm based in San Francisco, with a specialty in high-tech underwriting and advising, but without a major presence in either New York or London.

THE RELATIVE SIZE AND IMPACT OF INVESTMENT BANKING ACTIVITIES IN THE BIG FIRMS

To gain a better feel for what counts in this business among the bulge bracket competitors, consider the impact of various activities on several of the largest investment banks. Table 10.2 shows the impact of several categories of income and expense on the income statements of Merrill Lynch, Goldman Sachs, and so on.

What is quite noteworthy about all of the firms is that interest and dividend earnings dominate the income flows. This is typical for the largest investment banks, which manage large portfolios of investments in companies and securities for their own account. "Investment banking" income, which covers income from underwriting securities' issuance, arranging mergers and acquisitions, and other investment advice, ranks significantly lower as a contributor to total income than interest and dividends in all of the banks. Commissions earned from stockbrokerage and other trading activity are even smaller in impact on the income statement (though they are certainly not trivial). And asset management represents another small but growing segment of the income generated by several of the leading investment banks, though again this segment ranks far below interest and dividend earnings.

Table 10.2   The relative size and impact of investment banking activities in the big firms (bold figures in $US million and as of December 31, 2001 unless otherwise indicated; information relative to the investment banking subsidiary of each firm unless otherwise indicated)

Activity	ML	GS	MSDW	CSFB	Citi/SSB	UBS W	Deutsche AB	Dresdner KB	Lehman	JPM Chase
REVENUES	**38,757**	**31,138**	**35,445**	**17,887**	**19,406**	**34,090**	**74,640**	**20,780**	**22,392**	**17,991**
Commissions	13.6%	14.7%	8.8%	8.3%	19.0%	4.7%	4.7%	9.6%	4.9%	8.3%
Asset management and other fees	13.8%		5.2%	12.0%						
Interest and dividends	52.0%	53.4%	60.6%	64.6%	25.8%[a]	75.5%	67.2%	73.6%	65.5%	17.2%[a]
Principal transactions	10.1%	20.1%	14.6%	7.0%	16.7%	9.6%	18.8%	12.4%	7.3%	34.4%
Trading	15.5%	8.1%	2.7%	9.8%						
Investments	-0.9%	1.5%	16.1%	-2.4%						
Investment banking	9.1%	11.8%	9.5%	18.8%	23.3%	8.9%	7.2%			20.1%
Underwriting	6.3%									
Strategic advisory	2.8%									
Other	1.4%	1.4%	1.2%	2.0%	15.0%	4.5%	0.2%	1.7%		20.0%
EXPENSES	**37,380**	**27,442**	**31,815**	**10,578**	**23,254**	**27,367**	**72,837**	**19,549**	**20,644**	**8,978**
Interest expense	45.1%	55.9%	61.4%	57.1%		63.2%	61.6%	75.8%	51.3%	
Brokerage, clearing, and exchange fees	2.4%	3.1%	1.6%	1.8%		1.0%	1.5%			
Compensation and benefits	30.1%	29.8%	24.9%	26.2%	89.0%	66.8%	18.3%	24.2%	16.6%	64.4%
Office expenses	13.7%	11.3%	9.7%	10.5%		33.2%	12.4%	2.4%	4.3%	
Other	8.6%	0.0%	2.4%	4.4%	10.9%	6.1%	10.8%	1.7%	8.6%	35.6%
Net earnings	573	2,310	2,287	-144	2,627	6,723	167	1,153	1,255	9,013
Net earnings in $US	573	2,310	2,287	-144	2,627	4,019	148	1,022	1,255	9,013
Exchange rate (if applicable); local currency to USD						0.5978	0.8860	0.8860		

[a] Net interest expense from 2001 annual report.

Sources: figures for all banks were taken from their 2001 annual reports, except for the following: Salomon Smith Barney and J. P. Morgan Chase from "Investment banking puzzles," UBS Warburg, March 1, 2002; Dresdner Bank from 2001 Management Report.

COMPETITION IN INVESTMENT BANKING IN THE EARLY TWENTY-FIRST CENTURY

Why is it that investment banking is "at the crossroads"? The answer is that, as with many industries in the early part of the new century, external factors have changed the competitive environment such that previous strategies do not work as well as they did before, and new competitors are entering the market rapidly and successfully. The "traditional" firms of the sector face an enormous burden of reacting or proacting to the challenges of this new environment.

The most important features of competition in investment banking that have changed in the late 1990s and early 2000s are the two-pronged advances of *deregulation* and *technology change*. The first feature, deregulation, has accounted for a massive consolidation of the sector, since now commercial banks and insurance companies may offer investment banking services in the USA, just as they have done so in most of Europe and elsewhere for many years. As a result of the Gramm–Leach–Bliley Act of 1999[5], financial services giants such as Citibank and Chase Manhattan have been able to become major investment banking competitors. Citibank accomplished this through internal expansion of its corporate banking business, as well as through the merger with Travelers Group and Salomon Smith Barney in 1998. Chase accomplished this largely through the merger with J. P. Morgan in 2000.

And, of course, the permeation of Internet communications and ever more rapid computational capabilities into all aspects of the business has pushed investment banks to offer lower-cost and more rapid services to their clients, just as in all other financial services. The initial impact of this wave of technology change occurred at the retail stockbroker level, illustrated by the entry of E*Trade and AmeriTrade in the United States, and of Egg, Consors, and Comdirect in Europe. These initial forays of the Internet-only brokers have been followed by successful responses from the traditional brokers and commercial banks, such that in the early twenty-first century the largest providers of Internet-based brokerage are traditional houses such as Merrill Lynch, discount brokers such as Charles Schwab in the USA, and traditional universal banks such as Deutsche and Dresdner in Germany and HSBC in the UK. The Internet has additionally affected the brokerage business as more and more institutional trading moves to electronic platforms, where commissions are much lower. In 2002, it was estimated that automated investment funds accounted for about 30% of trading in the USA[6].

But this technological challenge has not stopped with retail brokerage. The traditional core of investment banking, the underwriting of securities' issuance, is now under attack. Issuers such as General Electric and IBM, as well as a handful of other blue-chip firms, are finding it feasible to issue their securities directly to the public without an investment banking intermediary – by offering new stock shares, bonds, and commercial paper directly to potential investors via the Internet. Given the high quality and high visibility of these issuers, Internet-based underwriting that avoids use of investment banks is a growing threat to at least a part of this business. Given that most companies are not as well known and trusted as IBM or GE, there remains a very large segment of underwriting that probably will remain in hands of the investment banks for many years to come. Even so, the traditional investment banks see the benefits of distributing new issues through the Internet, and they themselves can use this vehicle to reduce their own costs of arranging and selling new issues.

COMPETITION IN UNDERWRITING SECURITIES ISSUANCE

Despite the surge in new competitors in the underwriting area, the business is still largely confined to the bulge bracket investment banks. This seems likely to change in the future, as firms find more and more ways to attract retail investors as well as institutions to buy their securities through either discount-type intermediaries and/or the Internet directly. The shift will not be rapid or complete, for certain. Consider the case of one major blue-chip borrower, the World Bank, in this context.

An example: a World Bank eurobond issue

In January 2000, the World Bank issued a $US 3 billion, five-year eurobond entirely through the Internet. This was the first major issuer's electronic bond offering, and it was more than fully subscribed. This phenomenon illuminates some possible continuing characteristics for the use of the Internet in underwriting securities issuance. First, it certainly reduced the issuance cost to the bank, and it likewise made the bonds more widely available to retail investors than would have been the case through traditional distribution. At the same time, the issue was arranged by the traditional investment banks, Goldman Sachs and Lehman Brothers, which both underwrote and provided a secondary market for the issue. The World Bank did not go it alone to carry out the issue but, rather, took advice and distribution assistance from the big investment banks, which nonetheless gained a smaller income than they would have done with a traditional non-Internet issue. The geographic distribution of the placement of this issue was very interesting as well: half of the issue was sold to investors in the Americas, one-fourth to investors in Europe, and one-fourth to investors in Asia. Secondary market trading became available immediately upon issue, through Goldman Sachs' online trading system.

The inroads of commercial banks into underwriting and advising

The problems of traditional investment banks are certainly more noticeable for the firms that are not in the bulge bracket. Figure 10.2 shows that the largest investment banks have pretty much maintained their market shares in the key investment banking functions over the past few years – but that commercial/universal banks

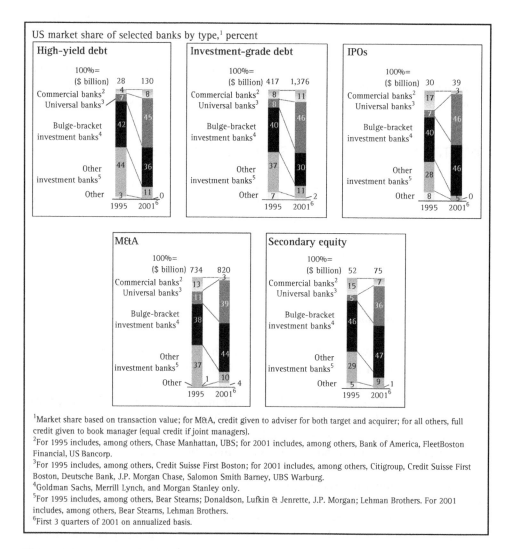

US market share of selected banks by type,[1] percent

Figure 10.2   An appearance of growth.
Source: Thomson Financial; McKinsey analysis as shown in Cairns et al. (2002), p. 43.

(such as Citibank and J. P. Morgan Chase) have taken large chunks of the business away from the smaller or more specialized investment banks.

The largest investment banks have not lost but, rather, have *gained* market share in functions including initial public offerings, mergers and acquisitions, and secondary equity issuance. They have lost share to commercial/universal banks in debt issuance, which may be due to the crossover possibilities for commercial banks to arrange debt financing through loans as well as bond or commercial paper issue.

COMPETITION IN RETAIL STOCKBROKERAGE

The world of stockbrokers has changed dramatically on several occasions in recent years. First, the discount brokerage service launched by Charles Schwab created a much more competitive business, with much lower charges to retail clients for securities trading. Schwab took literally millions of clients from the full-service brokerage houses in the USA, and forced them to respond with new divisions or arrangements for similar low-cost, low-frill brokerage service. This change in the environment was consolidated over several years, and then the environment produced another revolution – the Internet. In this case, the revolution was the advent of online or virtual brokers, with no offices and only a presence on the Internet. This revolution produced companies such as E*trade and AmeriTrade, both discount, Internet-based brokerage firms. While they appeared to cause a threat to the business models of the traditional brokers, time has shown that purely virtual brokers are not as widely accepted as the bricks-and-mortar firms (which offer their own Internet-based services), so the Internet brokerage business has evolved but has not replaced the leading firms.

Finally, the deregulation of securities trading progressed through the 1990s, culminating in the permission for commercial banks and insurers to enter the securities business directly. This revolution has produced a consolidation of brokers, the largest of which are now mostly affiliated with commercial banks or other broader financial services providers.

The incursion of the Internet in investment banking

In both retail and corporate markets for investment banking services, the Internet has made major inroads into the operations of the financial services providers, as well as into their relations with clients. From the huge growth of stock and bond trading on the Internet to the provision of transaction clearing and general record-keeping, the Internet has dramatically transformed the functions of information processing and distribution within investment banking. Figure 10.3 shows some of the players in these activities early in the new century.

While the more visible intermediaries here are retail stockbrokers such as E*Trade in the USA and Comdirect in Europe, the number of firms providing Internet-based services goes through the full range of investment banking functions. Firms such as Archipelago and Xetra have made major inroads into the market-making business for US and European equities, respectively. Likewise, Credit Trade and Creditex have taken important market shares in the provision of credit data and in dealing in credit-related transactions (such as loan conversions and credit swaps). These rapid changes in the stock/bond market infrastructure are shaking the traditional investment banks, as their hold on more and more services is being threatened.

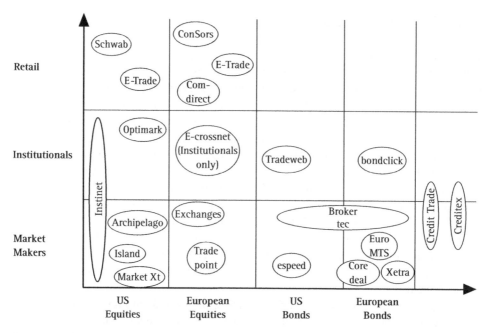

Figure 10.3   E-stock/bond markets.
Source: Zuhayr Mikdashi (ed.), *Financial Intermediation in the 21st Century* (London: Palgrave, 2001), p. 80.

THE DIRECTION OF COMPETITION IN INVESTMENT BANKING

Investment banking faces some of the same problems that plague the insurance sector, namely intrusion by commercial banks into formerly protected turf. A huge difference between the two sectors is that insurance deals with many more products (viz., many insurance policies and annuities) that are reasonably standardized, thus facilitating the entry of nontraditional players. Competition in investment banking is much more based on people skills and knowledge, and on specially tailored products, which are not as replicable as the insurance contracts. Thus, investment banking is inherently more defensible as a sector, and investment banks more likely to hold onto their business than insurance companies.

Nevertheless, the challenge to the firms that continue to concentrate in primarily investment banking functions, such as underwriting, M&A, and corporate finance, is that their competitors with broader services may continue to take business away from them. Particularly in debt instruments, the investment banks are clearly facing a severe challenge from commercial banks with deeper pockets. And this competition, especially in the area of funding client needs, may force even Goldman Sachs and Morgan Stanley to link up with a commercial bank[7]. Even without competition from commercial banks, investment banks face the rise of competition from in-house advice at large industrial companies such as General Electric, and at other deal-making firms such as Berkshire Hathaway, Viacom, and even Johnson & Johnson. To avoid investment banking fees, these organizations have hired former investment bankers to work as in-house employees on the same kinds of merger and acquisition advising[8].

FURTHER READING

Cairns, Alastair, Davidson, Jonathan, and Kisilevitz, Michael 2002: The limits of bank convergence. *The McKinsey Quarterly*, no. 2, pp. 41–51.

Gardener, Edward, and Molyneux, Philip (eds.) 1996: *Investment Banking: Theory and Practice*. London: Euromoney Publications.

Liaw, Thomas 1999: *The Business of Investment Banking*. New York: John Wiley.

Marshall, John, and Ellis, M. E. 1994: *Investment Banking and Brokerage*. New York: McGraw-Hill.

Rea, Alison 1998: *Global Investment Banking Strategy*. New York: Economist Intelligence Unit.

Smith, Roy C., and Walter, Ingo 2003: *Global Banking*, 2nd edn. New York: Oxford University Press.

NOTES

1 This, of course, is the challenge facing Goldman Sachs, the largest and most competitive investment bank that is not affiliated with either a commercial bank or a major retail stockbroker.

2 *Allfinanz* institutions provide investment banking, commercial banking, and insurance services. Universal banks provide investment and commercial banking services.

3 Morgan Stanley (through its stockbroker affiliate, formerly called Dean Witter) and Merrill Lynch might be considered in a different category, because with their enormous retail stockbrokerage businesses, they are in a very real sense "quais-banks" that take quasi-deposits (money market/cash management accounts). In principle, they should be able to leverage that major internal funding base to some extent.

4 Interestingly and unfortunately, BankBoston (which merged with Fleet Financial) was unable to fit Robertson Stephens into its organization, and in 2002 Robertson Stephens was disbanded and ceased to exist.

5 This is discussed in more detail in chapter 4.

6 "Banks Beaten," *Business Week*, June 14, 2003, pp. 74–5.

7 Merrill Lynch should be mentioned here as well, but I would not be surprised if Merrill were to merge with a major commercial bank before this book gets into print.

8 See, for example, Emily Thornton, Diane Brady, and Peter Burrows, "Bypassing the street," *BusinessWeek*, June 2, 2003, pp. 78–9.

11

FINANCIAL INSTRUMENTS AND FINANCIAL STRUCTURES

It is clear that the enormous changes that have shocked the global financial services market over the past decade are producing a new world of financial intermediation, risk management, and advising. Not only is competition becoming more global and more rapid, but the financial instruments and structures themselves are evolving into more agile and more user-adapted vehicles. The fitful starts and stops in Internet-based banking are probably the most visible sign of this evolution.

The Internet is certainly the most efficient means of distributing financial services such as deposits and loans, risk management contracts, and financial advice – not to speak of the transfer of funds itself. In fact, the problems with Internet-based banking have been largely in the realm of funds transfers, relating mostly to the assurance of confidentiality and accuracy of transfers. When these technical difficulties are resolved adequately, there will be a large-scale migration of financial transactions to this format, since it is extremely low-cost and rapid. Even with these concerns, by 2002 a significant amount of financial intermediation (deposit-taking and lending) had already moved to the Internet in many countries, including the United States.

What other financial services will move to the Internet in short order? Consider once again the panorama of financial services that was shown in chapter 1. Figure 11.1 below reproduces that view, adding shading in the boxes that are most susceptible to near-term shift to the use of the Internet.

This figure shows that the "virtualization" of financial services is proceeding throughout the range of financial services – though, as one would expect, with particular speed in those instruments and structures that are standardized. That is, when the financial instrument is standardized (such as a deposit or a loan, or a life insurance policy), this product can be packaged clearly in electronic form, with no need for negotiation between buyer and seller, so that the whole process can be

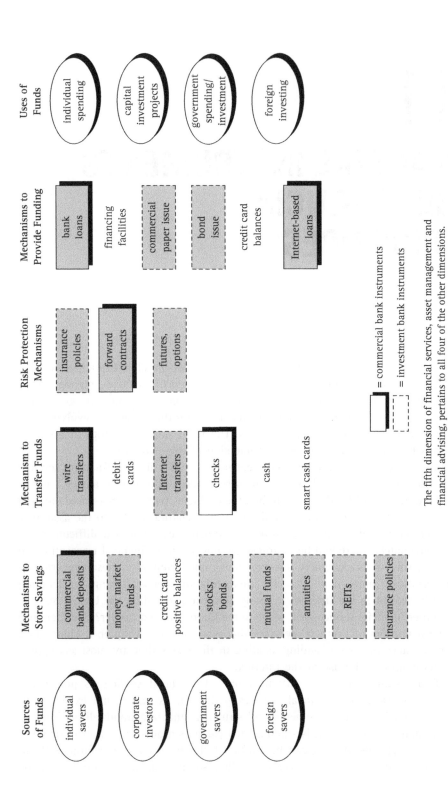

Figure 11.1 The financial services landscape once more.

mechanized. More individualized contracts and transactions are less susceptible to use of the Internet, because some level of interaction between buyer and seller, and some judgment about the client and the instrument, are both often required.

The process of financial instrument evolution is occurring also due to regulatory forces. As the barriers between investment banking and commercial banking fall – and likewise with the barriers to entry into insurance – the need for parallel instruments goes away. Why are annuities necessary as an insurance product, when they can be offered equally well by a commercial bank? Maybe the annuity instrument (with an initial investment and then periodic payout of equal-value coupon payments) is attractive to investors, but it certainly does not need different names to accomplish the same task. Annuities will (probably) not go away, but their character as insurance products will quickly fade away, as they are sold by banks and other intermediaries.

Some other financial instruments will simply disappear. If the system of electronic funds transfer can be protected adequately, there is no need for paper checks, since checks simply cause additional delays and expenses in the payment system. Internet-based payments and credit and debit cards can easily cover the function of checks, with dramatically lower costs and delays. The US administration is already moving full-force in this direction, requiring all financial dealings with the government to be handled electronically[1].

WHAT KINDS OF INSTRUMENTS ARE NEEDED?

There is no doubt that financial services will be needed in each of the areas identified before: storing savings, extending credit, transferring funds, managing risks, and offering financial advice. We can look at them one-by-one, and also see if there are any instruments or financial structures that are able to offer multiple services.

Mechanisms to store savings

Traditionally, banks have offered deposits and brokers have offered access to securities such as stocks and bonds. Clever brokers and other analysts discovered additional ways to channel savings into instruments that savers like: mutual funds that spread the investor's risk across various companies with one investment are a good example of this idea. Annuities that require a single initial investment, and which subsequently make periodic payments to the investor in equal amounts for a specified period of time (for instance, annually for ten years), are another[2]. Each of these innovations was able to tailor financial products better to client needs than traditional instruments. This does not mean that deposits and bonds have remained unchanged either. Deposits now exist that pay interest and still function as checking accounts; some of them may even be used to transfer funds into securities purchases. Bonds have evolved from "plain vanilla" to quite sophisticated hybrids, such as bonds that are convertible into equity shares, bonds that are redeemable (callable) by the issuer before maturity, variable interest rate bonds, and bonds that have different collateral or no collateral at all (junk bonds).

The likely mechanisms that will remain over the next 5–10 years include bank deposits, since these instruments both allow the saver to put funds into a financial institution and then to subsequently channel them into instruments of various kinds. They also include money market funds, since these stockbroker accounts allow most of the same functions as bank deposits, without the benefits (most importantly, deposit insurance) and costs (most importantly, the lower rates paid by banks and the more limited investments typically allowed to the commercial banking institution).

Beyond the bank deposits and money market funds, it is not clear what instruments will remain for storing savings. Certainly, stock shares must remain in a capitalist economy. But the shares may end up being quite differentiated – from preferred shares that pay fixed dividends and hold no voting rights, to convertible issues that allow investors to switch back and forth between equity and bonds, to other structures that may offer investors a superior set of characteristics versus the traditional instrument of ordinary shares. At present, it appears that there is a broad demand for straight equity shares, so this instrument most likely will be retained, and will remain important in the near future.

Bonds likewise have the attractive feature of higher returns than bank deposits, and for high-quality issuers, bonds may continue to face solid demand in the market. The primary market for issuing bonds, however, will likely shift to the Internet and away from stockbrokers. That is, issuers may go directly to investors through their own placements of bonds via the Internet, displacing the "intermediation" of the brokers. This phenomenon has begun to occur, although brokers are generally still involved in the issues, providing a sales effort beyond just posting the securities on the Internet.

Bonds also will likely become much more adapted to investors' interests. This adaptation will range from the currency of denomination – traditionally dollars, but increasingly euros, yen, Swiss francs, and pounds – to interest rates (traditionally fixed, but frequently variable today, with a rate adjustment every three or six months) – to collateral (usually the company's future earnings, or accounts receivable, but also real estate or other real property, and sometimes none at all).

I expect to see innovations such as deposit-like instruments that provide not only access to the purchase and sale of securities, but also ready access to markets in many geographic locations and conversion into additional financial instruments, such as insurance policies and real estate investments. Such instruments are not at all far-fetched – it just remains to be seen how much demand there will be for such tinkering with the traditional ones.

Mechanisms to provide funding

The range of funding structures available to firms today is enormous and expanding. Figure 11.2 presents an overview of the kinds of financing arrangements that are available, though of course not all alternatives are available to all firms.

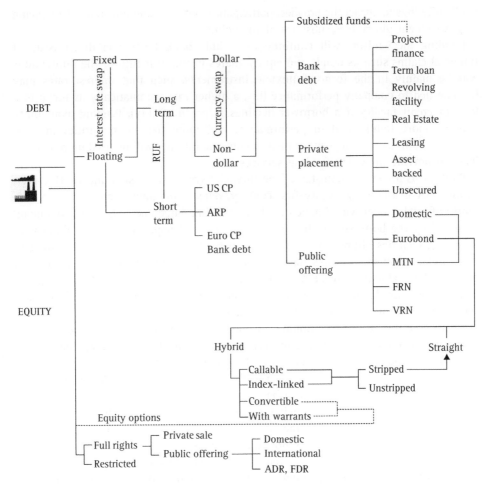

Figure 11.2   Financing alternatives available to major corporations.
Source: Gunter Dufey, unpublished manuscript.

Firms face the possibility of seeking funding through debt and equity alternatives, with some instruments even providing convertibility between debt and equity. On the equity side, there are fewer alternatives, though this may be due to the fact that such alternatives are more idiosyncratic (less generalizable) than the debt instruments, and thus they exist but are harder to specify in simple terms.

Notice that the debt instruments (mainly loans in the bank market and bonds in the broker market) are now available to allow borrowers to switch between fixed and floating interest rates; to allow conversion from one currency to another; and even to meet conversion needs from short-term to medium-term. Also note that funding can be obtained specifically from various target audiences: commercial bank loans and other instruments; private placements generally to large institutional investors;

public offerings to attract the broadest participation possible; and government financing or government guarantees/subsidies of financing.

Funding mechanisms will continue to include bank loans and direct issue of financial claims such as bonds and equity shares in the near future. The innovations will be mainly in the form of flexible instruments, such that interest rates may become tied to company performance (i.e., a higher rate automatically assigned to a loan or credit facility if a borrower declines in credit quality), funding availability may be more tightly tied to performance, and more flexible maturities may be arranged. And, as with depositary instruments, the Internet will be used more extensively to provide the credit/funding services.

Bank loans are still a mainstay of the financial system in most countries. However, in the USA in the early twenty-first century, bank loans have dropped below one-fourth of total system-wide financing. They are being outcompeted by direct financing arranged by the borrowers in the form of commercial paper and bonds, along with financing facilities offered by the investment bank intermediaries. In responding to this threat, commercial banks have cut interest rates and other charges, but they have not been able to stop the flow of activity to other instruments. What is equally true, on the other hand, is that bank loans remain the principal source of funding to small and medium-sized firms in the USA, so that the millions of such firms are likely to continue to use traditional bank instruments well into the future.

The instruments that banks use to keep themselves in the running will have to be loan-like arrangements that offer more attractiveness to the borrowers. One of the most successful of such instruments already in the market is the *financing facility* or *underwriting facility*, in which a bank or other intermediary commits funding to a borrower, and then seeks participation in the funding in the money or capital markets. Thus, a note issuance facility is a quasi-syndicated lending structure, in which the (investment) bank does not find co-lenders but, rather, finds investors in pieces of the total funding, as it is requested by the borrower. The bank remains as "lender of last resort," but the intent is to pass the funding on to investors who want to earn higher than deposit interest rates for taking on relatively low risk by buying claims on high-quality companies. Figure 11.3 depicts this financing structure.

This example is hypothetical and based on the assumption that straight commercial bank financing through a line of credit would cost more than that shown in the figure (say, LIBOR + 1%). The revolving underwriting facility costs the borrower slightly less (LIBOR + $3/4$%), and makes funding available for the four-year period just as with a bank's line of credit.

Banks will continue to be in the business of offering funding to companies and households that are not able to go directly to the market for this purpose, or that find bank intermediation to be less expensive (for example, due to credit quality that may make direct securities issue more costly than bank lending). And banks will fund themselves increasingly through sale of their loans in the form of loan-backed bonds. The "securitization" of mortgages in several countries, particularly the USA, has reached the level of trillions of dollars of such instruments, which are traded in securities markets (for more details on this subject, see chapter 12).

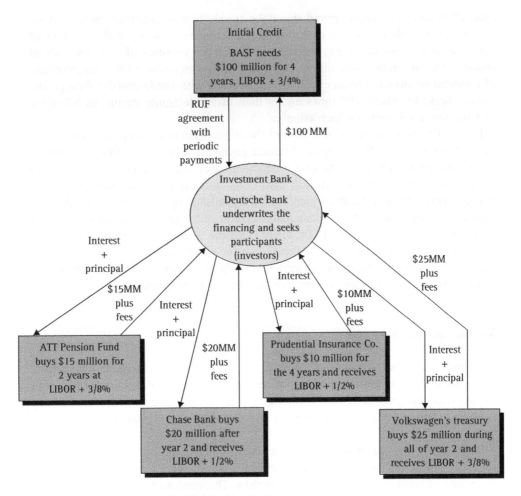

Figure 11.3   The RUF (Revolving Underwriting Facility).

Overall, it is logical to anticipate that financing in the USA will remain largely market-based – that is, outside of the intermediation of banks – in the years ahead. The mechanisms used to provide financing will evolve to reflect the borrowers' needs for flexibility in terms and the lender/investors' needs for evaluating repayment probability.

Mechanisms to transfer funds

Funds transfer is typically carried out through inter-bank electronic transfers. In addition today, checks and cash are used extensively, especially in the USA. Given the extreme difference in costs (checks and cash being much more expensive to process), financial systems around the globe are shifting to electronic means. These include debit cards that cause electronic funds transfers to occur at the moment of purchase to Internet-based payments such as via the websites of vendors such as amazon.com, and now many others. As shown in the discussion of the virtualization of financial services in chapter 3, the costs involved with funds transfer through the use of checks are about 100 times higher than using electronic means, so it is clear that the latter will win out increasingly.

In fact, the inescapable trend is toward the elimination of currency and checks for transactions, given the feasibility of electronic payments vehicles. Even for transactions that seemingly require cash, the new instrument called the "cash card" may prove to be an adequate replacement. (A cash card is an instrument similar to a credit card that contains virtual cash, and which can be replenished by being recharged through electronic connection to the holder's bank account or by adding cash through a cash card machine, just as Washington DC metro cards can be recharged to cover additional fare costs.) The equally inescapable fact is that for many situations away from major cities, and in emerging markets, the switch to electronic payments and the elimination of cash and checks will take longer, certainly into the next decade.

Mechanisms to manage risk

This area is perhaps the most likely to lead to institutional shocks in the near future, in the sense that traditional providers of risk management products are being forced to offer wider arrays of protection methods, and the products that are most standardized are being challenged by nontraditional providers. In short, the insurance industry is under attack.

Most likely, the outcome of the new environment will be to force insurance companies to become wider-scope providers of financial services, and also to broaden the range of tools available to deal with risks. The movement in this field is well under way, with a rash of mergers of insurance companies and banks (the Allianz purchase of Dresdner Bank and the Travelers Group purchase of Citibank being only the two largest and most visible examples of this process). But risk management is not limited to insurable risks.

To examine this issue more carefully, think about the scope of risk protection that firms would like to obtain or at least consider. There is property risk such as that relating to buildings and vehicles that the firm may own or rent; there is personal risk that life and health insurance usually covers; and then there are many other kinds of risks that must either be hedged or be borne by the firm – such as interest rate risk, exchange rate risk, political risk, and various others. The whole panorama of risks can be seen in figure 11.4.

These risks should be managed by the firm or the individual to achieve an optimal balance of risk exposure and risk protection, depending on preferences, costs, and the like. The key point for our discussion is that the risks are not independent of each other, so that an optimal risk management policy may involve futures contracts,

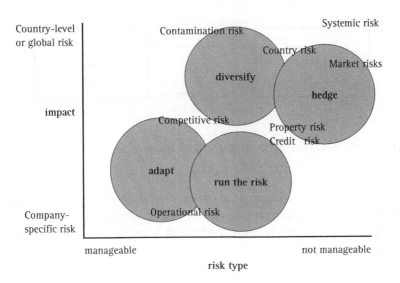

Figure 11.4   A risk management profile.

self-insurance, and even risk-running – without necessarily even including insurance contracts at all. This is the ultimate risk faced by insurance companies – that they become irrelevant if they do not offer a variety of risk management alternatives.

Which of the risk management tools are likely to remain in use in the future? In this case there are not many products that offer direct substitutability. Most of the risk management tools are tailored for a particular use, and thus are not generic enough to allow ready replacement, except by the same instrument offered by an alternative supplier (e.g., a bank instead of an insurance company). A number of futures and options contracts that are traded on stock exchanges have come and gone, so certainly more of this entry and exit of specific products such as futures on particular currencies or particular interest rates will continue. Individual health insurance policies have become less and less common, as such insurance is concentrated more in group policies covering entire firms, governmental organizations, and other common-interest groups.

In principle, global risk should be managed on a comprehensive basis, but given our inadequate understanding of the interrelations of various kinds of risks, it is safe to say that specialized risk management tools will remain in the near future. As more detailed understanding is developed with respect to risks such as combined foreign exchange and interest rate risk, or combined credit risk and country risk, then new instruments may be developed to directly deal with the combined risks.

Just on the subject of credit risk, a market has developed in the past decade for credit risk derivatives, passing credit risk from lenders to third parties who choose to run the risk in exchange for premiums, commissions, and other kinds of compensation. One credit derivative structure is described in figure 11.5.

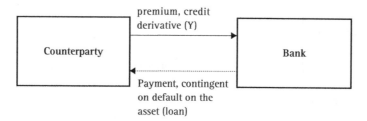

Figure 11.5   Credit derivatives: option on loan default. Taking a position on default risk.

In this credit derivative, which is an option on default risk, the option buyer (the counterparty) obtains a guarantee of payment in the event that the borrower defaults. The option seller (the bank) receives a premium from the buyer for taking on this risk, which is a contingent liability.

Asset management

This area has become an enormous part of the financial services landscape in recent years, mainly as the result of government policies around the world that have permitted the privatization of pension funds, and the resulting need to manage those assets. The starting point for most of such savings plans is to invest in long-term central government securities (Treasury bonds). As the social security and private pension plans become more open to alternative investments, the need for instruments to absorb these funds has grown dramatically. Logical diversifications include investments in other long-term instruments such as stocks and corporate bonds, as well as in such things as collateralized mortgage obligations (on this subject, see chapter 12).

In addition to domestic investments, the asset management communities in countries around the world are looking to international instruments to diversify portfolios. The most common choices of such investors are mutual funds, which in turn invest in multiple corporate issues of shares or bonds. Mutual funds specialize in investments just in stocks, or just in bonds, or just in issues from one country, or in one industry, and so on. The prospects for this type of investment are almost limitless, and the thousands of funds traded in major stock exchanges today attest to the significance of this phenomenon.

Which mutual funds are likely to survive the competition in the 2000s? Those that best serve the risk/return profiles sought by the investors in the market. This will range from money market funds, that take small investors' savings and pool them into multi-million dollar investments in eurocurrency bank deposits, high-grade commercial paper, and so on – to country funds that give institutional investors the opportunity to take on the risk of investing in a particular country without the (excessive) risk of one particular company. They also range from funds that pay no interest or dividends, accumulating earnings through price appreciation, to funds that pay regular dividends or interest – once again tailored to meet the interests of a particular class of investors. The limits on mutual funds that may survive are probably in the context that some investments dominate others, and so some funds may not offer the same return for a given level of risk, or other goal, that may be simply better served by one fund than another. For example, a country fund in Luxembourg stocks probably would be dominated by a country fund of Belgian stocks, since the economies are so tightly linked, and there are more choices of individual securities to include in the Belgian portfolio. Or a money market fund might invest only in eurodollar deposits, while another might include high-grade commercial paper, obtaining a consistently higher return for no added risk.

Another aspect of asset management that could structurally change the market is the choice of managing assets in-house versus contracting out this activity. There is no question that there are benefits of specialization in this activity, and that the knowledge and skills possessed by a high-quality asset manager may be worth buying. The question is: How beneficial are these skills? And how much is the cost of buying them? Judging from the millions of self-made investment "experts" who benefited from the stock-market boom of the late 1990s, there may have been little benefit to specialized skills. Obviously, with the dot-com crash of 2000, skilled investment advice is extremely valuable. And the reality in general falls somewhere in between these extremes – but the point is that there will be an ongoing institutional tension between the choice to farm out investment management to outside experts versus carrying out that function within a given company or other organization.

Methods of providing financial advice

This area is probably the least likely to experience wrenching changes in the near future. Financial advice is provided by stockbrokers, bankers, mutual fund managers, and many other categories of financial advisory firm. Other than the fact that such advice can now be distributed more rapidly via the Internet, the basic kinds of advice and advisor are not going through a process of radical change.

However, this simple commentary may no longer be so true in the USA after the crisis of confidence in investment banks during 2002. At that time, Merrill Lynch and then a dozen more leading investment banks were accused in New York State of providing misleading investment advice to clients in order to favor companies in which the investment banks had an interest. This was especially true in the dot-com arena, where Merrill's and Salomon's leading research analysts were heavily fined and banned from the industry for publicly lauding firms that privately (within the bank) they were criticizing. This led to a highly visible legal process and fines on Merrill Lynch, Salomon Smith Barney, and a dozen other major firms totaling $US 1.4 billion[3].

Given this history, there was quite a demand for independent investment advice, not contaminated with conflicts of interest between analysts and investment bankers.

This situation could well lead to the development of an important independent investment advisory business in the USA, though it is too soon to tell if such a business will become an important part of the market.

NOTES

1   The US administration is already well on this path toward checkless payments. See, for example, Bill Orr, "Uncle Sam goes digital," *ABA Banking Journal*, July 1997, pp. 62–8. Even so, the future of checks in the USA does not appear to be headed toward demise in this decade. See, for example, Joanna Stavins, "While more people are paying electronically, many of us still cling to checks," *Federal Reserve Bank of Boston Regional Review*, 4th Quarter 2001.

2   The education accounts designed by individual states in the USA are an annuity-like innovation. The investor periodically deposits funds into an account, typically managed by the state authorities but operated through a bank. Thus the pay-in is similar to an annuity structure. Payout takes place not all at once, but over the four years of college education of the investor's child, thus assuring availability of funds for that purpose. See, for example, Penelope Wang, "Yes, there's still college," *Money*, 30(13), December 2001, p. 172, 3p; and Wang, "Investing for college," *Money*, 31(5), May 2002.

3   See for example, Robert Grosse, "The trials of Merrill Lynch," *Thunderbird Case Series*, July 2003; available at http://www.t-bird.edu.

CHAPTER 12

THE GENERATION OF LONG-TERM INVESTMENT TO SUPPORT BOND AND STOCK-MARKET GROWTH

INTRODUCTION

Financial services provision is aimed at the fundamental needs of storing and safe-guarding savings and providing funds for investment and spending. This financial intermediation function, however it may be provided (through banks or via direct link-up of savers and investors), faces an interesting problem in most countries of the world. Although it is logical that some financial needs – such as bill paying and current spending – are short-term, it is equally logical that some financial needs are long-term, such as assuring and providing retirement funds in the future, or paying for a product or service that cannot be afforded in the current time period. These long-term needs are often inadequately served, and this is especially true in emerging markets, where long-term financial instruments are scarce.

This problem is understandable in many instances, where inflation and interest rates may be 20% per year or more, such that a long-term bond or a mortgage might have almost no present value of the future maturity payout, due to the steep discount factor. (A $US 100,000 mortgage, for example, if it matures in 15 years and carries a discount rate of 25% per year, has a present value of the final principal payment of $US 3,518 today.) However, even in more macroeconomically stable countries that have lower inflation and interest rates, and in fact in most countries in the past decade, there still is a very limited availability of such long-term financial instruments. Table 12.1 shows some of the characteristics of long-term financial markets around the world in the early twenty-first century.

Table 12.1   Long-term financial market characteristics

Country/ Feature	Number of listed firms	Mortgage- backed bonds?	Derivatives allowed?	Privatized pension fund management?	Government bond interest rate	Other
Argentina	756	Yes	Yes	Yes	12.221	15 yr
Australia	7,697	Yes	Yes	Yes	5.13	
Brazil	2,557	No	Yes	Yes	11.306	
Chile	557	No	Yes	Yes	4.835	
China	4,763	No	Yes	Very limited	4.381	30 yr
Czech Republic	1,974	No	Yes	Yes	4.0807	
France	6,096	Yes	Yes	Very limited	3.96	
Germany	6,542	Yes	Yes	Yes	3.9688	
Hungary	339	No	Yes	Yes	6.7021	
India	13,267	Yes	Yes	Yes	5.7169	
Indonesia	962	Yes	Yes	Yes	11.2673	8 yr
Japan	10,175	Yes	Yes	Yes	1.114	
Luxembourg	461	Yes	Yes	Yes		
Malaysia	2,742	Yes	Yes	Yes	3.52	
Mexico	1,529	Yes	Yes	Yes	8.7949	
Poland	767	No	Yes	Yes	5.1695	
Russia	18,466	No	Yes	Yes	6.9134	
Switzerland	2,563	Yes	Yes	Yes	2.3356	15 yr
UK	11,078	Yes	Yes	Yes	4.3011	
USA	88,986	Yes	Yes	Yes	3.7047	

Source: The company data come from Bloomberg. The pension fund data is from the countries' central banks, the OECD website, and news articles. Additional data come from national stock exchanges and national securities regulatory commissions.

The first question is: Why? Why are long-term financing and investing instruments so difficult to obtain in most countries? In fact, the reasons are becoming fewer over time, as more and more countries have stabilized their economies – or at least have moved to market-based economies. Traditionally, the main reasons have been as follows:

1   High inflation degrades the value of any principal involved.
2   High interest rates (usually but not always above the inflation rate) make borrowing too expensive for long-term commitments.
3   Default risk from borrowers is too high to attract lenders.
4   Political risks mean that the rules may change before maturity, to the possible detriment of the lender.
5   No issuers of long-term securities are available (that is, borrowers), other than the government.
6   No markets are available to buy and sell such instruments.

These reasons are all logical and relevant – but at the same time they are diminishing in importance today. First of all, as global inflation has dropped on average to 2.5% per year by 2002[1], both inflation and interest rates have dropped below their historic values, to levels more conducive to long-term financial contracts.

Still, with country risk, credit risk, and other risks remaining, lending rates do surpass 15% per year in many countries (for example, the prime lending rate was above 15% per year in Argentina, Brazil, Ukraine, Russia, Cambodia, and Indonesia – among many other countries – in 2002). So long-term borrowers in these countries would be facing the same kinds of principal-destroying rates as noted previously – and thus the global lowering of inflation still has not eliminated the risk features that keep interest rates high in many emerging markets. Nevertheless, the average interest rate on loans has declined significantly during the past decade, such that the average borrower in an emerging market paid interest of 15.5% per year in 2001, versus over 20% per year in 1991.

A central reason for high interest rates despite relatively low inflation is risk. Points 3 and 4 above refer to this problem, first from the perspective of the borrower directly and second with respect to the government and its policies. Default risk by borrowers, as measured by the spread over US Treasury bonds, was more than 60% in Argentina in 2002; this compares with 1–2% in the United States for the same year. Creditors charge their borrowers interest to reflect both the time value of money and the risk of not being repaid, so that the more difficult the financial position of the borrower, the higher is the interest rate[2].

Political risk similarly causes lenders to raise the interest rates that they charge borrowers, because the risk of nonpayment grows with political risk. Even if the borrowing company or individual has complete ability and willingness to meet debt commitments, external problems such as a downturn in the country's economy, or a conflict such as war, or domestic strikes or protests, may jeopardize the borrower's ability to pay.

This risk is even more striking in the case of foreign currency debt, in which the lender offers credit in, say, dollars to a borrower in some country other than the USA. If that country experiences a financial crisis, then the borrower may be simply unable to meet dollar debt servicing requirements, even assuming that the borrower's domestic-currency capacity to pay has not changed. (That is, when a financial crisis hits, the domestic currency devalues, and makes dollar debt payments that much more expensive. It is not at all uncommon to see 50% devaluations of emerging market currencies in the 1990s and early 2000s in conditions of financial crisis.)

A fifth reason for the shortage of long-term financial instruments is the frequent lack or limited availability of long-term financial markets. If a country either does not have a stock market, or it has one dominated 90% or more by issues of the government (typically long-term government bonds), then the opportunity to find long-term financing in this market is limited, and also the opportunity to find investment instruments other than government debt is limited. This phenomenon is extremely common throughout the world. In every stock market, the largest single issuer is the national government. This is true in the United States and the United

Kingdom, just as it is in Brazil and China. The difference is that in the industrial countries, usually the market also contains a wide variety of corporate securities such as stock shares and bonds, whereas in emerging markets the private-sector securities are far more limited. And additionally, the emerging market stock shares that are traded often constitute small percentages of a company's total shares – with the controlling majority in the hands of a small group of insiders. This makes the attractiveness of investing in such securities relatively low, and discourages the development of such stock markets.

A sixth reason for the global shortage of long-term financial markets is the somewhat circular argument that the lack of a market disallows the introduction of the financial instruments. That is, how could a company issue stock or bonds if the country does not have an organized exchange? While this problem is not pervasive in the sense that many emerging and all industrial countries do have stock exchanges (or belong to economic blocs that do, such as the European Union in the case of Luxembourg), the size and scope of most of these markets is extremely limited by practice and by law. In particular, while a stock market may exist, it is often limited to issues approved by the government, and thus not open to issues of innovative instruments or financial structures.

RESPONSES TO THE PROBLEM OF MARKET UNAVAILABILITY

A variety of responses to this problem of a lack of long-term financial instruments and markets have developed in recent years. These responses include the broad policy of economic opening and the promotion of private-sector development, including the development of stock exchanges. They also include the mobilization of savings through long-term investment vehicles such as pension funds, annuities, and mutual funds. In fact, the responses cover the spectrum of imaginable instruments to provide safe havens for savers' long-term holdings, to provide funding for borrowers' long-term financing needs, and to provide market structures that allow such instruments to operate increasingly more efficiently and more openly. Figure 12.1 shows the range of responses and suggests the directions available for further developments.

Government-led responses

The first line of attack to resolve the problem of weak or nonexistent long-term financial markets is for the national government to explicitly permit such markets to be established and to function. In Roman-law countries (such as in Latin America) this is an extremely important step, since otherwise the bond and stock markets simply cannot exist, regardless of the ability and willingness of financial institutions to offer them. Without any doubt, the government is the single most important actor in this entire process. Still, the financial institutions have to decide to provide the content once permission is given, so the whole outcome depends on both sides.

```
┌─────────────────────────────────┐   ┌─────────────────────────────────┐
│ Government-led:                 │   │ Bank-led:                       │
│                                 │   │                                 │
│ * creation of stock market      │   │ * sale of loans to investors    │
│ * permission to create          │   │ * development of forward        │
│   derivative instruments        │   │   contracts and options         │
│ * permission for pension        │   │ * access to foreign banking and │
│   funds to invest in            │   │   capital markets               │
│   nongovernment securities      │   │                                 │
└─────────────────────────────────┘   └─────────────────────────────────┘

┌─────────────────────────────────┐   ┌─────────────────────────────────┐
│ Investment-bank led:            │   │ Client-led:                     │
│                                 │   │                                 │
│ * collateralized mortgage bonds │   │ * direct issue of securities to │
│ * futures and options           │   │   global investors through the  │
│ * money market mutual funds      │   │   Internet                      │
│ * access to foreign capital     │   │ * direct arrangement of long-term│
│   markets                       │   │   financing with suppliers or other│
│ * financing facilities          │   │   intermediaries                │
└─────────────────────────────────┘   └─────────────────────────────────┘
```

Figure 12.1   Responses to long-term financial market unavailability.

The government can itself constitute and operate the stock and bond markets (as in China). Alternatively, the government can implement enabling legislation and leave the design, ownership, and operation of the markets to the private sector (as in the USA, the UK, and most industrialized countries). In either case, it is crucial for the government to establish the "rules of the game," so that the stock and bond markets can function transparently and without excessive costs to the users.

Even with these markets in operation, the government can add to the value of the markets by allowing additional instruments such as mortgages converted into bonds (discussed below), instruments for protection against unexpected price changes (forward contracts and futures contracts), and instruments that may operate contingent on price changes (such as options). And additionally, the government can promote the development of these markets by allowing social security and private pension plans to invest in such private-sector securities, and not just in government issues.

Commercial bank-led responses

Once government allows the introduction of long-term financial markets, the most logical intermediaries to offer services in those markets are commercial banks. (Realistically, in most countries, the commercial and investment banks operate under the same roof, so this commentary is really more focused on the type of instrument offered rather than on the company that offers it.) Banks can mobilize much more funding for clients if they can take long-term loans off their books. So, the institution of mortgage sales and creation of mortgage-backed bonds will transform a sluggish and often complacent banking system into much more of a dynamic and accessible source of funding for the private sector.

Also, with government permission, commercial banks can offer risk-protection instruments such as forward contracts on currencies and interest rates, allowing investors and borrowers alike to buy securities and operate in longer-term markets with some degree of protection available against these market risks.

Investment bank-led responses

Investment banks have been the main initiators of the financial innovations that populate capital markets today. They are the ones that developed futures and options exchanges in the United States, and they were the main arrangers of nontraditional financing such as commercial paper issue and leveraged buy-outs, among other vehicles. The investment banks also have been the main drivers in the securitization of bank loans, although in the USA the three specialized institutions – Fanny Mae, Ginnie Mae, and Freddie Mac – have played the single most important role in securitization of mortgages. And, similarly, a specialized institution plays the lead role in securitizing student loans (Sallie Mae). Credit card debt and car loans are more typical in that the investment banks (and commercial banks) are the main repackagers and leaders in this market.

Investment banks also have led borrowers in emerging markets to seek out investors in global money centers through the issue of eurobonds, American Depositary Receipts, and other innovative instruments that bring emerging market issuers to industrial-country financial markets. In this way, the investment banks are leading emerging markets away from the development of the domestic financial market to the concentration of long-term financing in a handful of global money centers (principally London and New York).

Client-led responses

The responses of clients, such as corporate borrowers, households, and savers looking for long-term vehicles to guard their wealth, have gone in both directions, seeking out access to the global money centers and trying to obtain funding and investments in their domestic markets through changes in rules and financial practices. Perhaps the most important response of clients has been to push governments to open up financial markets and thus to allow savers and borrowers to take advantage of overseas opportunities.

In only a few cases have borrowers themselves gone into financial markets to seek out funding or investments without intermediation of a commercial bank or an investment bank. Today, with the Internet providing global access to clients, a handful of blue-chip firms have issued bonds or commercial paper directly to investors worldwide, without arranging a listing on a particular stock exchange. This possibility exists theoretically for any borrower or investor anywhere, but the reality thus far is that only highly creditworthy firms have been able to sell securities through this medium without access through the local financial market. This reality may change in the future, but certainly not in the medium term of the next 3–5 years.

FINANCIAL INNOVATIONS THAT BUILD LONG-TERM MARKETS

Mortgage-backed bonds

A key example of limitations that preclude the development of a long-term market is the issue of housing/real estate finance. When banks lend to a customer for a home purchase or to a company for an office building or factory, the loan is typically long-term; for example, 10–15 years. Once the bank has loaned out its available funds from deposits, it is stuck with a fully committed portfolio. How can such a bank make additional loans? In principle, the bank may be able to issue its own bonds or take loans from other banks, but these are fairly costly funding sources. An even better way to handle this problem would be to sell some of the bank's portfolio of mortgage loans to a third party. In that way, the bank can get its money back, earn a profit on originating the mortgage loan, and "recycle" the funds to other borrowers in new mortgage loans. The third-party purchaser of a mortgage might not want to try to evaluate the creditworthiness of the original borrower. However, if a package of mortgages can be put together – grouping, say, 100 home loans – then the third party would have a fairly diversified risk and would presumably be more interested in buying (all or part of) the mortgages. Figure 12.2 depicts the securitization of mortgage loans.

This kind of creative structure can be developed in any country, if the government authorities are willing to permit the loan restructuring process. It is a concern to regulators in that housing finance is a tremendously important part of the national financial system, and any risks that might arise from banks selling the mortgage loans could create unacceptable risks for the financial system. Any number of payment-assurance guarantees can be created, but fundamentally the mortgage-backed bonds created by reselling these loans have the physical property to back them. Under normal conditions, these assets will provide more than adequate collateral to cover any loan defaults by individual borrowers. In the case of a country-wide financial crisis, real estate prices may fall significantly, and a large percentage of borrowers may default on their loan payments. The restructuring of mortgage loans as mortgage-backed bonds actually helps in this situation – because the losses from real estate price declines are shared by the bondholders as well as the borrowers and the banks that keep some mortgages on their books.

The idea of freeing up capital for additional loans is precisely the logic that has brought into being the huge market for CMOs (collateralized mortgage obligations) in the United States. Fanny Mae and Freddie Mac are mortgage-buying organizations

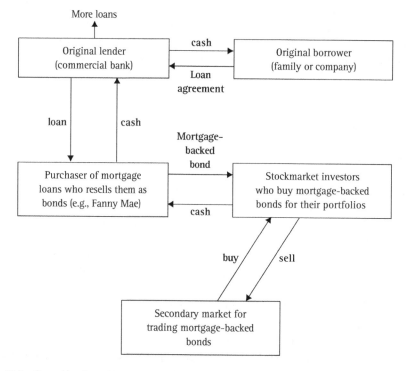

Figure 12.2 Securitization of mortgage loans.

that buy thousands of mortgages every day and package them into long-term bonds that are sold on the secondary market. In 2002, the US market in mortgage-backed bonds held over $US 1.5 trillion of mortgages, which are traded very actively on major exchanges.

This is one example of the general phenomenon of **securitization**, the transformation of bank loans into tradable financial instruments. While mortgage-backed bonds are probably the most commonly discussed type of securitization vehicle, in principle just about any kind of bank debt can be restructured in the form of long- or short-term bonds. In the USA today, trading also is active in bonds that are collateralized by credit card debt, by auto loan debt, and by student loan debt, for example.

Securitization of other loans

While mortgages are the single largest category of long-term loans that have been transformed into bonds through the securitization process, there are a number of other loan types that also have been and are being converted in this way. The overall result of securitization is to lower the cost of funding for issuers (because

Table 12.2   Securitization of debt in the USA, year-end 2002

Loan category	Value outstanding ($US billions)	Percentage of total
Mortgages	3,156.6	75%
Auto loans	221.7	5.5%
Credit card debt	397.9	9.5%
Home equity loans	286.5	7%
Manufactured home loans	44.5	1%
Student loans	92.7	2%
Total	4,199.9	100%

the standardization and tradability of the instruments make them more attractive to investor/lenders). And in the case of mortgages and other long-term debt, the asset-backed bonds may attract more long-term funding to the country than would be possible with conventional loans kept on the books of the initial lending bank. In the USA, by 2002 securitization of loans had reached the levels shown in table 12.2.

Auto loans are extensively securitized in the US market, with General Motors, Ford, and Chrysler Credit as the major issuers. This market has grown to close to $US 100 billion of new issues per year in the early 2000s. The process works exactly parallel to the mortgage-backed bond issuance, with packages of auto loans put together and sold as bonds, backed by the vehicles to which the loans apply. The auto-loan bonds have shorter-term maturities (typically five years) than mortgage-backed bonds, since the mortgages typically have maturities of 10–15 years, while car loans are typically for 3–5 years.

Credit card debt in the US has also become a major source of securitization by the lending banks. By 2002, credit card securitization accounted for about 10% of total securitization of debt in the US market. This financial structure actually uses accounts receivable rather than physical goods (such as houses or cars) to back the bonds. The maturities of credit card debt-backed bonds are shorter than the previous instruments, but are still multiple-year bonds.

Student loans are largely issued or purchased from banks and managed by the SLM Corporation (Sallie Mae) in the USA. This organization originates Federally guaranteed student loans and purchases student loans from banks, making the market for bonds backed by student loans. By 2002, the value of bonds held by Sallie Mae was about $US 90 billion. While bonds backed by student loans are traded in the secondary market, Sallie Mae itself maintains about one-third of total student loans in its own portfolio.

The Federal Family Education Loan Program, or FFELP, was authorized by Congress through the Higher Education Act of 1965. About 71% of all student loans, approximately $28 billion annually, is provided under the FFELP. Sallie Mae began operating in 1972 as a "government-sponsored enterprise," and is now in the process of full privatization (to be achieved by 2008).

In sum, securitization of mortgages in particular, and other forms of debt in general, has provided an immense boost to bank lenders' liquidity and to the ability of financial markets to spread risk much more widely than when loans remain with the lending banks. The mortgage-backed securities market alone holds more than 3 trillion dollars in bonds in the USA, making it one of the largest financial markets anywhere. If this kind of instrument can be further extended to more countries and greater volume, it will be one major step toward financial market development in emerging and well as industrial markets.

MOBILIZATION OF DEMAND FOR LONG-TERM INSTRUMENTS – PENSION FUND PRIVATIZATION

One of the most striking steps that has been taken toward building up the long-term capital markets in many countries, from the most advanced to the transitional economies of the former Soviet bloc, is the development of private-sector participation in the management of pension funds and other retirement programs. Even more than they intervene to try to assure the safety and solvency of commercial banks, national governments historically have intervened by owning and operating national retirement programs. The "social security" fund or national pension plan for most countries is held by the national government, and often is managed by a government body. This historical situation is changing around the world, as an increasing number of countries have chosen to allow either private-sector operation of major pension plans, and/or private-sector management of the public-sector retirement program.

This trend has moved further in Latin America than in any other region of the world. Beginning with Chile in 1981, when the government-managed retirement system was privatized, this allowed privately owned pension management companies (AFPs) to manage retirement savings for those who elected each firm. The government remained as manager of last resort, but most of public- and private-sector employees' pensions are now managed by the half-dozen AFPs that remain after mergers and acquisitions over the years.

The Chilean example was followed by Peru in 1993, by Argentina in 1994, Colombia in 1994, and Bolivia in 1997. In each case, the retirement system of the country has been freed up to invest in a broader portfolio of securities, and the returns on the retirement funds have increased dramatically, even with financial crises in many countries.

This is a very large source of potential investment in long-term financial instruments such as stocks and bonds, because the pension fund managers need to match retirement timing with maturity of investments. And with the average age in Latin American countries below 30 years old, this means that even 30-year investments can easily be included in the fund managers' portfolios. Not only corporate stocks and bonds fit this investment need, but also the asset-backed securities described above can feed directly into this new source of demand.

IN SUMMARY

The markets for long-term financial instruments in industrial countries are well established and strong in the early twenty-first century. The prospects for developing such markets in the emerging economies are improving with the creation and extension of financial mechanisms such as securitization and the opening of pension fund management to allow for investments in both asset-backed securities and in non-government securities in general. The record of the 1990s in emerging markets, though full of examples of financial crises, still shows a consistent and growing movement toward both development of supplies of long-term instruments (especially mortgage-backed bonds) and demand for such instruments (through pension fund management privatization).

FURTHER READING

International Finance Corporation 2003: *Emerging Stockmarkets Factbook* (annual). Washington, DC: World Bank.

Jobst, Andreas 2002: Collateralized loan obligations: a primer. CFS Working Paper #2002–13, Center for Financial Studies, Frankfurt, December.

Miyake, Mariko 1999: The dawning of the era of real estate securitization. Japan Research Institute *Monthly Review*, September.

Tavakoli, Janet 2003: *Collateralized Debt Obligations and Structured Finance: New Developments in Cash and Synthetic Securitization*. New York: John Wiley.

NOTES

1   Economist Intelligence Unit, *Country Forecast Main Report* (2003).

2   A simple measure of risk in an emerging market can be derived from that country's borrowing in dollar instruments. Any borrower from the emerging market can be compared to a similar borrower from the USA. Whatever degree the interest rate is higher for the similar emerging market firm is a reflection of the higher perceived risk by the market. For example, 20-year US Treasury bonds yielded about 5% in the year 2002. In the same year, Argentine government bonds denominated in US dollars yielded about 65%, Korean government bonds in dollars yielded about 6.7%, and Polish government bonds denominated in dollars yielded about 5.9%. These conditions mean that the "risk premium" for Argentinian borrowers was 60%, that for Korean borrowers was 1.7%, and that for Polish borrowers was 0.9%.

13

INTERNATIONAL FINANCIAL CENTERS

An international financial center is a location in which large values of foreign exchange, cross-border bank deposits and loans, cross-border securities issue and trading, and other international financial transactions take place. London is the world's leading international financial center, because it is by far the largest center for eurodeposit, cross-border lending, and foreign exchange activity – and it is even far ahead of New York in stock and bond trading by nonlocal firms. In addition, London serves as a leading center for the international insurance and reinsurance industry, with transaction values exceeding those in New York or any other location.

This definition of international financial center probably misses more than it captures, because of the range of financial activities that take place internationally from a variety of locations. For example, there is an enormous business of tax shelter finance done in the British Channel Islands, Nassau, and the Cayman Islands, as well as in a few other key tax havens globally. This business is a "shell" activity, existing most importantly in terms of financial record-keeping in those locations, rather than in large real-sector impacts such as jobs or active income generation. There are also international *banking* centers that do not have significant investment banking or insurance activity associated with their operations, as in the cases of Singapore, Panama, and until it became part of China, Hong Kong. In this last instance, Hong Kong may become a full international financial center as it moves to try to become the financial capital of China.

The first order of business is to demonstrate the leadership of various locations in various kinds of international financial service. Table 13.1 gives some idea of this situation in the early 2000s.

International financial centers can be ranked separately according to their importance in international banking (primarily deposits, loans, and foreign exchange trading), versus their importance in other international financial activities such as stock/bond and insurance underwriting and brokerage. On the banking side, centers such as the tax havens of Panama, Nassau, and the Cayman Islands play a significant role – at

Table 13.1   International financial centers, 2001 (in $US billions)

City	Value of forex transactions (April 2001)[a]	Value of international bank deposits (year-end)	Value of international bank loans (year-end)	Number of foreign listed firms	Number of international insurance syndicates
London	11,823.3	2,164.1	1,802.2	466	71[b]
New York	5,747.8	1,327.8	1,149.9	472	n.a.
Tokyo	3,593.1	491.6	493.6	34	n.a.
Zurich	1,553.7	670.0	718.8	149	n.a.
Frankfurt	1,952.3	953.1	922.1		n.a.
Singapore	2,256.4	356.1	330.9		n.a.
Hong Kong	1,600.2	241.9	290.1		n.a.
Paris	1,056.6	606.3	481.3	134	n.a.
Panama	n.a.	40.5	n.a.		n.a.
Nassau	n.a.	265.6	261.0	16	n.a.

[a] The original data for the value of forex transactions is from the BIS table called "Foreign exchange turnover by country and counterparty in April, 2001" (daily average in $US millions). Daily gross turnover is multiplied by 20, which was the number of work days in April 2001.
[b] This is the number of international insurance syndicates at Lloyds Reinsurance Exchange, the only international insurance market in the world: see http://www.lloyds.com/index.asp?ItemId=2605

least in the booking of transactions. On the stock-market side, these havens play almost no role, whereas traditional industrial cities such as Paris and Frankfurt are much more important. And finally, in the international insurance business, London is almost the only player in the market.

Questions that we want to consider in this discussion are as follows:

1   Will New York or London be the international financial capital of the twenty-first century?
2   Will London or Frankfurt be the (international) financial capital of Europe?
3   Will Tokyo or Hong Kong, or some other location, be the international financial capital of Asia?
4   Will the Internet and decentralized transactions replace a large part of the business that is currently centralized in these financial centers?

The answers to these questions are simple in one sense: London is the world's financial capital; Tokyo is well ahead of Hong Kong in Asia; and the Internet is only taking a small part of cross-border financial transactions from the traditional centers. These conditions will not change overnight. However, there are trends under way that could lead to a new distribution of financial leadership in the reasonably near future. The Internet certainly could draw away a huge part of the more standardized and routinized business from both securities exchanges and foreign exchange dealing. The leadership of Asia's financial market depends greatly on China's financial progress and rule-making, as well as on Japan's seemingly permanent recession. So there do seem to be enough doubts that it is worth an effort to look carefully at the current international financial activity in each place, and to speculate about where the current trends are leading in the next few years.

The greatest unknown in this discussion is the possible role of the Internet to disperse financial transactions around the world and away from any financial center at all. In principle, bank deposits and loans can be made from anywhere in the world to anywhere in the world, without the need for a physical central location. And likewise, the issue and trading of stocks and bonds only requires electronic communication between buyer and seller, without a physical location to unite them. However, financial services providers who offer skills to package and price securities, to rate the riskiness of securities and bank loans, to seek out potential buyers of new issues, and other nonstandardized, often complex skills, are largely still needed – and they operate most successfully from central locations where they can realize agglomeration economies (that is, reduced costs due to the existence of a large number of suppliers, customers, rivals, and infrastructure in the location – see the appendix). These two factors will push and pull financial activity worldwide in the years ahead, and a new constellation of financial services locations is already developing. The rest of this chapter weighs the main factors that are driving the location of international financial activities.

A CLARIFICATION – INTERNATIONAL VERSUS DOMESTIC FINANCIAL CENTERS

The discussion here focuses on centers of international financial activity, rather than domestic activity. This is a huge distinction in the case of a comparison between New York and London, since New York's stock market is the largest in the world, while London has a larger percentage of nonlocal companies traded. That is, the New York Stock Exchange is much larger than the London Stock Exchange, but New York's securities are largely domestic ones, while in London more non-UK firms trade than domestic firms. In London, the Stock Exchange in February 2002 held capitalized value of £1.07 trillion of domestic stock issues, versus £2.6 trillion of international issues. In New York at the same date, domestic issues were capitalized at a value of $US 13.5 trillion, while international issues were capitalized at $US 3.4 trillion.

If we reconsider the table 13.1 comparison of various cities as international financial centers, instead switching to a comparison of *domestic* financial activity, the results shown in table 13.2 are seen.

As shown in this table, New York and Tokyo, and even Frankfurt and Paris, are major financial centers in the domestic context. Given that a lot of the financial

Table 13.2 *Domestic* financial centers, 2001

City	Value of financial derivatives traded[a]	Value of domestic bank deposits or loans	Value of domestic stock issues[b]	Premiums of domestic insurance contracts[c]
London	390,313	1,600,763	2,173,330	218,381
New York	169,076	6,361,700	11,015,450	904,021
Tokyo	115,946	4,590,137	2,289,631	445,845
Zurich	52,951	303,166	527,576	31,442
Frankfurt	65,218	1,747,422	1,083,630	123,682
Singapore	69,258	97,071	179,563	4,005
Hong Kong	49,388	356,797	511,683	10,391
Paris	40,925	851,698	1,863,966	360
Panama	n.a.	8,847	n.a.	312
Nassau	n.a.	3,554	n.a.	113,595
Cayman Islands	40,925	851,698	1,863,966	n.a.

[a] Financial derivatives data are the daily averages of OTC FX derivatives turnover in April 2001 by country (BIS Triennial Central Bank Survey 2001).
[b] Data on domestic stock issues are from the Swiss Exchange 2001 Annual Report.
[c] Data are the sum of the premiums of both nonlife and life business insurance contracts in 2001. See http://insurance.about.com/gi/dynamic/
offsite.htm?site=http%3A%2F%2Fwww.internationalinsurance.org%2Fdefault.htm
Data are for whole countries rather than individual cities.

activity in both international and domestic centers involves domestic firms, except in the case of tax havens, some degree of competition will continue to exist between the largest domestic financial centers and the two global ones in London and New York.

QUESTION 1: LONDON VERSUS NEW YORK

The financial landscape has not changed with regard to the global leadership of London in financial services since before the US Civil War. Despite the United States' overtaking the United Kingdom as world economic leader at the time of World War I, London has still maintained its financial center leadership for another entire century. This may have been due partly to the historically slow process of shifting financial centers, which happens quite infrequently. Thus, even if New York should have replaced London in terms of global financial significance after World War I, the participants in using financial markets were and are very slow to change locations. The continued leadership of London may also have been due, after World War II, to the fact that London was a feasible[1] location to hold dollar-denominated loans and deposits, as well as securities such as stocks and bonds – without being subject to the oversight and possible interference of the US government. The concern for various

Table 13.3 London versus New York in banking activities over time (in $US millions)

	London daily forex trading[a]	New York daily forex trading[a]	London international bank deposits	New York international bank deposits	London cross-border loans	New York cross-border loans
1980			375,300	139,300	356,300	176,800
1985	90,000	50,000	625,800	366,300	589,800	417,900
1990	220,000	135,000	1,203,500	653,700	1,069,900	578,400
1995	463,769	244,371	1,399,800	870,200	1,123,600	600,700
1998	637,309	350,863	1,784,000	1,012,800	1,473,800	813,000
2000	n.a.	n.a.	1,960,100	1,159,000	1,591,600	951,400
2001	504,429	253,654	1,992,600	1,285,700	1,676,700	1,115,100

[a] The forex surveys were conducted in 1986, 1989, 1992, 1995, 1998, and 2001.
Source: Bank for International Settlements, Triennial Foreign Exchange Market Surveys, and Quarterly Reports on International Bank Activity.

financial market participants to escape US regulators and politicians led to rapid growth of the eurocurrency market in the late 1950s, and to continued growth of the foreign exchange market. These factors, along with the strong tendency for stasis, left London as the leading international financial center for the rest of the past century.

Another important issue is the amount of international business activity taking place at each location. Given the large size of the US market, there has been much less demand for foreign exchange there than in the smaller European nations, whose firms were actively involved in trading and investing between countries in that region. Even with the advent of the euro, European countries remain separate legal jurisdictions, so that some international financial concerns (e.g., taxes) require international services in a place such as London. For these several reasons, London has remained far ahead of New York as an international financial center.

In the twenty-first century, the possibility for New York to overtake London depends largely on how strongly Europe moves to place financial activities in Frankfurt. This would follow the EU decision to place the European Central Bank there (since 1999), and the efforts by continental European countries to wrest financial activity away from London. If another European location were able to take significant market share away from London in foreign exchange or eurocurrency bank deposits or loans, this could elevate New York to a higher status in comparison.

The likelihood of this kind of shift appears to be quite small, as shown in table 13.3, which compares forex market activity and cross-border bank deposits over time in London and New York.

Given New York's inability to build comparable forex activity in spite of the EU's decision to replace 12 currencies with the euro, and likewise New York's inability to eliminate the great margin of international deposit and loan activity held by London, it appears that London is headed for continued leadership in the international banking realm.

Stock exchange underwriting and brokerage

Moving from banking markets to securities exchanges, the picture is somewhat different. Although the New York Stock Exchange is the world's largest, and in domestic terms it outpaces the London exchange by a large margin, London is similar in size and importance for international issuers. As noted earlier, the New York Stock Exchange had a capitalization of more than $US 13 trillion in domestic stock shares, while London's exchange listed domestic shares worth $US 1 trillion in 2002. For foreign firms, the NYSE listings had a total value of $US 3.4 trillion, while in London the foreign shares listed had a value of $US 2.6 trillion in 2002. Thus, New York is the world's largest domestic and international stock market, though it is ten times larger than London in domestic terms, and just slightly larger in international issues. Even so, London has recently recorded twice as much international trading as Nasdaq, NYSE, Deutsche Borse, and Euronext combined. (For February–June 2002, the values of nondomestic trading were as follows: London Stock Exchange, $US 652.24 billion; Nasdaq, $US 80.36 billion; NYSE, $US 206.79 billion; Deutsche Borse, $US 32.84 billion; Euronext, $US 6.12 billion – source WFE/FESE.)

Insurance underwriting

In the insurance sector, very little of the policy-writing is cross-border. In other words, most international insurance business is done by foreign insurance companies that set up local subsidiaries and then offer local policies. The insurance policy business is generally highly regulated, and limited to locally incorporated insurers (to try to better protect the policyholders against possible failure of the insurers), so that international insurance companies write very few cross-border policies. Nevertheless, companies such as Allianz, AXA, and AIG are highly international, with affiliates in many countries, so the industry overall is not a purely domestic one.

The only really major international insurance activity is the operation of Lloyds Reinsurance Exchange in London. Lloyds is comprised of 123 participating insurance syndicates, which come from many countries. They underwrite new insurance contracts, buy and sell reinsurance contracts, and generally offer a market for insurers to trade existing insurance contracts among interested parties.

In summary, the reasons for London's commanding lead over New York as the world's key international financial center, and also the reasons for New York's inability to compete, are presented in table 13.4.

QUESTION 2: LONDON VERSUS FRANKFURT

This battle was joined when 11 European Union countries formed a monetary union and launched the euro as their single currency in 1999. Since the UK chose not to participate in the European Monetary Union, London was not eligible as a site for

Table 13.4   Competitive features of New York and London as international financial centers

Characteristic	London	New York
Headquarters of international banks	3	12
Branches and sub-branches of foreign banks	296	49
Volume of international lending	19% of global total	10% of global total
Headquarters of international insurers	2,490 "names" (at Lloyds); 460 (both domestic and international)	219 (both domestic and international)
Foreign exchange trading	31% of global total in 2001	16% of global total in 2001
Volume of international insurance activity	$20.0 billion in premiums in 2001	Negligible
Trading of foreign stock shares	56% of world total in 2002	26% in 2002
Trading of foreign bonds	60% of issues, 70% of trading	n.a.
OTC derivatives trading	36% of global total in 2001	18% of global total in 2001
Institutional equity holding	$2,460 billion in 2001	$2,400 billion in 2001
Country risk (*Euromoney* rating: higher = better)	92.70	95.15
Availability of skilled people (number of financial sector jobs)	376,000 people in London in financial services in 2001	741,000 in New York in finance, insurance, and real estate in 2001
Costs of operation Office rental per square foot	$112.91 in City of London	$57.13 in Mid-town Manhattan
Average financial-sector salary	n.a.	n.a.

Sources: Bank for International Settlements; London Stock Exchange, New York Stock Exchange; International Securities Market Association; World Federation of Exchanges; *Euromoney*, September 2002; Statistical Abstract of the U.S. 2002, Table 601–602; Dun–Bradstreet Million Dollar Database; http://www.lloyds.com/index.asp?ItemId=2946 (page three of six).

locating monetary policy authorities for the group. The European Central Bank was placed in Frankfurt, thus supporting Frankfurt's effort to wrest financial leadership in Europe away from London.

Frankfurt's attempt to build a competitive alternative to London for international financial activity in Europe made some sense, in that the eurozone clearly is the leading economic entity in Europe. However, the established financial infrastructure in London, and the highly open and transparent legal system for financial transactions, have combined to make it ever more difficult for a rival to take market share from London. During the four years since the launch of the euro, Frankfurt and Paris have fallen even further behind London as centers for foreign exchange transactions. And the London Stock Exchange has also gained ground relative to Deutsche Borse in attracting international company listings. Frankfurt has recently won the title of the world's leading derivatives exchange, after merging several national derivatives exchanges into the Eurex exchange. Even so, the main exchange in which derivatives on such instruments as German Treasury bonds are traded in Europe is the London-based Euronext.LIFFE, ahead even of the Eurex in Frankfurt in such trading.

In fact, the data in table 13.1 show that Frankfurt is far behind London in every category of financial service (except derivatives). And the trends during the past 20 years only show more of the same. The inability of Frankfurt to compete with London is based on several fundamental factors: an existing infrastructure, including the corporate headquarters of many financial institutions, that favors continuation of banks and exchanges in London; the use of the global language of business, English, in London; a regulatory environment that has been more open and more transparent in the UK than elsewhere in Europe (although this difference is diminishing); and the competitiveness of the banks and brokers based in London relative to their continental rivals. These advantages will be impossible to overcome in the next few years, although in a longer time frame such a change could potentially occur if conditions were to change dramatically.

QUESTION 3: TOKYO VERSUS HONG KONG

While the competition for a financial capital in Europe and North America is not leading toward any changes away from London and New York, the situation in Asia is much different. Historically, Tokyo has been the largest financial center in Asia, though it has been primarily focused on the domestic market. Hong Kong has been the international financial center that dominates dollar business in the region. With the return of Hong Kong to China in 1997, and the long-term recession in Japan since the early 1990s, conditions may be ripe for a change in financial leadership in Asia. The main competitors include the two incumbents, plus Singapore (with characteristics much like Hong Kong, except that Singapore remains an independent jurisdiction), as well as Shanghai.

The reasons for Tokyo's leadership as an (inter)national financial center in Asia stem largely from the size and economic leadership of the Japanese economy in the region. Tokyo also provides a base for yen financing and asset-holding, just as New York does for dollar-denominated financial instruments. And Tokyo also offers a locational advantage of being in a time zone opposite from New York, thus aiding financial services providers that look for the ability to carry out transactions at any time of the day or night. Even so, Hong Kong provides a similar time zone advantage, and Hong Kong historically has offered a much more open regulatory environment – thus equaling one and trumping another of Tokyo's purported advantages as an international financial center.

QUESTION 4: LONDON/NEW YORK VERSUS THE INTERNET

The real key to dramatic change in financial services provision over the next few years will come from the competition between financial centers and the Internet. The more activities that banks and brokers can figure out how to provide through the Internet, the less need there will be for financial centers. The US money-center banks have already contracted out loan servicing on mortgages to third-party suppliers, and have moved a number of their back-office operations (e.g., check clearing) out of New York to lower-cost locations such as New Jersey and Delaware. These trends will only continue, until banks retain core knowledge-intensive activities in their financial center locations and move most of the rest to other places, and sometimes to other providers.

The Internet itself is now being used as a retail financial services provision channel, for stockbrokerage and insurance policy sales and servicing, as well as traditional commercial bank activities of funds transfer, bill paying, and credit provision. How much further can this process go in replacing traditional banking and brokerage? It appears that at the retail level in the USA, by 1999, the point had already been reached at which more than one-third of retail stock trading transactions were being realized through the Internet. This does not mean that the Internet has replaced Merrill Lynch but, rather, that Merrill Lynch and other brokers are using the Internet to carry out an increasing percentage of retail transactions. Each of these formats provides strong positive attractions to users. The Appendix points out some of the relative benefits of using financial centers versus using the Internet for financial services provision.

APPENDIX: AGGLOMERATION ECONOMIES VERSUS BENEFITS FROM DISPERSED FINANCIAL SERVICES

Agglomeration benefits	Benefits from dispersed services
1 Information spillovers and learning from other experts in various financial activities, such as credit evaluation, creation of complex instruments, and underwriting	1 Use of the Internet lowers the cost of communicating information about contracts, prices, and so on
2 Availability of specialized equipment, such as trading platforms, clearing centers, back-office equipment	2 Low-cost rental space in locations selected by individual service providers
3 Ability to hire experts from rival close-by firms (liquid labor market)	3 Knowledge of local markets is spread around the world
4 Market liquidity, which leads to narrower bid-offer spreads, and thus better prices to market participants	

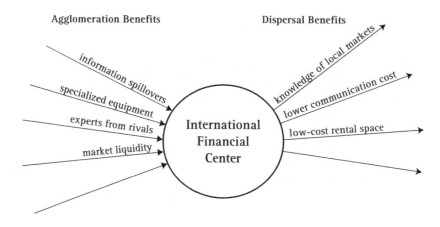

FURTHER READING

Choi, Sang-Rae, Park, D., and Tschoegl, Adrian 1996: Banks and the world's major financial centers, 1990. *Weltwirtschaftliches Archiv*, 132, pp. 774–93.

Choi, Sang-Rae, Tschoegl, Adrian, and Yu, Ch.-M. 1986: Banks and the world's major financial centers, 1970–1980. *Weltwirtschaftliches Archiv*, 122, pp. 48–64.

Gehrig, T. 1998: Competing markets. *European Economic Review*, 42, pp. 277–310.

Jeger, M., Haegler, U., and Theiss, R. 1992: On the attractiveness of financial centers. In N. Blattner, H. Genberg, and A. Swoboda (eds.), *Competitiveness in Banking*. New York: Springer-Verlag.

Kindleberger, Charles 1974: *The Formation of Financial Centers*. Princeton, NJ: Princeton University Press.

O'Brien, R. 1992: *Global Financial Integration: The End of Geography*. London: Royal Institute of International Affairs, Chatham House.

Park, Y. S., and Essayad, M. 1989: *International Banking and Financial Centers*. Boston: Kluwer.

Reed, Howard 1981: *The Pre-Eminence of International Financial Centers*. New York: Praeger.

Roberts, R. (ed.) 1994: *International Financial Centers: Concepts, Development and Dynamics*. Aldershot, UK: Edward Elgar.

Thrift, N. 1994: On the social and cultural determinants of international financial centers: the case of the City of London. In S. Corbridge, N. Thrift and R. Martin (eds.), *Money, Power and Space*. Cambridge, Mass.: Blackwell, pp. 327–55.

Tschoegl, Adrian 2000: International banking centers, geography, and foreign banks. *Financial Institutions, Instruments and Money*, 9(1), pp. 1–32.

NOTE

1   This is feasible in the sense that the law permitted such financial activities, and the rates offered by financial intermediaries were attractive.

14

SURVIVING THE TWENTY-FIRST CENTURY

Financial services provision around the world is growing and changing at such a rapid rate that both providers and regulators are greatly worried about the future of the sector. The stability of the global financial system may be in question, although the current safeguards and the historical ability of institutions to respond to crises should lead one to have at least some degree of confidence that we are not looking over the edge of a precipice with respect to financial risks.

Even if the overall system is resilient and reasonably protected by safeguards such as capital adequacy minima and deposit insurance programs, there is still plenty of room for crises at individual institutions that could lead to their downfalls. The recent bail-out of the Resona Group in Japan[1] is indicative of the possibility of failure of large institutions, which in turn can affect the stability of others and of the system overall. The Japanese government's response in this case was to bail out the bank with an injection of more than $US 17 billion of new capital – a hefty cost by anyone's measure, and unfortunately one that may be repeated for other large Japanese financial institutions in the near future.

In the United States, the most recent huge bailout was for the hedge fund Long-Term Capital Management, and that was back in 1998. That occasion, in which the institution took on enormous, supposedly low-probability risks, resulted in a bailout (by creditors, not by the government) on the order of $US 3.5 billion. In that case just as in Japan, the government displayed a willingness to intervene to the extent needed to stabilize the financial system, although not to support the continued existence of the particular institution (which was sold to creditors as part of the bailout to resolve the crisis).

These enormous incidents notwithstanding, our interest is primarily in examining how the firms involved in commercial banking, investment banking, and insurance will evolve in the near future. Assuming a continuation of the broad system as it now exists, there appears to be a large-scale convergence of the largest institutions toward the *allfinanz* model of providing all three types of financial service in the same organization. Despite comments from various analysts that such organizations are too diverse to succeed (e.g., that investment bankers and commercial bankers cannot operate well in the same organization), we have seen an inexorable wave of consolidations in this direction over the past five years. And outside of the United States and the United Kingdom, this *allfinanz* model was the norm rather than the exception for many years.

At the same time as the largest banks and brokers have been moving toward the multiple-service model, smaller niche players are alive and well in many countries. Specialized community banks and insurance brokers are the rule in the USA, with literally thousands of them competing in the early twenty-first century. There is no trend toward their disappearance, since they seem to provide the personalized service that attracts many retail clients, regardless of the costs or the limited set of instruments that they may offer. Since our interest has been in the international competitors, the discussion focuses on the large firms and on their international activities in particular.

As far as the individual segments of the financial services sector are concerned, the insurance segment is the most likely to disappear as an independent area in the near future. Insurance activities related to homes, automobiles, and individuals are relatively standardized, statistically stable businesses, and they are thus subject to competition based on price and availability. If a broader financial services provider can offer these kinds of insurance along with other services such as commercial banking, it is difficult to see what role there is for independent insurers. And this logic seems to be leading almost all of the major insurance firms to either buy banks (e.g., Allianz buying Dresdner; Citibank merging with Travelers Group) or to set up their own banks (as State Farm and the Prudential have done). There are some parts of the insurance business that are highly nonstandardized, such as reinsurance and insurance of nonstandard kinds of property – so there is room for providers of these specialized services to remain independent, as long as they continue to require specialized knowledge. Also, since insurers are major institutional investors themselves, there may be room for such firms to offer asset management services along with insurance, rather than necessarily entering into commercial banking.

A fascinating battle remains in investment banking, as the *allfinanz* pressure continues to buffet the largest investment banks – Goldman Sachs, Morgan Stanley, and Merrill Lynch. With Citigroup and J. P. Morgan Chase making inroads into their business, it will be interesting to see whether any or all of these three giants decide to "build their balance sheets" by acquiring or merging with a commercial bank. While the investment banking business itself (especially underwriting and M&A) tends to require specialized knowledge, and is not readily able to be copied, the benefits of offering more diversified services remain compelling. This may mean, as in insurance, that investment banks can become more active in asset management and perhaps other services, and not necessarily all move into commercial banking. Still, the pressure is on.

The financial services providers, even the largest ones, are decidedly nonglobal in their geographic locations. With the exception of Hongkong Bank, the rest of the world's major banks and brokers are either focused almost exclusively on their home regions (e.g., Bank of America, J. P. Morgan Chase, UBS, and the Mizuho Group) or on a couple of regions such as North America and Europe (e.g., Deutsche Bank, Credit Suisse, and Goldman Sachs). While most of the large players are present in London and Tokyo, the vast majority of their business is still in the home country or region. Thus, there is plenty of room for cross-border mergers and acquisitions, as these institutions move to become more truly global.

It appears that London will remain the world's financial capital for the foreseeable future. Despite all of the visibility of New York as the financial center of the world's largest economy, London is ahead on almost every measure of international financial service. And the competition between London and Frankfurt for the leadership in Europe is not even significant, except for some specific financial instruments such as German government bonds. As far as domestic financial centers are concerned, New York is much bigger than London, and other centers such as Tokyo are also very important. The most liquid and most extensive set of financial instruments at the international level will remain in London for the five-year horizon of our interest, and probably far beyond.

The intent of this discussion has been both to open readers' eyes to the realities of international financial services provision today, and to suggest directions for managers in financial firms to lead their firms in order to survive in the competition that exists and is coming. The competition certainly has become more intense with the dropping of regulatory barriers, and also with the advent of electronic means of competing. The number of large players is declining as national barriers to cross-border mergers and acquisitions are reduced, and as markets become more interlinked. Organizations really do need to be transformed to position themselves competitively and to take advantage of the new opportunities. This challenge will produce quite a few restructurings and realignments of competitors in the next several years. One very interesting question is whether or not the competition will become truly global.

To me, the most exciting feature of this financial services landscape is the way in which good ideas are now passed around the world rapidly and fully. It took a long time to overcome the barriers to international financial flows imposed by communist countries. Now that this economic model has been rejected, more and more countries are opening their economies to foreign investment and greater foreign lending. While this certainly implies a greater risk of destabilizing flows – as we saw with the Mexican, Asian, Russian, and Brazilian crises of the 1990s, and the Argentine crisis of 2001 – it also implies a much greater ability of emerging market firms to find financing internationally. And it means the ability of countries from Europe to Latin America to Asia to observe the benefits of mobilizing savings through the development of long-term capital markets – via privatization of pension/retirement fund management and securitization of mortgages in particular.

And as this process of financial market development takes place, it is equally important to see the creation and spread of risk-protection instruments, from futures and options to devices such as debt/equity swaps, credit derivatives, and many, many others. The counterpart to allowing markets to operate relatively freely is to offer participants the ability to protect themselves against potentially overwhelming risks.

Just as insurance markets developed to pass homeowners' risks and family income earners' risks on to third parties, so are new risk-management markets developing to enable greater participation in global financial markets to users who need risk protection in this more open environment. We are certainly blessed/cursed to live in interesting times!

NOTE

1   See, for example, http://www.asahi.com/english/business/K2003053100175.html and http://www.fpcj.jp/e/shiryo/jb/0330.html.

INDEX

Abbey 145
Abbey Life 145
ABN Amro Bank 24, 156
account transfers 36
Ace Technology of Korea 62
Aegon (The Netherlands) 59
Aetna Life Insurance 88, 97
AfDB 66
AFPs 188
AGF 79
agglomeration economies/benefits 193, 199–200
aggregators 36, 50
Agricultural Bank of China 63
AIG 42, 59, 196
Alcatel 42
Alex Brown 96, 156
allfinanz institutions 201–2
  Argentina 65
  competitive strategies 88, 90–4, 100
  France 77–8
  Germany 63, 73, 112, 113, 146, 157
  Japan 73, 148
  Korea 83
  management of 83–4
  Switzerland 62, 73
  TM process 127, 130–1, 133
  UK 60, 73, 145
  USA 29, 73–5, 117, 127, 130, 144, 154
  virtualization of services 35, 36, 42, 45
Alliance and Leicester 145

Allianz 29, 43–4, 60, 63, 73, 85, 88, 113, 146, 148, 150, 157, 174, 196
  TM process 128, 129–30, 131, 133, 135
Allianz Dresdner Bank 3, 63, 89–90, 92–3, 99–103, 113, 146, 157
  TM process 133, 135
Allstate 42, 59, 74, 148, 149
Allstate Federal Savings Bank 59
Alte Leipziger Europa 147
Amazon.com 174
American Depositary Receipts (ADRs) 21, 23, 184
American Express 76–7
American General 59
American Heritage Life 59
American International Group 148
Ameritrade 27, 35, 160, 163
annuities 29, 60, 141, 143, 169
anti-trust policies 59
Archipelago 163
Argentaria 28
Argentina 81, 188, 203
  regulation 56, 64–5, 66
Asahi Bank 18, 115, 116
Asahi Mutual Life Insurance 147
AsDB 66
Asia 18, 192, 193
  crisis 55, 68, 112, 203
  see also individual countries
Asia Recovery Bank 18
asset-backed securities 78, 156, 157

asset management   4–5, 62, 158, 176, 202
  competitive strategies   92, 93, 97, 99
  France   79, 80
  Germany   92, 93, 112–13, 146, 147
  Japan   114, 115, 147
  role of insurance companies   142–3
  Switzerland   97, 113, 114
  UK   110, 111, 145, 146
  USA   75, 97, 118, 143, 144
AT&T credit cards   91
auto insurance   141
auto loans   187
automatic teller machines (ATMs)   19–20,
    25–6, 36–7, 44–5, 47, 56, 81, 149
AXA   29, 42–3, 63, 74, 78–80, 85, 93, 128,
    143, 145–6, 196

Bamerindus   91
Banamex   47, 80–1
Banamex-Citibank   80–1
bancassurance model   88
Banco Bilbao   28
Banco Central   28
Banco de Crédito e Inversiones   44
Banco de la Nacion   64
Banco de la Provincia de Buenos Aires   64
Banco Edwards   91
Banco Santander   18, 28, 44
Banco Santander Central Hispano   23, 81
Banco Totta et Accores (Portugal)   18
Banco Vixcaya   28
Bancomer   80–1
Bancomer-BBVA   81
Banesto   28
Bank America   117
Bank of America   5, 24, 27, 31, 40, 74, 84,
    93, 116, 127, 156, 157, 158
Bank of England   60
Bank Holding Company Act   23
Bank for International Settlements   11–12,
    65, 67, 192, 194, 195, 197
Bank of Japan   8, 9
Bank of Montreal   24
Bank One   36, 40, 73, 75, 84, 93, 156
Bank of Scotland   110
Bank of Tokyo   18, 114
Bank of Tokyo-Mitsubishi   24, 94–5, 107,
    108, 111, 114–15, 116, 148

BankBoston   158
Bankers Trust   15, 18, 21, 31, 58–9, 63, 96,
    112
Banking Act (USA)   58
banks   16, 17
  competitive strategies   87–103
  globalization process   15–33
  government regulation   55, 56–65
  international centers   191, 195, 197
  loans   172, 184, 185
  performance/competitiveness   105–23
  TM process   13, 125–35
  virtual banking   44–7
  see also allfinanz institutions; commercial
    banks; community banks; corporate
    banking; investment banks; online
    banking; retail banking; wholesale
    banking
Banorte   80
Banque AGF   79
Banque Directe   79
Banque Finama   79
Banque National de Paris (BNP)   24, 42, 78,
    79, 156
Banque Paribas   79
Barclays Bank   24, 31, 42, 60, 61, 107,
    110, 111, 114, 121
Barclays Capital Grant   156
Barclays de Zoete Wedd (BZW)   114
Barings   21, 88
BASF   42
Basle Accord (1988)   64, 65–8
Bayerische Vereinsbank   113
Bayerische Vita   147
BBVA   81
BBVA Bancomer Seguros   80
Bear Stearns   154, 156
Benjamin Moore Paints   149
Berkshire Hathaway   146, 148, 149,
    165
Best Investment Bank   97
Big Bang deregulation (Japan)   8, 18, 114,
    115, 116, 121, 147
Bolivia   188
bonds   78, 100, 169–70
  collateralized mortgage obligations   176,
    183, 185–6
  global   61

growth (long-term investment) 179–89
Internet-based issuance 47–8
mortgage-backed 176, 180, 183, 185–6, 187
Brady bonds 56
Brazil 56, 66, 203
Brinson Associates 114
brokerage *see* stockbroking
bulge bracket investment banks 154, 157, 158, 161–2
Bundesbank 63

CA Asset Management 79
Cairns, A. 162
Caisse des Depots et Consignations 80
Caisse National des Caisses d'Epargnes, La 80
Camden Motors 61
CAN 59, 65, 148
Canada 22, 24, 66
Canadian Imperial Bank of Commerce 24
capital adequacy requirements 56, 201
Basle Accord 65–8
capital flight 22, 23
capital markets
deregulation 22, 23
long-term 35–6
Cardif 79
Casa de Bolsa BBVA Bancomer 81
cash 173–4
cash cards 174
Cash Management Account 11, 27, 75
casualty insurance 150
Argentina 65
France 79, 80
Germany 92, 101, 146–7
USA 60, 76, 78, 84, 140, 141, 148
catastrophe insurance 141, 142, 150
Cayman Islands 191, 192, 194
central banks 4
Argentina 64, 65
Bank of England 60
Basle Accord 64, 65–8
Bundesbank 63
European Central Bank 10, 11, 63, 195, 197
see also Bank of America

Central Europe 55
CGNU 145
chaebols 79, 82, 83
Champalimaud 23
Channel Islands 191
CHAPS 118
Charles Schwab 27, 35, 43, 73, 74, 75–6, 98, 160, 163
Charles Schwab Bank 76
Chase Manhattan 107, 111, 117–18, 121, 127, 160
checks 169, 173–4
Chemical Bank 117
Chicago 61
Chile 44, 188
China 44, 191, 193
regulation 63–4, 66
China Construction Bank 63
China Merchants Bank 44
CHIPS 118
Chrysler Credit 187
CIBC Oppenheimer 156
Citibank 3, 15, 18, 24, 27, 40, 44–5, 47, 56, 58–9, 63, 74, 82, 88, 93, 107, 111, 119, 159–60, 162, 174
TM process 126–9, 130–3, 134–5
Citibank-Mexico 80
Citicorp 116–17, 121
Citigroup 3, 5, 15, 31, 36, 45, 73–5, 77, 80–1, 84, 87–92, 98–100, 102–3, 150, 156, 202
TM process 130, 132–3, 135
Citigroup Corporate and Investment Bank 90
city banks (Japan) 8, 9
CJ Lawrence 112
Claessens, S. 51
Clarendon Insurance Group 146
client-led responses (market unavailability) 183, 184–5
CNA (Loews Group) 148, 149
CNP Assurances 78, 79, 80, 145
collateralized mortgage obligations (CMOs) 176, 183, 185–6
Cologne Re 146
Colombia 28, 188
Comdirect 43, 160, 163
Comision Nacional de Valores 65

commercial banks　4, 6, 12, 150, 168–9, 201–2
  Argentina　64–5
  China　63–4
  competitive strategies　88–9, 94, 96, 98–101
  competitiveness (factors)　105–23
  France　28, 78, 79
  Germany　8–9, 10, 11, 17, 63, 96, 112
  implications of globalization　23–7, 31
  Japan　8, 18, 115, 116
  key participants　73, 83, 84, 85
  Korea　81–2
  -led responses (market unavailability) 183–4
  Mexico　80–1
  regulation　57–8, 60–5
  rules　66
  Switzerland　62
  UK　28, 60–1, 110, 112
  underwriting/advisory role　161–2
  USA　7, 10, 17, 23–8, 31, 40–1, 57–8, 60, 74, 77, 78, 117, 118
  virtualization of services　35, 36, 40–1, 42, 46–7, 49
  see also allfinanz institutions
commercial paper　154, 177, 184
Commercial Union　145
Commerzbank　10, 11, 17, 24, 63, 93, 107, 111, 113
community banks
  Germany　84
  Korea　82
  USA　26, 40, 73, 74, 77, 84, 150
company-specific risk　175
competencies (core)　12, 88, 97, 99–103
competition　12, 13, 203
  investment banking　160–1, 164–5
  retail stockbrokerage　163–4
  underwriting securities issuance　161
competitive risk　175
competitive strategies　13
  banks (key countries)　105–23
  financial landscape　73–85
  insurance sector　148–50
  international financial institutions 87–104
ConSors　43, 160

consumer banks　25–6, 117
contagion effects　68
contamination risk　175
Controller of the Currency (FDIC)　57, 58
corporate banking　88
  Internet and　47–8
  Japan　116
  USA　75, 90, 93, 117
country risk　175, 181
Coutts　61
credit　67, 68
  extension　31, 47
  Germany　9, 10
  provision (mechanisms)　4, 5, 6, 168, 170–3
  risk　175–6, 181
  USA　17, 21, 25, 31
Crédit Agricole　78–9, 80
credit cards　31, 36, 37, 43, 75, 77, 90–1, 112, 117, 169, 187
Crédit Commercial de France　92
Crédit Lyonnais　79
Credit Suisse　24, 62, 107, 111, 114
Credit Suisse First Boston　61, 62, 114, 156, 159
Credit Trade　163
credit unions　78
Creditex　163
Czech Republic　66

Da Vinci Re　76
Dai-Ichi-Fuji-IBJ group　116
Dai-Ichi Kangyo Bank　9, 15, 18, 24, 94, 107, 111, 115, 147
Dai-ichi Mutual Life Insurance　147
Dai-Ichi Securities　116
Daido Life Insurance　115
Daimler Benz　42
Dairy Queen　149
Daiwa Bank　18
Daiwa Securities　116
Dean Witter　40, 59, 63
debit cards　31, 36, 43, 169
debt　156, 157, 162, 181
  Asia　8, 55, 68
  emerging markets　55
  government regulation　55, 56, 68
  instruments　171–2

Japan 8
Latin America 55, 56, 68
securitization of 184, 186–8
default risk 176, 180, 181
demutualization 143–4
deposit insurance 64, 66, 170, 201
global 57
government-backed 24–5
depositary institutions 26, 78
depositary receipts
American (ADRs) 21, 23, 184
Global (GDRs) 21, 23, 61
deposits 169, 170
deregulation 15, 22, 55, 56, 57
competitive strategies and 87, 96, 99,
150
Germany 96
global 23, 127
insurance sector 59, 147, 150
investment banking 160, 163
Japan 8, 18, 114, 115, 116, 121, 147
USA 26, 129
Design a Strategy (TM process) 127, 130–2
Deutsche–Bankers Trust 40
Deutsche Bank 10, 11, 15, 17–18, 24, 29,
31, 42–3, 45, 59, 63, 89–90, 92–3, 96,
100, 102–3, 107, 111–13, 147, 160
TM process 128, 131, 133
Deutsche Bank Alex Brown 96, 156, 159
Deutsche Borse 196, 198
Deutsche Morgan Grenfell (DMG) 112
Dexter Shoes 149
Dillon Read 59, 114
Dimon, J. 75
Direct Line 61
disintermediation process 17, 31, 40
dispersed financial services 199–200
distributed service provision 19–20, 26
distribution channels (insurance) 149
domestic financial centers 193–4
Donaldson, Lufkin and Jenrette (DLJ) 114
Dresdner Bank 10, 11, 17, 29, 59, 63, 84,
88, 92, 96, 107, 111, 113, 128, 131,
133, 146, 148, 157, 160, 174
Dresdner Kleinwort Benson 61, 113
Dresdner Kleinwort Wasserstein (DrKW) 84,
93, 156, 157, 159
Dufey, G. 171

e-commerce 36, 75, 84, 177
E*Financial 76
e-mail 19
e-payments 51
E*Trade 27, 35, 36, 49, 76, 160, 163
Economist Intelligence Unit 66
Edward Jones 74
efficiency ratios (international banks)
107–8, 109, 110, 118, 119–20
Egg 42, 43, 145, 160
EIB 66
electronic banking 19–20, 27, 36, 40–7,
48, 49, 50, 56
electronic bill paying 19, 44
electronic finance (providers) 48–50
electronic funds transfer 169, 173–4
Electrowatt Corporation 62
Ellis, M. E. 155
emerging markets 22, 23, 90, 91, 203
current supply chains 44
debt 55
government regulation and 55–6,
68
enablers (electronic finance) 51
Enron 91
Envision the Future (TM process) 126,
129–30
Equitable Life 148
equity 100, 109
derivatives (Switzerland) 113
instruments 171–2
securities (Germany) 112–13
see also return on equity
ERGO 147
Eurex exchange 198
euro 10, 195, 196, 197–8
eurobonds 156, 157, 161, 184
Eurohypo AG 96
Euronext 196, 198
Europe 55, 84
competitive strategies 89–90
current supply chains 42–4
virtualization of services 42–4, 49
see also individual countries
European Central Bank 10, 11, 63, 195,
197
European Monetary Union (EMU) 4, 18,
22, 196

European Union
  Central Bank   10, 11, 63, 195, 197
  globalization process   17–18, 22, 23, 28, 31
  government regulation   61, 62–3
  Second Banking Directive   42, 62–3, 66, 84
  virtualization   42
exchange rate risk   174, 175

Fanny Mae   184, 185–6
Farmers   148
Federal Deposit Insurance Corporation (FDIC)
  40–1, 57, 58
Federal Family Education Loan Program
  (FFELP)   187–8
Federal Reserve Bank   45
Federal Reserve System   7, 8, 17, 27, 31,
  40–1, 57, 58–9, 78, 130
Fedwire   118
fee-based services (US banks)   25
Fidelity   28
Fidelity Investments   89, 90, 98, 100, 102–3
Fidelity Management and Research   98
Fides Corporation   62
finance companies (in USA)   78
financial advice (methods)   167, 177–8
Financial Advisory Center (Merrill Lynch)
  94
financial engineering   21–2
financial innovations (long-term markets)
  185–8
financial instruments   4, 167–8
  long-term   179–89
  types needed   169–78
Financial Management Account   27
financial markets   16, 17
  long-term   179–80
  unavailability problem   182–5
financial portals   51
Financial Reconstruction Commission   18
financial services
  challenge of new economy   125–36
  characteristics   12
  competitive strategies   see competitive
    strategies
  current supply chains   39–44
  dispersed (benefits)   199–200

expected changes   201–4
  functions/roles   3–5, 6
  globalization of   15–33, 85
  instruments/structures   167–78
  international financial centers   191–200
  legal/technological shifts   13
  providers   5, 7–12, 73–85
  rules (selected countries)   66
  virtualization of   13, 35–54, 167
  see also financial systems/landscape
Financial Services Authority (UK)   60
Financial Services Modernization Act (USA)
  27, 57–9, 74, 127, 139, 160
financial structures   167–78
Financial Supervisory Agency (Japan)   8
financial systems/landscape   168
  allfinanz institutions (management)   83–4
  defining financial services   3–5, 6
  financial service providers   5, 7–12
  France   77–80
  future developments   84–5
  globalization of services   15–33
  government regulation   22, 55–70, 84
  Korea   82–3
  Mexico   80–1
  USA   74–7
  virtualization of services   35–54
financing alternatives (mechanisms)   168,
  170–3
financing facility   21, 31, 154, 172, 173
Finaxa   79
First Boston Corporation   114
First Chicago Bank   75
First Direct   19, 132, 135
FirstDirect.com   36, 43, 132
First Union   40, 156, 157
fiscal policy   22
float (funding source)   19–20
Ford   187
foreign exchange trading   47, 61, 64, 191,
  192, 193, 195
France   42, 66
  financial market/landscape   73, 77–80
Frankfurt   43, 89, 192, 193–4, 195, 196–8,
  203
Freddie Mac   184, 185
Fuji Bank   15, 18, 94, 115
funding mechanisms   4, 5, 6, 168, 170–3

funds
  sources of 6
  transfer 19–20, 44, 167, 168, 173–4
future (TM process) 125–35
futures 21
Fxall 47

Gartmore 110
General Accident 145
General Cologne 146
General Electric 160–1, 165
General Electrical Capital Corporation 32
General Motors 187
General Motors Acceptance Corporation 32
General Re–New England Asset Management
  146
General Reinsurance 146
Generali 63, 65, 93
Germany 22, 42, 203
  bank performance 106–7, 108, 112–13,
    118–19, 120, 121
  economic growth rates 108–9
  financial landscape 73, 84
  financial system 8–12
  globalization process 15, 17–18
  government regulation 62–3, 66
  insurance sector 29, 63, 146–7
  international financial center 192,
    193–4, 195, 196–8
  investment banking 156–7, 159, 160
  reunification 108
  universal banks 8–9, 11, 73
Ginnie Mae 184, 185
Glaessner, T. 51
Glass–Steagall Act 27, 41, 114
Gleacher & Co. 110
global bonds 61
Global Capital Markets (Goldman Sachs) 97
Global Depositary Receipts (GDRs) 21, 23,
  61
global distribution of virtual financial
  services 15–33, 85
global lender of last resort 68
global risk 175
globalization of financial services 15–33, 85
Goldman Sachs 24, 61, 74, 82, 84, 88–90,
  93, 97, 99, 101–3, 154, 156, 158–9,
  161, 164, 202

Good Morning Shinhan Securities 82
government
  -backed deposit insurance 24–5
  bail-outs 201
  bonds 56, 180, 181, 203
  -led responses (market unavailability)
    182–3
  regulation see regulation
Gramm–Leach–Bliley Act (USA) 27, 57, 58,
  59, 74, 127, 139, 160
Grand Bank 59
Greenhill & Co. 154, 156, 158
Greenwich Capital Markets 110
Groupama 79
Groupe Caisse des Depots 78
Grupo Financiero Bital 91

Haftpflichtverband der Deutschen Industries
  (HDI) 146
Hamel, G. 12
Hanaro Merchant Bank 82
Hankyu Group 115
Hanover Life Re 146
Hanover Re Advanced Solutions 146
Hanover Rückversicherungs 146
Hanvit Bank 82
Hartford Life 65, 148
HC&B Bank 82
HDFC Bank 44
HDI Reinsurance (Ireland) 146
health insurance 80, 92, 101, 141, 148,
  174, 175
hedging 21
hidden reserves (German banks) 109,
  112
Higher Education Act (USA) 187
Hitachi 115
Hokkaido Takushoku Bank 18
home equity loans 187
home insurance (USA) 141
Hong Kong 63, 66, 191, 192, 194, 198–9
Hongkong Bank of CCF (France) 18
Hongkong and Shanghai Banking
  Corporation (HSBC) 3, 19, 24, 31, 36,
  42–3, 45, 60–1, 73, 87–93, 96, 99–103,
  156, 157, 160
  TM process 129, 130, 132, 133–4, 135
Household Finance Corporation 91

HSBC see Hongkong and Shanghai
    Banking Corporation (HSBC)
Hypobank 113
HypoVereinzBank 10, 11, 63, 92
Hyundai Fire and Marine 83

IADB 66
IBM 31, 160–1
ICICI Bank 44
implementation plan (TM process) 126,
    127, 134–5
India 44, 66
Indonesia 23, 68
Industrial Bank of Japan 9, 15, 18, 94,
    115
Industrial and Commercial Bank of China
    24, 63
industry structure
    government regulation 55–70
    virtualization of services 35–54
inflation 179, 180, 181
information technology 95
ING see Internationale Nederlanden Group
    (ING)
Initial Position (TM process) 126, 127–9
initial public offerings (IPOs) 162
innovations, financial 185–8
Insurance Information Institute 142
insurance sector 5, 12, 191, 192
    Argentina 65
    China 63, 64
    competitive strategies 88–9, 92, 93, 98,
        99–101, 148–50
    disappearance/survival of 139–51
    France 78–80
    Germany 29, 63, 96, 112, 146–7
    implications of globalization 28–9
    Japan 114, 115, 147–8
    key participants 73, 83–5
    Korea 82–3
    Mexico 80, 81
    regulation 58–65
    risk management see risk management
    Switzerland 62, 113, 114
    UK 61–2, 110–12, 145–6
    underwriting (London/New York) 196
    USA 28–9, 41–2, 49, 58–60, 74, 77–8,
        117, 139–44, 148–9

virtualization 41–2, 43, 46, 49
    see also allfinanz institutions
interest rates 66, 171–2, 179–80, 181
interest risk 174, 175
internal management information systems
    20–1, 36, 38
International Bank for Reconstruction and
    Development (IBRD) 66
international financial centers 203
    agglomeration/dispersal benefits 199–200
    definition/role 191–3
    domestic centers and 193–4
    London 191, 192, 193–8, 199
    New York 191, 192, 193–6, 197,
        199
international financial institutions 87–104
International Monetary Fund (IMF) 68
International Securities Market Association
    197
Internationale Nederlanden Group (ING)
    79, 80, 88–90, 96–7, 99, 101, 102–3
Internet 74, 97, 98, 99, 125, 129, 184
    -based payments 169
    -based services (strengths and weaknesses)
        38
    -based underwriting 160–1
    corporate banking and 47–8
    globalization and 17, 19–20, 25–6, 27,
        31
    government regulation 56
    insurance services 140
    international financial centers and
        192–3, 199
    investment banking and 163–4
    online banking 3, 19–20, 27, 36, 40–50,
        56, 76, 92, 132, 163–4, 167
    online brokerage 35, 36, 43, 49, 50, 56,
        75–6, 92, 163
    virtualization of financial services 13,
        35–54, 167
intranet 20
investment 17, 22
    financial advice 76, 77, 167, 177–8
    long-term 179–89
    management 5, 10, 61, 142–3, 145
investment banks 12, 168–9, 172, 201–2
    activities 153–4, 155, 158–9
    Argentina 65

bulge bracket 154, 157, 158, 161–2
China 63–4
Colombia 28
competition 160–5
competitive strategies 88–91, 93, 96, 97, 99–101
France 28, 78
Germany 10, 17, 63, 96, 112, 113
implications of globalization 27–8, 31
Internet and 163–4
Japan 8, 18, 28, 115–16
key participants 73–4, 75, 77, 78, 82, 83, 84
Korea 82
-led responses (market unavailability) 183, 184
major firms 154, 156, 157–8
Mexico 80, 81
regulation 58–65
rules 66
Spain 28
Switzerland 62, 95, 113, 114
UK 28, 60–1, 110–11, 112, 156, 160
USA 10, 17, 27–8, 42, 58–9, 74, 75, 77, 117, 118, 177
see also allfinanz institutions

J. O. Hambro Magan and Co. 110
J. P. Morgan Chase Bank 5, 24, 27, 40, 65, 74, 93, 107, 111, 117–18, 121, 156–7, 159, 160, 162, 202
Jackson National Life 145
Japan 49, 90, 201
bank performance 105, 106–7, 108, 114–16, 118–19, 120, 121
commercial banks 8, 18, 115, 116
deregulation 8, 18, 114, 115, 116, 121, 147
economic growth rate 108–9
financial landscape 73, 84
financial system 8, 9, 18
globalization process 15, 18, 28
government regulation 58, 66, 68
insurance sector 114, 115, 147–8
international financial centers 192, 193–4, 198–9, 203
investment banks 8, 18, 28, 115–16
Johnson and Johnson 165

joint stock companies 144
junk bonds 170

keiretsu 8, 18, 79, 84, 109, 114, 147
Kleinwort Benson 113, 157
Klingebiel, D. 51
Koa Fire and Marine Insurance 115
Kölnische Rückversicherungs-Gesellschaft (Cologne Re) 146
Konoike Bank 115
Kookmin Bank 82
Korea 22, 62, 68, 91
financial market/landscape 75, 82–3
Korea Exchange Bank 91
Korea Life 83
Kwangju Bank 82
Kyocera 115
Kyongnam Bank 82

landesbanks 10, 11
Latin America 23, 55–6, 68, 84, 188–9
see also individual countries
Lazard 154, 156, 157, 158
legal environment/shifts 13
Lehman Brothers 154, 156, 157, 159, 161
lender of last resort 172
global (argument for) 57, 68
LendingTree.com 36
leveraged buy-outs (LBOs) 116, 184
LG Fire and Marine 83
LG Investment and Securities 82
life insurance 174
allfinanz institutions 83, 88
France 79, 80
Germany 92
globalization process 28–9
government regulation 60, 65
Japan 115, 147–8
Korea 82
Netherlands, The 96–7, 101
Switzerland 113
UK 110, 145
USA 78, 140–1, 143, 148–9
Lincoln Life 42
liquidity 21
Lloyd's of London 61
Lloyds Reinsurance Exchange 192, 196

Lloyds TSB Bank   24, 42, 60–1, 107,
    110–12, 121
loans
    bank   172, 184, 185
    securitization of   184, 186–8
    see also mortgages; savings and loans
    (S&L) sector
LoansDirect   36, 76
Loews Group   148, 149
Loews Hotels   149
London   43, 61, 89
    international financial center   191, 192,
    193–8, 199, 203
    Stock Exchange   23, 193, 196, 197,
    198
Long-Term Capital Management   21, 201
Long-Term Credit Bank   18
long-term instruments, demand for   188–9
long-term investment   179–89
long-term markets   185–8
Lorillard Tobacco   149

McFadden Act   23
Malaysia   66
management information systems   20–1,
    36, 38
manufactured home loans   187
Mapfre   65
Marine Midland Bank   3, 31, 91, 129, 132
market
    long-term (innovations)   185–8
    risks   175
    unavailability problem   182–5
Marshall, J.   155
MasterCard   37, 77, 149
MBNA   43
MEAG Munich ERGO AssetManagement
    147
Meiji General Insurance   147–8
Meiji Life Insurance   147–8
mergers
    and acquisitions   90, 93, 116–17, 154,
    157, 162, 164, 165, 203
    globalization of services   15–33
Merrill Lynch   17, 24, 30, 35, 40, 61, 63,
    65, 74–7, 82, 84, 89–90, 92–4, 100,
    102–3, 134, 156, 158–60, 177, 199,
    202

Metropolitan   42
Metropolitan Life Insurance Company   59,
    65, 147, 148
Mexico   22, 47, 66
    crises   56, 68, 81, 91, 203
    financial market/landscape   73, 80–1
Microsoft   31
Midland Bank   60, 91, 129, 132, 133
Mikdashi, Z.   164
Ministry of Finance (Japan)   8, 9
Misubishi   147
Mitsubishi Bank   18, 114, 115
Mitsubishi Tokyo Financial   18
Mitsui   147
Mitsui Bank   116
Mizuho Bank   94
Mizuho Corporate Bank   94
Mizuho Group   15, 18, 24, 89–90, 94–5,
    100, 101, 102–3, 115, 147
Mizuho Holdings Financial Group   94
"Mom & Pop" organizations   26, 40, 73,
    150
monetary policy   22, 31, 63, 64, 197
money (role/uses)   4
money management
    at Credit Suisse   114
    at Deutsche Bank   112
money market   17, 30, 39–40, 78, 170
Montgomery Securities   158
Morgan Guaranty   27, 58
Morgan Stanley   59, 61, 63, 74, 82, 84, 93,
    156, 164, 202
Morgan Stanley Dean Witter   159
mortgages   36, 76, 82, 110, 111, 179
    -backed bonds   176, 180, 183, 185–6,
    187
    CMOs   176, 183, 185–6
    securitization of   172, 184, 185, 186,
    188, 201
Münchener Rückversicherungs-Gesellschaft
    63, 92, 96, 146–7
mutual funds   7, 8, 10, 28, 39–40, 78, 95,
    98, 100, 143, 169, 176–7

Nasdaq   196
Nassau   191, 192, 194
Natio Assurances   79
National Bank Act (USA)   58

National Bank of Detroit   75
national champions   31
National Housing Fund (Korea)   82
National Westminster Bank   60, 107, 110, 111
Nationale-Nederlanden   97
NationsBank   75, 116, 117, 127, 158
Nationsbank v. *Vatic*   60
Nationwide   148
Nationwide Life   148
NatWest   60, 61, 110
negotiable order of withdrawal (NOW)
    accounts   40
Net.B@nk   36
Netherlands, The   22, 80, 88–90, 96–7, 99, 101, 102–3
New York   89
    as international financial center   191, 192, 193–7, 199, 203
    Stock Exchange   23, 56, 193, 196, 197
New York Life   65, 148
Nichido Fire and Marine   147
NIFs   21
Nikko Securities   18
Nippon Credit Bank   18
Nippon Fire and Marine Insurance   115
Nippon Life Insurance   29, 147
Nippon Trust Bank   18
Nissho Iwai   115
NMB Postbank Groep   97
nonbank firms (financial market model)
    17, 18, 31
Northwestern Mutual   148
Norwich Union   145

O'Connor Associates   114
OECD   66–7, 109
online banking   3, 19–20, 27, 36, 40–50, 56, 76, 92, 132, 163–4, 167
online brokerage   35, 36, 43, 49–52, 56, 75–6, 92, 163
online lenders   50
online stock/bond markets   163, 164
operational risk   175
options   21
Orix   115
ownership (insurance sector)   139

Pacifica   79
Paine Webber   59, 75, 114
Panama   66, 191, 192, 194
Paris   192, 193–4, 198
payment mechanisms   4, 47, 51
Peace Bank   82
pension funds   78, 81, 157
    privatization   176, 180, 188–9, 203
pensions   145
People's Bank (USA)   91
Peru   23, 188
Pincus Warburg   114
political risk   174, 180, 181
portfolio investments/management   28–9
Portugal   23
Postal Savings system
    Germany   10, 11
    Japan   8, 9
Poste, La   80
PPP healthcare   145
Prahalad, C. K.   12
Predica   79
Private Wealth Advisers (Merrill Lynch)   94
privatization   23, 157
    of pension funds   176, 180, 188–9, 203
Procter and Gamble   21
profitability (banks)   107–9, 110, 112, 113, 118, 119–21
Property Claims Service   142
property insurance   29, 150, 202
    Argentina   65
    France   79, 80
    Germany   92, 100, 101, 146–7
    USA   60, 76, 78, 84, 140–1, 142, 148
property risk   174, 175
Prudential   42, 43, 74, 145, 148

quasi-deposits   30
Quotesmith.com   36

Raymond James   65, 74
Reed, J.   135
regulation   84, 85
    Argentina   56, 64–5, 66
    Basle Accord   64, 65–8
    China   63–4, 66
    Germany   62–3, 66

regulation (*cont.*):
   implications of globalization   22–3
   Switzerland   62, 66
   systemic risk   68
   UK   60–2, 66
   USA   55, 56, 57–60, 66, 68
   virtual financial services   48
   see also deregulation
reinsurance   29, 61, 141–2, 146, 191, 196,
      202
Reliastar Insurance   97
RenaissanceRe   76
Renault   42
Republic Bank of New York   3, 31
Republic National Bank (USA)   132
Resona Group   18, 201
retail banking   101
   France   78–9
   Germany   112, 113
   Mexico   81
   UK   110–12
   USA   74–5, 76, 90, 117, 118
retail stockbroking   93, 100, 113, 114, 154,
      160, 163–4
return on assets   107–8, 109, 118
return on equity   119, 121
   Germany   112, 121
   Japan   121
   performance data   105, 107–8
   Switzerland   113
   UK   110
   USA   109, 118, 119
Revolving Underwriting Facility (RUF)   21,
      172, 173
Ripplewood Holdings   18
risk   21, 83–4
   assets   66–7
   default   176, 180, 181
   political   174, 180, 181
   protection mechanisms   168, 184, 203–4
   reinsurance   29, 61, 141–2
   securitization of   142
   systemic   68, 175
risk management   5, 29, 91, 95, 117, 150,
      154, 167, 204
   Germany   10–12, 100
   mechanisms   174–6
   profile   174–5

Robertson Stephens   158
Rothschild   154, 156, 157
Royal Bank of Canada   24
Royal Bank of Scotland   60, 61, 110
Russia   56, 66, 203

Safra Banks   91
St. Gobain   42, 79
Sakura Bank   18, 115, 116, 147
Sallie Mae   184, 187–8
Salomon Brothers   59, 63
Salomon Smith Barney   90, 117, 159, 160,
      177
   see also Smith Barney
Samsung Fire and Marine   83
Samsung Securities   82–3
Santander Serfin   81
Sanwa Bank   18, 107, 111, 115–16
Sanwa keiretsu   147
Sanwa Securities Company   116
Sanyo Securities   18
savings   17, 182, 203
   mechanisms to store   4, 5, 6, 168–70
savings and loans (S&L) sector   26, 40, 60,
      78, 139
SBC Warburg   63
Schroders   117
Scottish Mutual   145
Scottish Provident   145
Scudder Investments   96
Second Banking Directive   42, 62–3, 66,
      84
securities   60, 78, 97, 101, 156–7, 196
Securities and Exchange Commission   58
Securities and Investments Board   60
securitization
   of loans   184, 186–8
   of mortgages   172, 184–6, 188, 203
   of risk   142
Security First Network Bank   36
Seguros Banamex   80
Seguros BBVA Bancomer   81
Seguros Comercial America   80
Seguros Santander Serfin   80
self-insurance   150, 175
Sell that Future (TM process)   127, 132–5
Serfin   80
SG Warburg   114

Shanghai 198
Sharp 115
Shearson Lehman Brothers 40
Shinhan Bank 82
Signal Iduna 145
Silicon Valley 75, 158
Singapore 191, 192, 194, 198
SK Life 83
SLM Corporation 184, 187–8
smart cards 26, 31
Smith Barney 40, 59, 63, 76, 80, 88, 90, 132
    see also Salomon Smith Barney
Société Générale 42, 79, 156, 157
Sogecap 79
Spain 22, 23, 28
State Farm 42, 59, 73–4, 76, 148, 149
stock exchange 23, 56, 75, 182, 193, 196–8
stock market 192
    growth (long-term) 179–89
    UK 181–2, 193
    USA 68, 75, 181–2, 193
stockbroking 42, 153
    Germany 17
    Japan 18
    Mexico 81
    USA 27–8, 40, 75–6, 196
    see also online brokerage; retail stockbroking
strategic alliances 37, 49, 94
strategy design (TM process) 127, 130–2
student loans 187–8
Sumitomo Bank 18, 21, 116
Sumitomo Mitsui Banking Corporation 18, 95, 147
Sun Life and Provincial Holdings 145
Suntory 115
SunTrust 74
supply chains (services) 39–44
swaps 21
swaptions 21
Swiss Bank Corporation 62, 95, 108, 111, 113–14, 118
Swiss Life 113
Switzerland
    bank performance 106–8, 113, 118–21
    economic growth rate 108–9

financial landscape 73
government regulation 62, 66
systemic risk 68, 175

T-bank 44
Taiyo Life Insurance 115
tax havens 191–2, 194
technology 95, 160
    globalization and 15, 17–19, 31–2
    shifts 13, 19–22
    virtualization of services 13, 35–54
Telebanc 36, 76
telephone banking 45, 56
Tequila Crisis 80, 81
Thailand 56, 68
Threadneedle Investments 96
TIAA–CREF 42, 74, 148
time deposits 4
Tokai Bank 18, 116
Tokyo 192, 193–4, 198–9, 203
Tokyo-Kobe Bank 116
Tokyo Marine and Fire 147, 148
Tokyo Sowa Bank 18
Towa Securities 116
Toyo Trust Bank 18, 115
transaction costs 45
Transamerica 59
Transformational Management 13, 125–35
Travelers Group 15, 59–60, 84, 90, 93, 116, 130, 132, 134, 148, 160, 174
Treasury bonds 176, 181, 198
treasury management 5, 91, 117–18
trust (in Internet services) 38–9
TSB Savings Bank 110

UBS Paine Webber 95, 114
UBS Warburg 59, 61, 95, 114, 156–7, 159
underwriting 27–8, 43, 172, 196
    securities issuance 100, 154, 160–2
    stocks and bonds 101, 154
Union Bank (USA) 129
Union Bank of Switzerland 95, 108, 113–14, 118
United Bank of Switzerland 24, 62, 89, 90, 95, 100, 102–3, 108, 111, 113
United California Bank 79
United Financial of Japan 18, 95

United Kingdom
  bank performance   106–7, 110–12,
    118–19, 120, 121
  commercial banks   28, 60–1, 110, 112
  economic growth rate   108–9
  financial landscape   73
  globalization process   28
  government regulation   60–2, 66
  insurance sector   61–2, 110–12,
    145–6
  international financial centers   191, 192,
    193–8, 199
  investment banks   28, 60–1, 110–11,
    112, 156, 160
  virtualization of services   42–3, 45
United States   22, 201
  bank performance   105–10, 116–20,
    121
  challenge of new economy   126–35
  commercial banks   7, 10, 17, 23–8, 31,
    40–1, 57–8, 60, 74, 77–8, 117–18
  competitive strategies   89–90
  economic growth rate   108–9
  financial market/landscape   73–8, 84
  financial system   5, 7–8, 10, 17
  globalization process   15, 17, 23–9,
    31–2
  government regulation   55–60, 66, 68
  insurance sector   28–9, 38, 59–60,
    139–44, 148–9
  international financial centers   191, 192,
    193–6, 197, 199
  investment banks   156–7, 158–63
  supply chains   39–42
  universal banks   117, 130, 134–5
  virtualization of services   35–6, 39–42,
    49
universal banks   91, 154
  Germany   8–9, 11, 73
  Japan   114, 115
  Korea   82
  Mexico   80
  TM process   130, 134–5
  USA   117, 130, 134–5
  see also allfinanz institutions
Universal Securities Company   115, 116

Vanguard   28
Venezuela   23
Viacom   165
videoconferencing   19, 20, 25, 44–5
virtualization of financial services   13, 167
  banking models   44–7
  corporate banking   47–8
  current supply chains   39–44
  global dispersed activities   48
  impact of Internet   35–7
  insurance sector   29
  limits and opportunities   37–9
  providers of electronic finance   49–52
  virtual banking (models)   44–7
  see also Internet
Visa   26, 37, 77, 149
Visa International/VisaNet   19
Vivendi   79

Wachovia   74, 157
Warren Buffet   146
Wassestein Perrella   59, 113, 157
wealth management   93, 94, 97, 145
Weill, S.   75, 134
Wells Fargo   40, 74
Wells Fargo Nikko Asset Management   110
wholesale banking   46–7
  Germany   112
  USA   26–7, 74, 76, 118
Wingspan.com   36
Winterthur   62, 114
Woolwich Ltd.   43
Woori Bank   82
World Bank   51, 109, 161
World Federation of Exchanges   197
World Trade Organization   64

Xetra   163

Yamaichi Securities   18

Zurich   192, 194
Zurich Financial Services   62
Zurich Group   96
Zurich Insurance   75, 114
Zurich Scudder Investments (ZSI)   96

Printed and bound by CPI Group (UK) Ltd, Croydon, CR0 4YY

16/04/2025

14658512-0005